THE ORANGE ORDER

BOOKS BY TONY GRAY

FICTION

Starting from Tomorrow

The Real Professionals

Gone the Time

Interlude
(Based on an original screenplay by
Lee Langley and Hugh Leonard)

The Last Laugh

NON-FICTION

The Irish Answer

The Record Breakers
(with Leo Villa)

Psalms and Slaughter

THE ORANGE ORDER

TONY GRAY

THE BODLEY HEAD

LONDON SYDNEY

TORONTO

Tony Gray is an Irish journalist and author who now lives and works in London. His anatomy of Ireland, *The Irish Answer*, had the rare distinction of being greeted as objective by reviewers on both sides of the border. His mother comes from an Ulster family of Scots-Irish settlers called McKee; his father's family was Anglo-Norman in origin and Church of Ireland by persuasion; and he married an Irish Catholic. So, as he says, he has been exposed to three of the main strains in the Irish situation and *The Orange Order* is probably as objective and unbiased as any book on this curious institution could be.

ISBN 0 370 01340 9
Printed and bound in Great Britain for
The Bodley Head Ltd
9 Bow Street, London WC2E 7AL
by Richard Clay (The Chaucer Press) Ltd., Bungay, Suffolk
Set in Monotype Baskerville
First published 1972

CONTENTS

I The Glorious Twelfth, 7
II Long Knives . . . and Long Memories, 27
III United Ireland—a Contradiction in Terms, 43
IV Down, Down, Croppies lie down, 55
V The United Kingdom of Great Britain and Ireland, 73
VI Orangeism in Trouble over the Water, 89
VII The Dog Days—and the New Menace, 97
VIII Catholic Emancipation—the Orange Backlash, 109
IX Orangeism in Trouble in England Again, 121
X The Great Famine—and its Aftermath, 135
XI Roaring Hanna and the Demagogues, 147
XII Ulster will Fight . . . and Ulster will be Right, 159
XIII The Troubled Times: 1916–1923, 173
XIV The Loyal Orange Institution of Ireland, 193
XV The Arch Purple and the Black, 209
XVI Religion and Politics, 221
XVII What Went Wrong?, 241
XVIII Orangeism outside Ulster, 257
XIX Jesuits in the Jam?, 275
Acknowledgements, 281
Suggestions for Further Reading, 283
Index, 286

It's old but it is beautiful,
Its colours they are fine,
It was worn at Derry, Aughrim,
Enniskillen and the Boyne.
My father wore it when a youth
In by-gone days of yore,
So on the Twelfth I proudly wear
The Sash my father wore.

—From *The Sash My Father Wore,*
a traditional Orange ballad.

I

The Glorious Twelfth

The date is July 11th. The year? Well, it could be any of what might be described as the peaceable years, before the present troubles in Northern Ireland started late in 1968—the late 'thirties, perhaps, or the early 'fifties.

The scene is Belfast. It is five-thirty in the evening and men and women are pouring out of the offices and factories, the shipyards, mills, shops and warehouses. There is a holiday spirit in the air as they jostle along the narrow pavements through streets decorated with Union Jacks and Orange garlands. In the Protestant areas, like the Sandy Row and the Shankill Road—where the houses carry splendid permanent murals of King William of Orange on his white steed, crossing the River Boyne (sometimes covering the entire end-wall of a terrace of houses, from the apex of the roof to the ground), pledges of loyalty to the Crown and various other less creditable sentiments (NO SURRENDER, TO HELL WITH THE POPE, R.C.S AND FENIANS OUT, DOWN WITH POPEHEADS, and so on)—there are elaborately constructed archways, decorated with Orange signs and symbols, and surmounted by yet more representations of King Billy on his white charger.

From dozens of Orange Halls and Church and community centres of one sort or another, bands can be heard practising—the final practice before the next day's great march. There are more bands per acre and per head of the population in Ulster than in any other part of the United Kingdom, if not of the world.

Occasionally, over the general din, can be heard the unmistakable and unforgettable fusillade made by the Lambeg drum, that enormous, ancient, intimidating bass drum, peculiar to this corner of the world. The Lambeg drums are beaten or 'chapped' with cane saplings, to a curious broken rhythm which can whip the listener—as well as the drummer—into a frenzy of excitement or fear. 'No one—Catholic or Protestant—who has heard the Lambeg drums can ever forget the experience or feel quite the same way again,' a Dublin Catholic photographer, who has covered the Glorious Twelfth on countless occasions for the *Irish Times*, told me. 'Though naturally,' he added, 'how you feel about them depends on which side of the fence you are on. At times,' he went on to say, 'the drumming reaches the intensity of Zulu tribal tom-toms before an attack, and the drummers get so carried away that they ignore torn knuckles and bleeding wrists and sometimes have to be separated from their sapling drum-sticks with cold water and a great deal of patience after the big parade.'

In the narrow side streets—and one of the surprising things about the city of Belfast is that the slums seem to start one block away from the smart shopping centres—where the population has always lived largely *in* the streets, the children are already putting the finishing touches to the great bonfires that light up the skies in and around Belfast every July 11th, frequently setting fire to tinder-dry slum houses and giving firemen their busiest night of the year. Bonfires are lit on the hills around Belfast, too, as well as in the other towns and villages throughout the Province, and a very festive sight they would make if it were not for their sectarian significance. As they build the bonfires, the children chant their own separatist slogans. 'Give us enough rope and we'll hang the bloody Pope' was the chant one year; recently they have become a bit more trendy. 'Yippy, yippy, yippy, the Pope's a bloody hippy' was a recent reincarnation of a ritual that has always carried a curiously 17th century flavour, harking back to the London Apprentice boys hauling effigies of Popes and Cardinals through the City to the stakes at Smithfield at the time of the Restoration.

Some of the women are indoors, ironing their husbands' white shirts and laying out the Orange collarettes and other insignia for the big march next day. Until recently, the uniform for the parade was standard and universal; company director and docker turned out alike in dark city suit, white shirt and bowler hat, carrying a rolled umbrella, and wearing the orange collarette with war medals and badges of various kinds, and sometimes Orange Order cuffs and white gloves. Latterly, some of the Lodges have dropped the bowler hat. 'We've got a lot of younger members in the Order who insist on wearing their hair long,' an Orange official told me, 'and long hair just doesn't go with a bowler hat. It looks ridiculous. So we let them march bare-headed, or wear berets. But most of the older members regret the passing of the bowler.'

The umbrella is rolled with meticulous care so that it looks almost like a sword, and is carried stiffly with military precision, though Orangemen insist that it is there purely for practical reasons and not as a weapon substitute. 'It often rains in Belfast on the Twelfth,' one man said to me, 'and we wouldn't want the sash to get wet.' Orangemen still refer to the collarette as the sash—originally the Order wore an Orange sash—and there are two versions: a small, token collarette which is worn at Lodge meetings, and the larger, ceremonial version which is worn during public parades. Most Orange sashes are passed from father to son, so that the phrase 'the sash my father wore' in the popular Orange ballad is no empty boast. Indeed, I have met young Orangemen who told me that their main reason for joining the Order was because they wanted to march on the Twelfth, wearing their fathers' collarettes and other emblems.

The women who have finished preparing the uniforms stand about in the streets waiting for the bonfires to start. The men have already started in on what is the main business of the evening of the 11th—drinking—and it is one of the many ironies of the situation in Belfast that the Orangemen celebrating their national three-day commemoration of the victory of the Protestant King Billy over the Catholic King James at the Battle of the Boyne on July 12th, 1690, thus ensuring the Protestant Ascendancy in the British Isles, are obliged to do so in pubs mostly owned and run by Catholics. The reason for this is that a strong streak of Puritanism in the Ulster Protestant made him reluctant to take out a licence or run a pub, though he is every bit as partial to a jar as his counterpart in the South; consequently he must, as a rule, take his refreshment in a pub run by Catholics with the knowledge that the profit is going to 'the other side'.

This streak of Puritanism has pockets within the Orange Order. There are many temperance Lodges, and some Orangemen will assure you—and apparently believe it themselves—that no drop of drink ever passes the lips of an Orangeman during the three-day ceremony in honour of King William III of Glorious, Pious and Immortal Memory. To suggest that 40,000 to 50,000 Irishmen—many of them shipyard and factory workers—would spend a three-day holiday which includes a five-mile march, often in hot sunshine, and a picnic in a field at Scarva, without as much as sipping a bottle of Guinness is asking too much of human credulity. The pubs never do better business than on the night of July 11th, and whatever the temperance Lodges may claim, the vast bulk of the rank and file Orangemen are in the pubs, knocking it back, while their wives prepare their gear for the march. And as they get drunk, they start to sing. They are great singers, the Orangemen, and they have plenty of stirring traditional songs, many of them, ironically enough, sung to ancient Republican airs. Some of them are highly humorous, too. Here is a typical sample:

THE OULD ORANGE FLUTE

In the County Tyrone, near the town of Dungannon,
Where many a ruction myself had a hand in,
Bob Williamson lived, a weaver by trade,
And all of us thought him a stout Orange blade.
On the Twelfth of July, as it yearly did come,
Bob played on his flute to the sound of the drum.
You may talk of your harp, your piano or lute,
But there's no sound on earth like the ould Orange flute.

But this treacherous scoundrel he took us all in,
For he married a Papish named Bridget McGinn,
Turned Papish himself, and forsook the ould cause
That gave us our freedom, religion and laws.
Now the boys of the townland put some stir upon it,
And Bob had to fly to the region of Connaught;

He fled with his wife and his fixings to boot,
And along with the rest went the ould Orange flute.

At the Chapel on Sundays, to atone for past deeds,
Bob said Paters and Aves and counted his beads,
Till after some time, at the priest's own desire,
He went with his ould flute to play in the choir.
He went with his ould flute to play in the Mass,
But the instrument shivered and sighed, Oh alas!
When he blew it and fingered, it made a great noise,
*But all it would play was 'The Protestant Boys'.**

Bob jumped and he started and got in a flutter,
And threw the ould flute in the Bless'd Holy Water;
He thought that this charm would bring some other sound;
*When he blew it again it played 'Croppies, lie down'.**
And for all he could whistle, and finger, and blow,
To play Papish music he found it No Go,
'Kick the Pope', 'The Boyne Water',* and such it would sound,*
But one Papish squeak in it could not be found.

At a council of priests that was held the next day,
They decided to banish the ould flute away.
For they couldn't knock heresy out of its head,
So they bought Bob another to play in its stead.
Then the ould flute was doomed, and its fate was pathetic,
To be fastened and burned at the stake as heretic;
While the flames roared around it, they heard a strange noise:
'Twas the ould flute still whistling 'The Protestant Boys'.

Other songs beloved of the more militant Orangemen are less amusing and more inflammatory, but during the peaceable years the Orangemen contented themselves with singing songs like 'The Ould Orange Flute', and if there were occasional aggressive outbursts, and the odd brick heaved through the odd Catholic window, the Catholics mostly kept indoors on the night of the 11th and let the Protestants work off their steam by singing and shouting.

* All titles of other well-known Orange ballads.

But even in the most peaceful of the peaceable years there were incidents which an Englishman would find difficult to credit in a part of the United Kingdom. The same *Irish Times* photographer told me that one July 11th, as he was walking down one of the main Belfast streets with a reporter from one of the local papers, a huge bully of a man lurched over towards them and struck him viciously in the chest, cracking a couple of his ribs. His friend, an Ulsterman, turned on the attacker and asked, 'What did you do that for?' The answer: 'Because he smells like a Catholic. And the only reason you didn't get it too was because you smell like a Protestant.'

When the last of the ballads has been sung, and the last pint has been downed, the Orangemen stagger home, threading their way through gangs of children still chanting round the embers of the bonfires, make sure that all is laid out in readiness for the 'walk', and repair to bed.

2

As early as seven o'clock on the morning of July 12th, small groups of Orangemen in full regalia can be seen making their way to the various assembly points all over the city. With their fife and drum bands, brass bands, accordion bands and pipe bands, they form up, with banners and bannerettes carrying the name and number of the Lodge and decorated with portraits, mottoes and symbols. For example, the Protestant Boys L.O.L. (Loyal Orange Lodge) No. 693, is purple with an orange border, and is decorated with formalized sprigs of some herb or plant and carries a painting of King Billy landing at Carrickfergus. The McComb Memorial Total Abstinence L.O.L. has a purple and orange border surrounding a portrait of the Reverend Samuel McComb, founder of Agnes Street Presbyterian Church. Other banners feature churches and castles in Ulster, or scenes from King William's Irish campaign, and of course a great many of the banners, like the Portavogie True Blue L.O.L. No. 552, feature paintings of King William on his white horse. In addition to the Orange Lodges of Ulster, contingents of Orangemen from the Republic, England and

Scotland, notably Liverpool and Glasgow, as well as from Canada and even Australia and New Zealand—who arrange package tours to include the celebrations of the Twelfth—can be seen forming up at assembly points at or near Carlisle Circus, a roundabout at the junction of the Crumlin and Antrim roads.

At the same time, crowds of spectators, many of them wearing Orange favours, or red, white and blue rosettes of one sort or another, begin to gather all along the route of the March. Like the St Patrick's Day procession on Fifth Avenue in New York, the occasion seems to bring out a curious kind of one-upmanship, with the result that you find people vying with one another to show ever more spectacular outward and visible signs of their loyalty. In New York on March 17th you will see men wearing bright green shoes and green bowler hats drinking green beer—obligingly emerald-tinted by patriotic or profit-conscious publicans—and women with bright green hair rinses and green lipstick; in Belfast on July 12th you will see children carrying Union Jacks twice as big as themselves, women wearing overalls made from Union Jacks over their coats, and men wearing hats sprouting up to half a dozen sizable Union Jacks.

It would be a mistake to assume that the vast crowd which assembles to watch the parade is exclusively composed of Protestants; I have met Belfast Catholics who wouldn't dream of missing the March, and who say that whatever its religious significance it is one of the most exciting spectacles in the world.

As ten o'clock approaches, the first contingents of the procession begin to converge on Carlisle Circus. Led by their banners—some of them so big that they have to be held by four men, with others holding 'stays' to prevent them from blowing down in the wind—the Orangemen, preceded by their officials, as often as not in limousines, walk four, five and sometimes six abreast, with a band every hundred yards or so. Nor is it an exclusively male event; there are girls' pipe bands, and girls' accordion bands and even American-style drum majorettes wearing boots and mini-skirts (and they wore the mini-skirts at a time when the ordinary Belfast girls' skirts came well down below the knees; nowadays the skirts and kilts of the drum majorettes are no briefer than those of many of the girls among the spectators, for Belfast, unlike London, has stuck firmly to the mini). The Ladies' Orange Lodges also march on the Twelfth, behind their own banners, and wearing their collarettes but over ordinary clothes; unlike the Orangemen, the Orangewomen do not adopt any 'uniform' for the parade.

From Carlisle Circus, the parade marches down Clifton Street, Donegall Street, into Royal Avenue, around the City Hall, on through the centre of the city and then out along the Lisburn Road to Finaghy Field, on the far side of Balmoral. It takes nearly four hours to pass any given point, and there are fresh banners and bands every few hundred yards. In the centre of the city, where the crowds always tend to slow up the march, the air is thick with the flapping of banners and the beat of the marching feet and the boom of bass drums and the rattle of kettledrums and the curious, menacing cannonade from the Lambegs. In recent years, the Lambeg can be heard only in country areas; it was felt that the gigantic instrument, which as often as not requires a lad to march ahead of the drummer to help him bear its great weight, was slowing up the Belfast march too much. But even without the Lambegs, the din is considerable and in a primitive way, it is generally agreed, curiously exciting.

The march on the Twelfth is completely taken for granted by the Ulsterman as something which has gone on, unchanged and unchanging, since the beginning of time. He knows that the festivities have their origin in the commemoration of the victory of King William at the Boyne, but somehow instinctively feels that the real origins of the Orange Order are lost in the mists of antiquity. There is a story which aptly illustrates this point. An Englishman who found himself in Belfast one July 12th was standing at a barrier among the crowds, absolutely mystified at what he saw going on before his eyes. He turned to a small man wearing a mackintosh beside him who was watching the procession with rapt attention. 'Excuse me,' he said, 'could you tell me what's going on?' The man in the mackintosh, without taking his eyes off the parade for an instant, and speaking out of the corner of his mouth, snapped: 'It's the Twelfth.' 'I beg your pardon,' the Englishman said. 'I don't think I heard what you said.' 'I said it's the Twelfth,' the man in the mackintosh replied, again without taking his eyes off the procession. The Englishman was silent for a moment, and then made yet another attempt. 'I'm afraid you must think me very stupid, but I'm afraid I still don't understand.' This time the little man in the mackintosh turned and faced the Englishman squarely. Enunciating very clearly, he said: 'It's the Twelfth of July.' 'Oh, I know that's the date all right,' the Englishman said. 'But what's all this about?' With a gesture of utter disgust, the Ulsterman dismissed him: 'Ach away home and read your Bible, man,' he said.

3

If that Englishman had persisted in his inquiries he would have discovered that what it was all about is simply this: the Orangemen 'walk' on the 12th of July every year as a demonstration of their loyalty to the Crown and the 'constitution', to show their determination to maintain the Protestant Ascendancy and to commemorate the victory of King William over King James's Catholic forces at the Boyne. The Orange Order is a semi-secret society—that is to say, a society with secrets as opposed to the sort of sworn secret society from which it developed—organized in a system of Lodges more or less on the Masonic pattern. No more—and yet a lot more, as I hope to demonstrate.

But we left the march on its way out to Finaghy Field. For years—certainly ever since the State of Northern Ireland was set up in 1921—it has been assumed (and faithfully reported, year after year, in the newspapers, on the radio and latterly on television) that between 40,000 and 50,000 Orangemen take part in the annual parade through Belfast to Finaghy Field. Last year (1971) the BBC decided to make a systematic count, employing students of Queen's University working at various check points along the route and throughout the province. The result: a total of 12,200 Orangemen and 2,889 bandsmen (and women) in Belfast, and in the province as a whole, a total of 46,000 Orangemen and 17,000 bandsmen. So 40,000 to 50,000 looks like a more realistic figure for the whole province than for Belfast city, and since the procession has always taken roughly the same length of time to pass a given point (at a point near the beginning of the march from 10.00 a.m. until about 1.30 p.m.) it can be assumed that the BBC's 1971 figures would hold good for most of the years since the foundation of the state.

Finaghy Field has no significance in itself; it is simply a convenient place to which to march, bought or rented, I was reliably assured, from the Catholic Bishop of Down and Connor. I could not find anyone who would confirm or deny this, but it seems not unlikely; it is also said that the Ancient Order of Hibernians (a Catholic association which holds its own parades and processions) frequently lend their banner poles to the Orange Order, on condition that if they are repainted in Orange colours the Orangemen will repaint them again, after the procession, in their original colours. Before they walked to Finaghy, the Orangemen used to walk to Craigavon (the estate of Lord Craigavon, formerly Sir James Craig, one of the founders of the state of Northern Ireland) which is in roughly the same direction but a bit further out; and recently the Order purchased a new field at Shaw's Bridge, on the Lagan, to which future Orange processions will march.

On arrival at Finaghy Field, the Orangemen break up and 'fall out'. They are joined by their wives and families who arrive in cars and charabancs, with picnic baskets, and the whole affair begins to take on the flavour of a folk festival. There are stalls selling ice-cream and other refreshments, and a platform has been erected at the end of the field for those who wish to address their fellow-Orangemen. The proceedings open with a prayer and a few formal speeches, after which the platform is taken by a wide variety of speakers.

'It's all very disorganized,' a photographer told me. 'It seemed to me to be an open forum where anybody could make a speech. Mostly the speeches I heard were diatribes against Fenians, R.C.s and Republicans.' He was talking about some years back; Orangemen say that in latter years it has been very much more organized. Although rabble-rousing speeches of the vintage Paisley type, full of references to the Roman Church as the Scarlet Woman, the harlot prowling for saints, are a lot less common now than they used to be, a prominent Orangeman admitted to me that they could still fairly be described as sectarian and anti-Catholic. 'The plain truth of the matter,' he said, 'and it's not realized either in England or in the Republic, is that the ignorant Orangeman still has a deadly fear of the Church of Rome. Even today at this very minute (we were talking in May 1972), many Orangemen are convinced that there is a committee sitting in Dublin which consists of Jack Lynch, the Papal Nuncio and representatives of both wings of the IRA, all plotting together to overthrow the Protestants and recapture Ulster on behalf of the Church of Rome.'

The same photographer—not the *Irish Times* one—assured me that one year at Finaghy Field he saw a sideshow which consisted of a large plastic effigy of the Pope, and Orangemen were paying a shilling a go for the privilege of having a kick at the Pope in effigy. When you ask the Orange officials about this kind of thing you become aware of a curious form of double-think which is part of their make-up of which perhaps they are not even themselves aware. On this, a very prominent Orangeman replied: 'Well, if that's true, and I must say I've never seen anything like it, but if it is true, isn't it better that a few of the Orange roughnecks should get a bit of the sectarian violence out of their systems by kicking an old effigy? It doesn't do anybody any real harm and isn't it far better than kicking live Papishes down the Falls Road?' Which is true enough, though it is begging the question; for if the sectarian bitterness were not kept alive by men such as the speaker, from various economic, social and political motives, the Orange roughnecks would not want to kick an effigy of the Pope, much less a live fellow-Christian.

Again a story to illustrate the sectarian hatred. A man walking home through the streets of Belfast on July 11th saw a small boy in the gutter, playing with horse dung. 'What are you doing?' he asked the little boy. 'I'm making a priest,' the child replied. 'Why don't you make a bishop while you're at it?' the man asked. 'I haven't enough shit here to make a bishop,' the child replied.

What else goes on at Finaghy Field? The men eat sandwiches and drink . . . well, here again, the accounts vary widely. I have been assured by temperance-orientated Orangemen that they have never seen a single bottle of intoxicating liquor at the field. I have heard other stories of camp-followers supplying the marching men with open bottles of Guinness for consumption on the hoof, so to speak, and I have been assured that more bottles of Guinness are drunk at Finaghy Field on the average Twelfth than in all the pubs in Belfast on any ordinary Saturday night. They sit in the sun, they eat their sandwiches, they applaud the speeches, and they listen to the bands; they take off their jackets and roll up their shirt-sleeves if the weather is warm; but the bowler stays put, and so does the collarette.

In the cool of the evening, the Orangemen form up and march back into Belfast, not in one big, formal procession but with each Lodge or Preceptory making its own way back to its headquarters, where they break up and, according to most sources, repair to the pubs and continue drinking. I believe this to be in general true, because whatever else about them the Ulster Orangemen are very human. Above all, they are Irish. The Irish in the South, convinced that the Orangeman's extravagant loyalty to the Crown indicates that he is really some strange hybrid species of Englishman or Scotsman, have never appreciated this simple fact: that the Orangeman loves the soil and scenery, the flora and fauna, the folk-lore and the folk songs of Ireland every bit as fervently as the Southern Republican does, and doesn't see anything incompatible in this. Nor, in a sense is there; the Scotsman can love Scotland without being disloyal to the Crown and, indeed, before the 19th century, when the whole concept of Irish Nationalism developed, generations of Irishmen saw nothing incompatible in a love of Ireland coupled with loyalty to the Crown. Even Butt, Parnell and Redmond would have been more than satisfied with some form of Home Rule under the Crown.

Four surprises await the Irish Republican who ventures north of the Border for the first time. He finds the scenery, outside the city of Belfast, every bit as beautiful as the scenery in the South, particularly, as in the South, around the coast line. He finds the Ulsterman every bit as keen on his pint as he himself is, and he finds the conversation in the pubs—'the crack', as it is called—just as entertaining. And he finds the Ulsterman warm, friendly and hospitable—every bit as hospitable as the 'true' Irishman from the Republic.

To emphasize this point, a number of Catholics who have reported and photographed the celebrations of the Twelfth for various papers have assured me that although they were aware of the sectarian feeling behind the whole ceremony they did not find it in any way objectionable and were treated with the greatest of courtesy. A Southern Irish Catholic reporter described it as a 'folk festival, a day out, which was simply great fun'. The *Irish Times* photographer said he was taken round the field and introduced to various Orange dignitaries as 'the only Papish in a field with fifty thousand Orangemen—there's a brave man for you'.

4

July 12th is the Orangeman's Day; on July 13th at Scarva, near Loughbrickland, County Down, the Blackmen have their day. That is a statement which requires immediate elucidation. Within the Orange Order, various degrees have developed over the years. There are the Purple Marksmen, with whom I shall deal later, and the Black Preceptories, or the Blackmen, as they are commonly called; their official title is the Imperial Grand Black Chapter of the British Commonwealth. To call the Black Institution the élite of the Orange Order is a common error; it is a separate, though not superior, institution, *within* the Orange Order in the sense that the Blackmen usually meet in Orange Halls, though on different nights, and in the sense that you cannot become a member of the Black Chapter without first being an Orangeman. I shall go into the delicate relationship between the two institutions and the various degrees within the institutions in more detail later; at this stage it is perhaps enough to say that between fifty and sixty per cent of the 100,000 members of the Orange Order in Ireland are also in the Black. And since the closing years of the last century the Blackmen have taken over the Sham Fight at Scarva on July 13th as one of their days. The date, incidentally, has no significance for the Orange Order or for the Blacks, 'apart from its convenience in the fact that it immediately follows the Twelfth', I was informed. 'Convenience from what point of view?' I asked. My informant—an Orangeman who is also prominent in the Black Chapter—replied: 'Well, in the streets of Belfast there's a saying that on the Twelfth the Orangemen goes out and kills the Papishes and on the Thirteenth the Blacks ates them.' He was joking, of course; but I don't suppose you would find the joke all that funny if you lived in the Falls Road or the Ardoyne and had recently had your house burnt down in a sectarian riot.

If the date has no significance for the Orangemen, the place has; for here, in the grounds of Scarvagh House, is an old oak tree under which King Billy is supposed to have camped for a couple of nights on his way from Carrickfergus to the Boyne.

But the sham fight which takes place at Scarva every year ante-dates the foundation of the Orange Order and stems from a faction fight which took place between Protestant and Catholic gangs some years earlier. (The Rev Dr M. W. Dewar, one of the official historians of the Orange Order, puts it at 1672, eighteen years before the Battle of the Boyne; Aiken McClellan of the Ulster Folk Museum believes it was a fight between Protestants celebrating the victory of the Boyne about a year after the Boyne battle and Catholics who attacked them.) In any event, the Protestants were the victors, and the Sham Fight is held every year in commemoration of this victory.

What happens at Scarva? Busloads of Blackmen and their ladies arrive in the village from all the neighbouring townlands and from as far away as Belfast and Derry; Dr Dewar, who was Rector of Scarva between 1955 and 1960, puts the figure at the magical 40,000 to 50,000, but my guess is that it is probably a lot lower. In the village, they get out of the buses and the men march, wearing their regalia—cuffs, collarettes with various emblems to denote which degree within the Black Institution they have reached, and the same dark suits and bowler hats as the Orangemen—down to the demesne, where the dignitaries of the Black Institution take the salute, as it were, open the proceedings with a prayer, and then repair into Scarvagh House for lunch.

In the meantime, the marchers' families and thousands of spectators, both locals and charabanc passengers from Belfast and Derry, have encamped in the field with picnic baskets and flasks of tea and some say Guinness and some say soft drinks only and again I know whom I believe. There are marquees where sit-down luncheons and refreshments may be purchased or are provided, out of Preceptory funds; and side-shows of all sorts. When the march-past is over, they are joined by their menfolk and around 1.30 p.m. the sham battle starts. It consists of two horsemen on each side, one pair representing King James II and Patrick Sarsfield, his chief general, and one representing King Billy and Schomberg, *his* chief general, plus their troops. The leading figures wear makeshift uniforms with a vaguely period flavour, and tricorne hats with enormous cockades of orange and green respectively; the troops are on foot and wear orange or green football jerseys and white slacks. As the field on which the 'battle' takes place is jammed tight with people, it is difficult to know what is going on. It is staged by the local lads, who have no great feeling either for history or pageantry, and a series of confused and confusing manoeuvres representing the four battles of William's Irish campaign—Derry, Enniskillen, Aughrim and the Boyne—are acted out in different parts of the field, with much firing of blank cartridges and a lot of good-humoured horseplay. I have heard that at one period live ammunition was used for the final phase of the battle, which officially ended when King James's green flag was 'all shot away to hell'.

One year when the fight had appeared to be more genuine than sham, and the chief actors had sustained more than one fall apiece from their horses, a visitor inquired, long after the fight, how King James and King Billy were getting along. 'King James is down below in the hottest hob of hell, being poked into the flames at this very moment,' was the reply, 'and King Billy is up in Heaven, where he has every right to be.' 'You mean both of those poor men were killed in that fight?' the visitor asked, horrified. 'Oh, you're talking about the actors? I thought you meant the real ones. The actors are away down the pub having a jar together.' It would be nice to think that this story is true, but I cannot think it is, because there is no pub in the village. Perhaps their horses were still fresh enough for them to ride all the way to Loughbrickland.

5

And throughout the three-day celebration, whether they are drinking Guinness, or whiskey, or Seven-Up, or milk, the Orangemen have a 'loyal' toast which is so flagrantly partisan and sectarian that Englishmen find it hard to believe that grown men anywhere today could utter or even listen to such nonsense.

There are many versions. One runs as follows: 'To the glorious, pious and immortal memory of King William III, who saved us from rogues and roguery, slaves and slavery, knaves and knavery, from brass money and wooden shoes: and whoever denies this toast may he be slammed, crammed and jammed into the muzzle of the great gun of Athlone, and the gun fired into the Pope's belly, and the Pope into the devil's belly, and the devil into hell, and the door locked, and the key forever in an Orangeman's pocket.'

The reference to brass money concerns the debased coinage issued by James II in Dublin. 'Wooden shoes' is a reference to the French, who persecuted the Huguenots and supported King James.

Another version of the toast—this one is issued by the Orange HQ in Belfast, which is situated, again ironically, on the Dublin Road—goes as follows: 'To the Glorious, Pious and Immortal Memory of the great and good King William, who saved us from Popery, Slavery, Priestcraft and knavery, brass money, and wooden shoes, and who allowed a debtor to walk on Sunday, and he who will not drink this toast shall be rammed, crammed and jammed down the Big Gun of Athlone, and shot up against the Rock of Gibraltar, and his bones made into sparbles to make boots for decent Protestants, and a fig for the Bishop of Cork.'

The reference to debtors concerns an edict of King William's allowing those imprisoned for debt to go out on parole every Sunday. The privilege was abused and withdrawn. Sparbles were small wooden nails used by old-fashioned cobblers and the toast ends with 'a fig for the Bishop of Cork' because at the time when this particular version was introduced (1715) the then Protestant Bishop of Cork, Peter Browne, had been preaching against the practice of toasting the dead, which he regarded as akin to the Popish practice of saying Mass for the dead.

The Orange Toast seems to be infinitely variable, though it normally opens in roughly the same way; the difference tends to come towards the tail, and, according to one edition of the *Encyclopaedia Britannica*, usually concluded 'with grotesque or truculent additions according to the orator's taste'. Here are a couple of samples: the version of the toast I quoted first follows the 'key forever in an Orangeman's pocket' phrase with 'and may we never lack a Protestant Boy to kick the arse of a Papist; and here's a fart for the Bishop of Cork.'

Another, much longer, toast is quoted in the Rev H. W. Cleary's *The Orange Society*, published by the Catholic Truth Society in 1899 ('It's written by a Roman Catholic priest,' a leading Orangeman told me, 'but he's not far out on a lot of his facts as to what goes on in the Orange Order') with discreet Victorian gaps: 'The glorious, pious and immortal memory of the great and good King William—not forgetting Oliver Cromwell, who assisted in redeeming us from Popery, slavery, arbitrary power, brass money and wooden shoes. May we never lack a Williamite to kick the . . . of a Jacobite! and a . . . for the Bishop of Cork. And he that won't drink this, whether he be priest, bishop, deacon, bellows-blower, grave-digger or other of the fraternity of the clergy, may a north wind blow him to the south and a west wind to the east! May he have a dark night, a lee shore, a rank storm and a leaky vessel to carry him over the River Styx. May the dog Cerberus make a meal of his r--p, and Pluto a snuff-box of his skull; may the devil jump down his throat with a red-hot harrow, with every pin tear out a gut, and blow him with a clean carcass to hell!'

The same writer appends the following alternative conclusion: 'May he be rammed, crammed and jammed into the great gun of Athlone, and blown on to the hob of Hell, where he'll be kept roasting for all eternity, the devil basting him with melted bishops and his imps pelting him with priests.'

I tackled several leading Orangemen about these savage and bloodthirsty toasts and asked whether in fact they were used today. Again I encountered this curious double-think which is such a feature of the movement. Sitting in his comfortable rectory surrounded by books, and with a civilized cup of coffee in his hand, a clergyman, who also happens to be prominent in the Orange Order, assured me that they were certainly used in some Lodges but 'purely in a jokey sort of way, and to keep up an ancient tradition'. Which again may be true for him, and for the better educated and more liberal-minded members of the Order. But I wonder if the grass-roots rabble of the Order in the Protestant slums regard these toasts in quite the same 'jokey' light; certainly, they can't sound very funny to the Catholics who make up slightly more than one-third of the community in Northern Ireland.

This double-think runs through the whole fabric of the Orange Order from top to bottom. The Laws and Ordinances of the Orange Institution specifically state that every Orangeman should abstain 'from all uncharitable words, actions or sentiments towards his Roman Catholic brethren' yet the very people who rule the Orange Order will admit that nowadays, as in the past, the Lodges are allowed considerable freedom in their interpretation of these laws and ordinances because to impose them too rigidly would be to risk destroying the driving force behind the movement—which is, of course, sectarianism.

The peak of insanity to which Orange double-think can lead is again best illustrated by a very common Ulster story. In a tiny Antrim village, where the population was roughly half Protestant and half Catholic, a member of the Orange Lodge fell ill. Rumour reached the District Master that the Catholic priest had been seen attending the old man's house. He hurried around to the sick man's bedside and questioned him about it.

'I hear tell,' he said, 'that the R.C. priest has been visiting you.' The old man replied: 'That's true. I'll not tell you any lies.' The District Master turned pale. 'You wouldn't be thinking of going over to the other side? And you a loyal Orangeman all your life.' The old man nodded his head. 'That's it,' he said. 'I'm taking instruction. But I'm doing it for the sake of the Order. You see, I've had a wee word with the doctors and they say I'm not long for it. And I thought that as we are pretty finely balanced in the village as it is, if someone has got to go it had better be one of the other sort.'

One final story, almost certainly apocryphal but very apt: in a BEA plane, just about to land, the air hostess makes this announcement over the public address system: 'Good afternoon, ladies and gentlemen, we are just about to land in Belfast. Please extinguish all cigarettes and fasten your safety belts. All clocks and watches should be put back three hundred years.'

* * *

A it stands for Aughrim, where blood flowed on the plain,
B is for Boyne Water, where bones do still remain,
C it is for Culmore, where crossing it we often had our falls,
D I'm sure for all know well, our Maiden Derry's Walls;
Bold E is for Enniskillen, where nobly they did join,
And F is for our Fathers bold, who conquered at the Boyne.

—From *The Orange A.B.C.*,
a traditional Orange ballad.

II

Long Knives . . . and Long Memories

There must be something in the Ulster air that produces formidable fighting men. Long before the province was inhabited by the present mixture of Scots and English Protestant settlers and dispossessed and disillusioned Irish Catholic nationalists—long before the birth of Christ even—it had a reputation for producing fiercely intransigent warriors. And in all the years between, and despite all the political upheavals, it has never changed: from Cuchulain, through Owen Roe O'Neill, to Field-Marshal Sir Henry Wilson, Lord Alexander of Tunis and Viscount Montgomery—and whatever else about them you would have to include both the Rev Ian Paisley and Bernadette Devlin as doughty fighters—there stretches a long, unbroken line of Ulster militants.

Recorded Irish history doesn't begin until the Christian era, but from the legends and epics which have survived, passed down the generations in song and story until they were eventually written down in the early Christian period, we know something of the early rulers of Ireland, the Gaelic Celts, a race from somewhere around the source of the Danube, who defeated the earlier Bronze Age inhabitants of the island with their iron weapons. They were much given to fighting and it is probably no coincidence that the most famous Celtic warrior was Cuchulain (pronounced, very roughly, Coohullan), the Hound of Ulster, who killed his own illegitimate son in a sword fight and died, according to one legend, after spending four days trying to fight the sea.

To start the history of the Orange Order in the mists of Celtic mythology may seem to be going very far back, but the

Irish, north and south of the border alike, are so much prisoners of their own past that it is impossible to understand what has created the mentality of the Orangeman without taking a quick flip, however cursory, through Irish history before the Order came into existence.

It is even, I believe, necessary to go back as far as the Roman occupation of Britain. For I have always held that if the Romans—who knew about Ireland and even did some trading with the Irish—had covered that small stretch of water between Holyhead and Dun Laoghaire and had occupied the island for the four centuries during which they ruled Britain, the Irish Question might never have arisen. Surely four centuries of firm but fair Roman administration—facilitated by a system of long, straight Roman roads—would have made the Irish a far more law-abiding, tractable race of people, accustomed to the whole idea of colonization. However, it didn't happen, though the Romans inadvertently did make another contribution to the Irish Question when, at the very end of their sway in Britain, a young British Roman citizen was captured by a gang of Irish pirates and sold into slavery in Ireland. Patrick escaped to the Continent, became a priest and returned to preach Christianity to the savage Celts among whom he had worked as a slave.* The Celts took avidly to Patrick's Christian message and Ireland soon became an ecclesiastical centre of learning famed throughout the Continent, though the pattern of monastic Christianity—which tended to be autonomous and independent of Rome—did not always meet with the approval of St Peter's successors in the Lateran Palace, yet another factor which contributed something to the Irish Question.

For, although the first Anglo-Norman invasion of Ireland was largely unofficial and characteristically came about as a result of a quarrel between two Irish Kings—the King of Leinster, Dermot MacMurrough, defeated and banished by the High King, went to England to raise an army of Norman auxiliaries to help him recover his kingdom—it was not long before King

* This is according to popular legend. There are authorities who claim that St Patrick never existed and others who claim that he was a combination of two or three different men.

Henry II decided that he had better prevent those Norman auxiliaries from setting up an independent Norman Irish Kingdom of their own by invading the country himself. The Normans—like the British today—were great sticklers for legal formality, and he did not want to invade Ireland without some authority. This he got from the Pope, who had issued a Bull bestowing the island on the British. The Pope in question, Adrian IV, happened to be an Englishman—indeed the only English Pope, Nicholas Breakespear—but he would probably have issued the Bull anyhow as the Vatican felt that Ireland was in need of some correction as the only Christian country which had not taken part in the Crusades, and he also probably felt that strong feudal government would make the Irish Church more likely to toe the Roman line.

Ignoring the Irish High King, Henry parcelled Ireland out between various of his own barons and a few native provincial kings who agreed to pay annual tributes to Britain. This, in a sense, was the beginning of British colonialism as it was to develop through the centuries; a system at least partly designed to enrich England at the expense of the conquered colonies.

The Anglo-Normans settled down happily enough in Ireland and began to adapt themselves to the Irish way of life. This development was viewed with deep suspicion by successive English monarchs, who feared an alliance between the barons and the old Gaelic chieftains and kings. To prevent it, they set up a parliament (which conducted its business in English and French and rigorously excluded the native Irish) and passed a series of laws forbidding the colonists to intermarry with the Irish, or speak Gaelic, or recognize the ancient Irish 'Brehon' laws, or even wear Irish clothes or hair styles. Thus, right from the beginning, the colonists were forced by England into the position of a recognizably 'foreign' ascendancy set amid a hostile population of under-privileged 'natives'.

The Reformation, when it came, emphasized this division and added the element of religious bitterness to the enormous gulf that now existed between the Anglo-Norman landowners and the English merchants and traders who had settled in the ports and principal cities on the one hand, and the 'mere' Irish on the other. One reason, incidentally, why the Reformation failed to alter the religion of the Irish people was the fact that the Tudor officials and churchmen who were sent over to achieve this objective spoke no Gaelic and the Irish spoke no English, and furthermore, most of the schools and monasteries—the only places where the conversion might effectively have been carried out—had been dissolved. Some of the Anglo-Normans or 'Old English' retained their Catholic faith, of course, and played a prominent part in some of the subsequent risings.

When a simple order in the name of the boy king Edward VI made the celebration of Mass illegal, it was inevitable that there would be religious clashes in Ireland. It was also inevitable that Ireland's rebels would look for help among England's Catholic enemies on the Continent.

One of the first clashes came in 1579 when a Munster Earl called Fitzgerald went to the Continent, raised a mixed force of Italians and Spaniards financed by the Pope and the King of Spain, and accompanied by priests who preached rebellion as a sacred duty returned to Kerry and engaged the British forces briefly and unsuccessfully. It had no great significance except that Fitzgerald's rebellion was followed by savage reprisals which set the pattern for generations to come. These included the destruction of most of the food in Munster and the confiscation of vast tracts of Catholic-held land which was handed over to loyal English subjects. In many cases the English did not work the land themselves, but allowed the Irish to creep back illegally and pay high rents for the privilege of farming their own land as tenants to absentee landlords. But it established the policy of land confiscation as a punishment for rebellion.

Curiously, this policy was not Elizabeth's innovation; it had been started by her Catholic half-sister, Mary, who tried to extend the peaceful 'Pale'—the area around Dublin largely occupied by English and Anglo-Normans—westwards into Leix and Offaly by banishing two rebellious tribes and replacing them with docile English settlers.

So far, I have not mentioned Ulster. Up to this time, Ulster had remained the most consistently Celtic part of the country.

Here the ancient Brehon laws still held sway, and although there had been settlements of Scots and English emigrants along the coast of Antrim and Down, and Monaghan had been broken up and planted in the 1590s, the remainder of the province was Gaelic-speaking and fiercely Celtic in outlook. It was here that the last stand of the ancient Gaelic aristocracy against the British invaders took place. Hugh O'Neill, Earl of Tyrone—an ancestor of Captain Terence O'Neill (now Lord O'Neill) as well as a descendant of the most famous of all the High Kings of ancient Ireland, Niall of the Nine Hostages—had been brought up in England at Elizabeth's court and knew the English inside-out; he held the English title of Earl of Tyrone but called himself The O'Neill, in the old Celtic style. His ally was Hugh O'Donnell, Earl of Tyrconnell; between them they controlled most of Ulster. In 1587, Hugh O'Donnell was kidnapped and imprisoned in Dublin as a hostage. He escaped, raised an army and went to war with Elizabeth's troops. O'Neill joined him and for nine years they held out; their revolt spread to the Gaelic chiefs all over the country. They brought in a force of Spaniards to help them, but in the end were defeated by superior arms and organization. O'Donnell immediately fled to Spain. O'Neill and O'Donnell's successors were pardoned and confirmed in their estates, but they never really settled down after the insurrection and felt certain that there would be reprisals sooner or later. In 1607 they chartered a ship and left for the Continent, taking with them into exile ninety-eight other Ulster Celtic Catholic chieftains.

This 'Flight of the Earls', as it was called, was held to be treason and opened the way for yet another plantation, the one which has caused and is causing more trouble than all of the others: the Plantation of Ulster. Throughout the province, the Irish were thrown out of their lands, and the whole area repopulated with Lowland Scots Presbyterians, English Protestants and English soldiers who were owed large arrears of pay. Derry (then capital of a county known as County Coleraine) was sold to a consortium of City of London Guilds, which explains why the name was changed to Londonderry; the Guilds were permitted to 'develop' the territory and take the profits, though a share in these profits had to go to the English government, and in return they undertook to fortify the towns and protect them against the native Irish.

What to do with the native Irish of Ulster was a problem—though less than might be imagined, for during the nine years of the O'Neill uprising, partly as a result of the Irish scorched earth policy and partly as a result of English reprisals, many of the towns and fortresses and even some of the houses in Ulster had been destroyed and the province was very largely a wilderness. Sheer starvation had driven most of the population elsewhere in search of food—for the moment. There is a widely-held theory that some never settled anywhere again and that it is from them that many of the tinkers, who still roam the Irish roads and are often confused with Gypsies, are descended.

One section of the native population of Ulster who were to cause a genuine problem were the swordsmen. Under the old Celtic system every chieftain had a number of armed men in his entourage; indeed it was by the number of swordsmen in his private army that his status was judged. These were the men who raided for cattle or hamstrung the cattle of their chieftain's enemies. They had formed the basis of O'Neill's armies. And when the Earls fled to the continent, leaving them behind, they tended to huddle around such of the minor dispossessed, disgruntled chieftains as remained in the province. These private armies are important because the tradition of private armies in Ireland never died; and in fact the Orange Order grew out of just one such private army.

2

By 1641 the province of Ulster had largely recovered. The Ulster planters, whatever else may be said about them, were sober and industrious workers and soon set about rebuilding the forts and blockhouses, draining and cultivating the land, felling timber for export—which in turn enabled the forest lands to be used for farming—and developing the towns.

Irish Catholics who had been expelled from their lands now began to seep back to work as labourers or in some cases to become small tenant farmers. Another generation had grown up since the Plantation; but they were a generation who had been taught at their mothers' knees that it would be their duty, one day, to fight to get their parents' lands back from the foreign invader.

In Dublin a plot was hatched to seize Dublin Castle, capture the arms stored there, and simultaneously stage an uprising of the Catholic chieftains and peasants in Ulster which would enable them to take back their old holdings, and which would eventually spread, they hoped, throughout the rest of the island. Through drunken incompetence, the plot leaked out, the ring-leaders were arrested and the rebellion was called off. Nobody, however, told the conspirators in Ulster anything of this. Consequently, soon after dawn on the appointed day, gangs of armed Irishmen descended on the homes of planters and bundled them out into the fierce October weather stripped of everything they possessed, including, in many cases, their clothes.

The affair is still remembered in Ulster as the 'massacre of the Protestants' and since a great deal of the Orangeman's almost paranoic hatred and fear of Catholics stems from the events of that winter it is worth examining what happened. There is no doubt whatever that terrible atrocities were committed in the wake of those first evictions. Neither man, woman nor child was spared; everything English was destroyed—houses were burnt down, horses hamstrung, cattle slaughtered, even the dogs of the English settlers were disembowelled.

The point that is missed by the Orangemen is that although it is true that the Irish who descended on the English and Scots settlers in 1641 and slaughtered them in thousands were all Catholics, the reason they did so was not because they were Catholics and the settlers were Protestants but purely because they wanted their lands back.

When Owen Roe O'Neill—a descendant of Hugh O'Neill, in exile on the Continent—heard of the rising, he arrived in Ireland from the Netherlands with two hundred trained officers and three boat-loads of arms and ammunition. Immediately, he tried to organize the marauding gangs of dispossessed Ulster farmers and swordsmen into an army, and the 'massacre of the Protestants' turned into a rebellion which spread throughout the whole island, dragged on for six years and was further complicated by the outbreak of the Civil War in England. Some of the Catholic gentry threw in their lot with the rebels and formed an all-Catholic Confederate Parliament which attempted to run the country from Kilkenny.

But to the Ulster Protestant settlers the years from 1641 to 1649 were years of peasant Irish Catholic terrorism. They were acutely conscious of the fact that if and when they got their lands back they would forever afterwards have to hold them in a state of siege against the Catholic terrorists all around them. By 1641, of the three and a half million acres of Ulster about three million belonged, by English law, to the settlers, although they numbered only about half a million in a province which also contained about three million dispossessed Irish-speaking Catholics. This fact—and the assumption that the massacres of the winter of 1641 and the years immediately following had been a deliberate Catholic plot to massacre them purely because they were Protestants, with the blessing of the Pope of Rome and the Bishops and priests of the Catholic Church, and that unless they were rigorously suppressed and kept down the Catholics would repeat the process at the next opportunity—produced in the Ulster Protestants what has often been described as a 'siege' mentality.

3

As soon as he had disposed of Charles II, Cromwell came to Ireland with an expert army and rapidly pacified the country, taking an undisguised pleasure in the slaughter of what he regarded as barbarous Papish wretches, no better than animals; atrocity stories about the 1641 massacres of the Protestants had been published both in London and in Dublin and there is no doubt that many of Cromwell's soldiers believed that they were punishing the perpetrators of those terrible crimes—although in some cases they were merely finishing off England's Civil War by mopping up isolated enclaves of Royalist supporters, some of them even English Protestants.

The entire garrison of Drogheda was slaughtered, other towns reduced with comparable cruelty, and there were about 200 executions, but most of the 30,000 Irish soldiers who surrendered were allowed to go into exile on the Continent. And there were still further confiscations of land to repay a loan floated in the Westminster Parliament to fight the war in Ireland and to pay arrears owing to many of the soldiers from the Civil Wars in England. An Act of Settlement decreed that every person in Ireland would lose his property unless he could prove that he had been constantly faithful to the English Parliamentary cause; the basic idea behind this was to clear the Catholics out of the other three provinces and herd them all in the wild and infertile fields of Connaught, to the west of the Shannon river. 'To Hell or Connaught' was the choice offered to Catholic landowners, and the result was that less than half the arable land of Ireland now remained in Catholic Irish hands. Catholics were also expelled from the towns and cities.

For a time after the Catholic King James II came to the throne of England it looked as if the Irish Catholics might get some of their lands back, but James himself did not last long enough to achieve anything permanent. After the bloodless revolution of 1688, when James fled first to France and thence to Ireland with a French Army, he did summon a Parliament which repealed the Act of Settlement. This would have had the effect of taking from the Protestant settlers all the lands given to them during the Cromwellian confiscation, but in the event it never became law.

Irish Catholics from three of the provinces flocked to King James's support. The one province which abstained, was, of course, Ulster, which remained as intransigently anti-Catholic as ever. Some time earlier, towards the end of 1688, rumours of another uprising of the Catholics had begun to fly around the province and the settlers flocked to the fortified cities where they proclaimed William and Mary King and Queen. They had no army to put into the field against King James, but they did control a number of strategic points where William's army might land. They held Enniskillen and Londonderry, the chief port of the province since Belfast in those days was no more than a village.

Tyrconnell, the Viceroy of Ireland—and the first Catholic one since the Reformation—had already sent some of King James's troops north to prevent any movement in sympathy with the Protestant bloodless revolution which had brought William and Mary to the throne of England. In August 1689 he withdrew a Protestant regiment from Londonderry and ordered Lord Antrim, with a Catholic regiment, to replace it. As Antrim's troops were approaching the city walls, along the east side of the Foyle Estuary, a group of apprentice boys seized the keys of the city and locked the Ferry Quay Gate in the face of the Catholic troops. This event, which has been celebrated by a march of the 'Apprentice Boys' every August since then, is really the beginning of the story of Orangeism in Ireland.

In *The Battle of the Bogside*, Russell Stetler writes: 'For the Protestant population of Northern Ireland, Derry is an ancient symbol of an embattled people, besieged by Papists and threatened by treason from within . . . in 1689 an army under the Catholic King James marched across Ulster, and large numbers of Protestants fled before them. The Orangemen of today quote approvingly the description by Lord Macaulay:

> All Lisburn fled to Antrim; and, as the foe drew nearer, all Lisburn and Antrim together came pouring into Londonderry. Thirty thousand Protestants, of both sexes and every age, were crowded behind the bulwarks of the City of Refuge. There, at length, on the verge of the ocean, hunted to the last asylum, and baited into a mood in which men may be destroyed but will not be easily subjugated, the imperial race turned desperately to bay.*

'The governor of the city, Lundy, was literally loyal to the Crown. Since the Catholic King James was the legitimate ruler, he intended to deliver the city to him. Ever since, his name has been a synonym for traitor, and Protestants do not hesitate to apply it to any politician whose "loyalty" to Britain fails to

* They would be a lot less enamoured of Macaulay's reference to their beloved King Billy as an 'asthmatic skeleton'.

conform to more sectarian interpretations. Derry city was "saved" from the traitor Lundy by thirteen young apprentice boys who closed its gates when the Catholic armies were first sighted on the horizon. The slogan of the ensuing siege, "No Surrender", has been the battle-cry of Ulster Protestants ever since. Revived in the twentieth century during the Ulster crisis, it continues to evoke great emotion today, scrawled on walls throughout the province. It recalls confrontation, heroism and victory.'

The troops who had been locked outside Derry's walls threw a boom across the River Foyle to prevent relief from reaching the city by sea, and settled down to starve the garrison and inhabitants into surrender. The townsfolk suffered terribly from hunger and thirst but held out for 105 days until a naval frigate and three provision ships, which had been standing off in full view of the starving garrison for over three weeks, burst through the boom and lifted the siege. In *Orangeism: A New Historical Appreciation*, a grisly extract from the diary of the Rev George Walker, one of the Defenders of Derry, indicates how desperate things were by listing the inflated prices quoted (on July 27, 1689) for the only food on sale: 'A quarter of a dog fattened by eating the bodies of the slain Irish, 5*s* 6*d*; A dog's head, 2*s* 6*d*; a cat, 4*s* 6*d*; a rat, 1/–; a mouse 6*d*.' And 6*d* in 1689 would be roughly equivalent to 22½p today.

To quote Macaulay again, although 'five generations have since passed away . . . still the Wall of Londonderry is to the Protestants of Ulster what the Trophy of Marathon was to the Greeks'. Those lines were written over a century ago. Another five generations have since passed and the Apprentice Boys still march around what remain of the Walls of Londonderry every August 12th, the anniversary of the lifting of the Siege.

4

The four battles commemorated in so many of the Orange ballads and songs are Derry, Enniskillen, Aughrim and the Boyne—Aughrim, County Galway, that is, not the much better-known Aughrim in County Wicklow.

Enniskillen was, however, not so much a battle as a whole series of guerrilla skirmishes fought throughout the counties of Fermanagh, Monaghan, Cavan and Sligo. Enniskillen controls the lakes which separate Connaught and Ulster, and the commander, Gustavus Hamilton, was determined to permit 'no Popish garrison' to cross the water. He declared: 'We stand upon our guard and do resolve by the blessing of God rather to meet our danger than expect it.' In other words, he had decided on a strategy of defence through attack.

One of these attacks, carried out by his successor, Colonel Wolseley, won a resounding victory over an army of Jacobite troops under a commander called McCarthy in the course of which many of McCarthy's men were driven into Lough Erne and drowned. The Ulstermen have as long memories as the Southern Irish; Lord Cushendun recalls, in a typically dry Northern story, how some years ago a Fermanagh man remarked to him that there were plenty of men at the bottom of Lough Erne 'and plenty of room for more'.

In August 1689 a Williamite army under Schomberg landed at Bangor Bay, established a base at Dundalk, and spent much of the winter in sporadic fighting in County Down and around Belfast Lough.

In June 1690, King Billy himself landed at Carrickfergus on the Antrim side of Belfast Lough with troops from England and the Netherlands and a few Danes.

To quote *Orangeism: A New Historical Appreciation* again: 'The two heroes, the aged Huguenot and the Dutchman in his prime, met by Whitehouse on the shore . . . So to Belfast, where began a long "affair of the heart" between its citizens and the Dutch Prince-President, whose homely virtues of thrift, courage and sincerity of purpose were so similar to their own. The Dutchman and the Ulsterman had, and have, more than a little in common.'

Since the sham battle of Scarva is another important celebration in the Orange hagiography, it is worth mentioning in passing that on King Billy's route southwards one assembly place was Loughbrickland in County Down. It would seem that the wings of the army were extended from Loughbrickland to

Poyntz Pass in County Armagh, which would leave the centre at roughly the site of the present Scarvagh Demesne. Scarva Presbyterian Church dates from 1756 and the Parish Church from 1850, so clearly Loughbrickland included much of what is now the site of the Scarva sham battle. The annual celebration of July 13th 'takes place close to the Spanish chestnut beneath which that Williamite "White Horse" is believed to have been tethered. [The horse was actually black or possibly bay, but is always depicted as white on Orange banners and emblems, because the emblem of the Protestant House of Hanover was a White Horse]. The Black Banners and the Royal Black Preceptories filing up Barrack Hill at Scarva to the Demesne are following in the footsteps of those regiments of Huguenots and Hollanders, Danes and Germans, Scots and English, as well as the veterans of Derry and Enniskillen, who encamped beneath the trees that midsummer.'

A couple of days later they moved southwards through Newry and on the last day of June reached the northern slopes above the River Boyne. On the south bank, James with some 30,000 men, most of them French under Lauzun but including some Irish under Patrick Sarsfield, waited to meet him. William had about 40,000 troops. On the eve of the battle William was shot in the right shoulder as he reconnoitred the position with his staff. 'This did not prevent the intrepid invalid from riding around his entire army,' writes the Rev M. W. Dewar. 'We have a mental picture of him, in the torchlight, wearing the Star and Garter, as he went on the rounds of the Camp before dawn on the fateful First of July, like another Henry V before Agincourt. At no time did he forget to say his prayers or to find time to write to Queen Mary, whom he had committed to the care of his Chaplain, Dr Gilbert Burnet. It was not easy for him to wage war against his wife's father and his own uncle. But destiny and duty had called him to this hour and place.' (In point of fact, King William was never happier than when fighting a battle and throughout their married life his wife had the greatest difficulty in trying to tempt him home from various battle-fronts.)

Between nine and ten o'clock on the morning of July 1st (old style) the Battle of the Boyne began. To the strains of Lilliburlero, with its insulting lyrics,* the Dutch Blue Guards, the men of Derry and Enniskillen, the Huguenots, the British and the Danes forded the Boyne. King James watched the action from the church tower at Donore, but his son-in-law, King Billy, was in the saddle, according to some accounts of the battle, for seventeen hours. With Schomberg's son holding the bridge at Slane, and Schomberg himself surrounded and cut down by French and Irish cavalry, King Billy bore the brunt of the fray. The Jacobite Army was driven from its position with about 1,500 casualties, while King Billy lost only about 600 of his men. Sarsfield fought a rearguard action and might have regrouped to fight another day, but James fled, carrying the news of his own defeat to Dublin and arriving there before his own retreating troops. On July 6th, King Billy entered Dublin, and gave thanks in Christ Church Cathedral. His third and greatest Orange victory had been won: only the west of Ireland remained to be subdued.

James had already fled to France where he tried unsuccessfully to persuade Louis XIV to give him another French Army to win back his kingdom. The Irish Jacobite army fell back on Limerick and relieved Athlone which was under siege. The French-led section of the Jacobite Army withdrew to Galway

* Recently Robert Graves, the poet and a member of an Irish Protestant family from County Meath, protested in a letter to *The Times* at the use of this tune to introduce the BBC's Overseas News. The lyrics as he recalled them sung by his father, ran as follows:

There was an old prophecy found in a bog,
Lilliburlero, bullen a la,
That we should be ruled by an Ass and a Dog,
Lilliburlero bullen a la.

And now is that prophecy clean come to pass,
Lilliburlero bullen a la.
For Talbot's the Dog and James is the Ass,
Lilliburlero, bullen a la.

He added: 'Lilliburlero had been whistled and sung in 1686 by Protestant Ulstermen when the Catholic King James II nominated General Talbot as Lord Lieutenant of Ireland. . . . Both Lilliburlero and Bullen a la had been used by the Loyalists as passwords during their struggle.'

and King Billy attacked Limerick. After a prolonged siege and a series of battles in Athlone, Galway and Aughrim—William himself having returned to England after the first siege of Limerick—Sarsfield decided to negotiate for peace when the Protestant forces under Ginkel again laid siege to Limerick. Cork and Kinsale had already capitulated to Marlborough, ancestor of Winston Churchill and the future victor at Blenheim.

The last stand of the Irish Catholic Army took place at the tiny village of Aughrim, near Ballinasloe, County Galway; 20,000 of them under a French General, St Ruth, were routed by a similar number of Dutch, Huguenots and Ulstermen from Derry and Enniskillen.

The Treaty of Limerick, signed on Thomond Bridge in August 1691, allowed those Irish soldiers who wished to enter the French service a pardon and a free passage to France. Sarsfield also asked for full toleration for Catholics and the restoration of their confiscated estates. Ginkel's assurance of 'such privileges as are consistent with the laws of Ireland, or as they did enjoy in the reign of Charles II' was framed in terms so vague as to be quite worthless and was in any event completely ignored.

With a Protestant King and Queen safely on the English throne, and the best and bravest of Ireland's Catholic soldiers leaving to fight in France, the Ulster Protestants began to breathe more freely; for the moment at any rate, the Orange was in the ascendancy, and they were determined to keep it that way.

* * *

Now Armagh County still hold dear,
Grand secrets there were found . . .
Old Erin's shore we'll still adore,
And that grand spot you know,
Where our true Order first saw light,
One hundred years ago.

—from a ballad written by an anonymous member of Loyal Lodge No. 124, to celebrate the centenary of the Battle of Diamond

III

United Ireland—a Contradiction in Terms

After the Treaty of Limerick, when the Catholic army left to serve in France, the population of Ireland as a whole was between three and four million, three quarters of them Irish Catholics and the remainder English, Scots or old Anglo-Norman, and mostly of mixed Protestant faiths, the latter confined very largely to two areas, the Pale around Dublin, and Ulster; there were, of course, English landlords scattered all over the country, most of whom spent a great deal of their time in England.

With their army in exile, the Irish Catholics no longer had any military power. The Irish Parliament—which was at this period, in effect, subordinate to the Parliament at Westminster and obliged to accept its rulings—now set about trying to ensure that they would never be able to achieve any political or economic power either. This was done by passing a whole series of Penal laws which virtually removed all their civil rights as citizens. They could not vote, nor hold civil or military posts or become lawyers or teachers or stand for Parliament. And although they were not and could not be strictly enforced, the Penal Laws had one important side effect; since the ablest of the Catholics emigrated, and those who remained were prevented by the laws from playing an active part in the life of the community, such leadership as there was fell into the hands of the clergy. This is important in relation to the history of the Orange Order because when the next rebellion broke out nearly a century later, some of the rebel brigades were led by priests, a circumstance which confirmed the Orangemen in the belief they already held that Rome was behind all attempts to overthrow the establishment. In fact, nothing could be further from the truth; throughout history and throughout the world, Rome has always been on the side of the establishment and firmly against rebellion, revolution and *coups d'état*; but you would be hard put to convince any Orangeman on that point. Nor could you convince an Orangeman that the Pope supported King Billy and not James at the time of the battle of the Boyne, because James was an ally of Louis XIV of France, who was becoming altogether too powerful for the Pope's liking.

Irish agriculture was in a deplorable state. Further confiscations had left only about one-eighth of the arable land in Irish hands and the Penal Laws required those Catholics who did own land to subdivide it among all their sons in ever-diminishing and increasingly uneconomic plots. Agricultural crime was rife; armed brigands with names like the Tories, the Rapparees and Whiteboys roamed the country rustling cattle, burning and looting. Tenants had no security of tenure and no rights in law; if they improved their holdings their rents were racked up, and if they could not pay they were evicted and their cottages burnt down.

This did not apply in Ulster where what was known as the 'Ulster Custom' prevailed. This was a quite unofficial but widely-accepted system which gave the tenant security of occupancy and allowed him to sell his tenancy to the highest bidder, provided the landlord approved the new tenant. Although this condition was primarily designed to keep out Catholics, it had the side-effect that it provided the tenant with a strong incentive to improve his holding. The result was that the farms in Ulster were markedly more prosperous than elsewhere in Ireland, another factor which tended to accentuate the growing gulf between Ulster and the rest of the island.

One reason for the grinding poverty that bedevilled Ireland at this period was that successive English Governments had destroyed whatever few industries the Irish had managed to develop (with the exception of linen, and again the linen industry happened to be sited in Ulster). The trouble was that, unlike Britain's now rapidly expanding colonies overseas, Ireland produced, with the single exception of coal, exactly the same things as England. As early as the reign of Charles II, Ireland had been forbidden to export goods to British possessions or import goods from them except through British ports, which increased freight costs and hampered the development of an Irish shipping industry. No livestock could be shipped to England for fear the Irish produce would reduce the English farmer's profits. And when, as a result of this prohibition, Irish farmers started sheep farming for wool, and there were signs of a competitive wool trade developing, Ireland was forbidden to export wool anywhere other than to England. Another Irish industry—small but profitable—was glass manufacture: suddenly Ireland was forbidden to export glass. Even the importation of hops was heavily taxed to make Irish brewing uneconomic and to force the Irish to drink imported British beer.

When the Tories came to power in 1702 some of the Penal Laws were applied to all Dissenters; Puritans who held public office had been in the habit of taking the Sacrament according to the Church of England rites once a year as a pure formality to pass the sacramental test; now an 'Occasional Conformity Bill' was introduced which meant that Puritans would have to take the Sacrament regularly or lose office. This and other niggling measures combined with the restrictions on trade—which affected the prosperous Protestant merchants and traders far more than they affected the starving Irish peasants—had two results. The first was a large-scale emigration of Ulster Protestants to North America, whither they transported not only their deep grievances against the British Government but also the ruthlessness acquired in so many years of fierce fighting with the Irish Catholic peasants. Between 1730 and 1770 about 200,000 of them emigrated, pioneering the great move westwards and treating the indigenous Red Indians as they had learned to treat the Irish Catholic peasants. Later they were to provide the most militant and determined elements in Washington's armies in the American War of Independence, and no fewer than ten future American Presidents.

The other result of the extension of the religious restrictions to the non-conformists and of the restrictions on trade was to draw, for a time, the Irish Catholics and Presbyterians a little closer together so that for a period, towards the end of the 18th century, it almost looked as if a society of United Irishmen might be made to work.

Throughout the century, a new middle-class element had been emerging both in Ulster and in the rest of the country. In Ulster, trade and commerce were almost exclusively in the hands of the Protestants; Belfast, now rapidly becoming the commercial centre of the province, was almost 100 per cent Protestant and the ban on Catholics entering towns and cities was sometimes enforced in Ulster. Elsewhere in Ireland, this was not so. In cities like Dublin, Cork, Galway and Limerick, the majority of professional and businessmen were Protestants certainly, but there were some Catholics among them and the ban on Catholics entering the cities had failed; indeed it was never seriously implemented. But Ireland remained, nevertheless, very largely a Protestant country in the sense that the bulk of the Irish Catholics were too poor and wretched to know or care what was happening in trade, commerce or politics. Apart from constant agrarian crimes, the country was quiet for almost a century; even the Jacobite uprisings in England and Scotland in 1715 and 1745 provoked no reaction among the Irish Catholics.

By the middle of the century the final wave of settlers had been living in Ireland for half a century, and like their precursors, the Cromwellian settlers, were beginning to identify themselves with the country which they very largely owned and which owed to them what little prosperity it now had. They began to resent more and more the fact that this country was being run by and from England, very largely for England's benefit.

The nucleus of what might be described as a Protestant Patriot Party had started to develop around men like Flood and Grattan, both members of the Opposition in the Dublin Parliament. The outbreak of the American War of Independence provided these Protestant Patriots with an army with which to press their claims for a fair deal for Irish trade. When the British realized that Washington's armies were going to prove a surprisingly formidable adversary, they withdrew troops from Ireland to fight in America and when the British Government refused to grant an Irish Militia to replace them, the Protestant Patriots raised their own Volunteer force—initially to preserve law and order and protect the country from a possible French invasion. However, as soon as the force had been raised—and in no time at all almost the entire male Protestant population of Ireland, dressed in a wide variety of highly elaborate uniforms, was drilling and marching and parading behind military bands—the Irish Parliament realized that this amateur army could be used to force the British Parliament, now losing the American War of Independence, to accede to some of their demands. In Ulster, the Volunteers were exclusively Protestant at first and were often led by their Presbyterian ministers who wore their uniforms even in the pulpit (a fact which may partly explain the presence of so many Ulster clergymen in prominent positions in the militant Orange Order today); in some companies in the South a few Catholics were admitted, though this was strictly against the law since Catholics were still forbidden, under the Penal Laws, to carry arms.

Shaken by what had happened in America, the British caved in and acceded to most of the demands of what was known as Grattan's Parliament: free trade was granted and the Irish Parliament was given power to make its own laws for Ireland without the approval of Westminster, though in practice it proved impossible to get commercial legislation affecting both countries through both Parliaments, and in any event, the Dublin Parliament was still effectively controlled by the Executive, through bribes and patronage.

Constantine Fitzgibbon says of this: 'The immediate result was a sharp decline in interdenominational hatred, and particularly in Belfast, where by 1784 Roman Catholics were being admitted into the Volunteers in some numbers. Lecky quotes from *Thoughts on the Volunteers* from that date: "The Papist with an Orange cockade fires in honour of King William's birthday. He goes to a Protestant Church and hears a charity sermon . . . The Catholic who wishes to carry arms proposes himself to a Protestant corps. His character is tried by his neighbours. He is admitted to an honour and a privilege; he receives a reward for his good conduct . . . Thus are the best of the Catholic body happily selected, the whole of the Catholic body satisfied, and the two religions marvellously united.'"

It was, however, to be a union of very brief duration.

2

Immediately in the wake of the success of the Protestant Patriot Irish Parliament, came a new dream: United Ireland, then as now, a contradiction in terms. The dream was imported from France; its creed was taken from Tom Paine's *The Rights of Man* and its prophet and martyr was Theobald Wolfe Tone, a Dublin Protestant lawyer. Rank and religion alike, he believed, would vanish in the United Ireland of his dreams.

In a sort of euphoria that is difficult to credit in view of events before and since, the anniversary of the Battle of the Boyne was celebrated in 1784 in a most extraordinary way; the Protestants paraded to the only Roman Catholic Church in Belfast, St Mary's, Chapel Lane, and from there they sent a petition to Lord Charlemont, titular head of the Volunteers and Governor of Armagh, demanding Catholic emancipation and freedom for Catholics to join the Volunteers and carry arms. Charlemont turned down the petition on the grounds that it was premature, and there was the inevitable grassroots backlash. Rumours spread among the Ulster Protestants that the Catholics were arming again and it was up to the Protestants to protect their homes from attack. Oakboys and Steelboys began once more to raid Catholic homes, ostensibly searching for the arms that they were rumoured to be storing, but more often with the idea of intimidating them into clearing out of Ulster; since these raids normally took place at dawn, the various raiders came to be known collectively as the Peep o' Day Boys. To defend themselves against such attacks, the Catholics formed their own private army, the Defenders, though inevitably, despite their title, many of their exercises were offensive rather than purely defensive. It is worth pointing out, perhaps, that at this period there was no police force as such in

Ireland; each parish had its constable who theoretically kept order by calling on loyal citizens to assist him in dealing with miscreants. This system, which worked well enough in England where the population as a whole was behind the forces of law and order, did not work at all in Ireland, for obvious reasons.

Violence in Ulster, and particularly in Armagh, rapidly escalated, and soon there were large parties of men marching and brawling and raiding and looting.

In 1789 the French Revolution burst over Europe and produced a chain reaction of repercussions all over the world; and nowhere more strongly than in Ireland. In the clubs in Belfast the anniversary of the Fall of the Bastille was celebrated with enthusiasm in 1791 and again in 1792. The Volunteers held processions and the Northern Whig Club toasted 'Thomas Paine and the Rights of Man' and 'The Majesty of the People', and despite the sectarian riots that were going on almost nightly in County Antrim, the Volunteers called, in the Linen Hall, for 'an abolition of the Popery Laws and an extension of privileges to Roman Catholics'.

To quote the Rev John Brown: 'For it was believed that the Roman Catholics might be active allies in securing a reform of the Irish Parliament, and in taking political power out of the hands of the upper-class groups that dominated it. For years now they had been pressing, through their standing committee in Dublin, for a formal relaxation and ultimate repeal of the "Popery laws". Both the British and Irish Governments, and the Patriots and the Volunteers, had bid for their support during the American War. Some of the restrictions had already been removed. Now the revived corps of Volunteers admitted more and more Roman Catholics to their ranks; resolutions of amity and tolerance passed to and fro; and Mr Theobald Wolfe Tone, paid Secretary of the Roman Catholic Committee, gave up what little work he did at the Irish Bar to write on behalf of Roman Catholic Emancipation, and, in the autumn of 1791, to help in establishing a "Society of United Irishmen" in democratic, dissatisfied Belfast. Soon throughout the North, in Dublin and elsewhere, United Irishmen were forming a "brotherhood of affection", resolving that Protestant and

Catholic should join in political action to change the established order as had been done in France . . .'

But everything changed the moment Britain declared war on France in 1793. Under pressure from Pitt, the Irish Government raised a largely Catholic militia. Tone travelled to America and thence to France to persuade the French to send a force of 150,000 men to supplement his own estimated 150,000 United Irishmen in a rising that would throw off the British yoke for ever.

In Ulster, a wave of loyalty to the British Crown cancelled out all previous notions of liberty, equality and freedom. Furthermore, some of the Ulster Protestants had been growing alarmed at instructions which had been appearing in the United Irishman's newspaper, the *Northern Star*, on how to make gunpowder and on the use of weapons and military tactics. Furthermore, pikes similar to those used by the French were being manufactured in large numbers in forges throughout the province, and it began to occur to the Ulster Protestants that these pikes could very easily be used to make another attempt to unseat them. Many who had originally looked on the French Revolution favourably now drew back nervously.

Agrarian crimes and clashes between the Peep o' Day Boys and the Defenders continued to increase both in frequency and in severity. Many of these encounters seemed to take place in the neighbourhood of the Diamond, a crossroads village near Loughgall, County Antrim, and matters reached a crisis there during the summer and early autumn of 1795.

In the spring of 1795 a cockfight at Dan Winter's inn in the village resulted in a brawl during which a Defender was badly beaten up by Peep o' Day Boys. Alcohol has always played a major role in cases of violence among the lower class Irish (except curiously enough, during the Easter Week Rising, when even hardened, heavy drinkers abstained for the week) and, as Constantine Fitzgibbon remarks '. . . it is not hard to visualize the dreary pub, the blood lust aroused by the cruel sport, the tension mounting as the drinks were lowered'. The reaction to the incident was normal; on the following day gangs of Defenders and Peep o' Day boys assembled. Insults were exchanged, shots were fired. There was a confrontation some time later when a party of Defenders returning from a wake clashed with a party of Peep o' Day Boys returning from a dance. Again, both groups had almost certainly been drinking, and again there were casualties. The authorities later intervened and arrested fifty Defenders and two Peep o' Day Boys. The Defenders realized—as so many Catholic minority groups in Ireland before and since have realized—that they could expect no impartiality from the authorities. They began to organize and talked openly about an attack on Dan Winter's pub, a recognized meeting place of the Peep o' Day Boys, as soon as the harvest was safely in.

Accounts of the action are understandably confused. However, there seems to be general agreement that towards the middle of September 1795, parties of Defenders moved into the vicinity of the Diamond where they looted Protestant houses, occupied a gravel pit, manning it with an least 500 men and flying a white flag. Inevitably the Peep o' Day Boys also turned up and the two armies appear to have taken up positions on hilltops facing one another, the Peep o' Day Boys on Diamond Hill and the Defenders on Faughart Hill opposite. At this stage two local Protestant landlords and three priests intervened and undertook to stand surety—the landlords (who were also magistrates) for the Protestants and the priests for the Catholics —in the sum of £500, the money to be forfeited by whichever party broke the treaty by a breach of the peace.

Meanwhile the news of the battle had spread to other districts and fresh forces were converging on the Diamond. Some of these were turned back by the Militia, but other parties of Defenders arrived who did not consider themselves bound by an agreement made before their arrival and early on the morning of September 21st Dan Winter's pub was attacked. It is hard to get any accurate figures but it seems likely that the Catholic attackers amounted to about 400 and the Protestant garrison to about a dozen. The crucial moment in the encounter, according to Orange versions of the affair anyway, occurred when their ammunition was running low and the garrison was sorely pressed. A party of Protestants who had served in the Volunteers stepped out in front of the pub, dressed their line according to the drill books, and fired a destructive volley at short range straight into a disorganized mob of Defenders. This was the decisive turning point; the Defenders poured back through the Diamond, still under heavy fire, and the Protestants followed and cleared them off Faughart Hill.

Estimates of the casualties vary greatly and, because the Defenders carried their dead away with them, could not be verified; but it seems likely that about 40 of the Defenders were killed and many more wounded, for one Protestant casualty.

It was a decisive victory for the Protestants, but it had been a close thing. At one point the Protestants believed that it was the Defenders' intention to make a permanent stronghold of both Diamond and Faughart Hills, which between them command key roads which might have enabled them to dominate the whole neighbourhood and expel the Protestants or at least make life extremely unpleasant for them. The very fact that the despised Irish Catholics could raise an organized armed force that could and would fight even if so ineffectually, came as a rude shock to them.

And the result of the shock was the immediate formation, that same evening at the Diamond, of a new secret army known initially as the Orange Boys which eventually became the Orange Order, a semi-secret society which through Freemason-type Lodges—a society to which many of the original members also belonged—has largely shaped and controlled, and until March 1972 still shaped and controlled, that curious anomaly known variously as Ulster, Northern Ireland and the Six Counties.

* * *

Poor Croppies, ye knew that your sentence was come,*
When you heard the dread sound of the Protestant drum;
In memory of William we hoisted his flag,
And soon the bright Orange put down the Green Rag.
Down, down, Croppies lie down!

—Traditional Orange Ballad.

* 'Crop-heads' is an Orange term for Catholic 'rebels'.

IV

Down, Down, Croppies Lie Down!

Just as some confusion still clouds the sequence of events at the Diamond that September over 170 years ago, a similar sort of confusion surrounds the transformation of the Orange Boys into the Orange Order as it now exists.

The Rev John Brown, one of the three co-authors of *Orangeism: A New Historical Appreciation* (upon which I have drawn substantially as it is the most recent 'official' history of the Order, published by the Order) admits as much: 'Can we reconcile picturesque tradition that resolute men, their hands and faces still blackened with powder from the Diamond's battle, made solemn vows in a field near Dan Winter's house, and initiated the first Orangeman at a bush beside a spring well in Dan's garden, with the other statement that the first Orange Lodge was formed in James Sloan's inn at Loughgall? And what had James Wilson and the men of the Dyan near Caledon in Tyrone to do with it, and why was Warrant No. 1* given to them, and neither to the Diamond nor Loughgall?'

No doubt these details are of far more interest to the members of the Orange Order than they are to the general public, but it seems likely that the news of the Diamond affair spread very rapidly through the province, and in time the more prominent landlords and merchants and traders, many of whom were Freemasons, decided that there was the nucleus here for a popular movement which could be used to preserve and

* A warrant, which cost one Irish guinea, was required before anyone could open a new Orange Lodge; these warrants were initially issued at the first Orange HQ at Loughgall and the table on which they were signed is preserved in the Orange Museum on the site of Sloan's Inn.

maintain the Protestant Ascendancy in Ulster, provided that it was controlled and organized along the right lines. And since so many of them were Freemasons, development along the Masonic Lodge pattern seemed the most logical. Right from the beginning, membership was strictly limited to 'those born and brought up in the Reformed religion'; there would be no question, as there had been with the Volunteers, of admitting Catholics and thereby giving them access to arms which could be used against Protestants.

It was probably at the meeting in the ruins of Dan Winter's pub after the Battle of Diamond that the idea of a secret system of signs and passwords was first discussed, and the details were probably hammered out later in James Sloan's Inn at Loughgall. Certainly there is no evidence that the Peep o' Day Boys had any systematic method of recognition or any rites or formalities, though the Defenders had secret recognition customs.

Several years before the Battle of Diamond a man called James Wilson of Dyan, a member of a Freemason Lodge at Caledon, Co. Tyrone, had attempted to persuade the Masons in his Lodge to intervene on behalf of some Protestants who were being roughly handled. When they refused, he formed another organization which would be less scrupulous in interfering in such matters. Wilson and his associates, who probably called themselves the Orange Boys, were certainly at the Battle of Diamond, and it is possible that the Orange Order as it now exists grew out of his organization. And it is logical, especially since Dan Winter's inn was badly damaged in the fighting, that they might all have repaired to nearby Loughgall to James Sloan's inn, to continue their discussions. James Sloan was also a Mason.

There is a tradition that Wilson insisted that the first Orange warrant 'should not be written by anything made by the hand of man' and took a sprig from a tree of hyssop which grew in the garden and gave it to Sloan, who made out the warrant with this novel pen. But Orange historians are by no means agreed on this; nor is it even certain that the warrant for Loyal Orange Lodge No. 1 went to Wilson and the Dyan. Constantine Fitzgibbon states categorically that Wilson never joined the

Orange Order. Hereward Senior also states that Wilson left the Diamond without joining the new movement, but in the latest official 'historical appreciation of Orangeism', the Rev John Brown states equally categorically that the warrant of Loyal Orange Lodge No. 1 went to Wilson and the Dyan (which Senior spells Dian).

The choice of the title 'Orange' for the Order was almost a foregone conclusion. Long before the Orange Order came into existence there were men who described themselves as Orangemen*—loyal followers of William of Orange—and a couple of the Masonic Lodges in Belfast and Londonderry also carried the additional title 'Orange'. Officers of the Fourth Foot regiment belonged to the 'Loyal and Friendly Society of the Blew and Orange' (the 'Blew' presumably refers to King Billy's Blue Dutch Guards). In most Protestant gardens in Ulster the orange lily and the sweet william grew side by side; indeed, Ulster's devotion to William of Orange was really, as the Rev M. W. Dewar remarked, 'an affair of the heart' and is as difficult for a non-Ulsterman to understand as is the Ulsterman's fanatical devotion to the Crown today.

The Orange Order, when it was organized, simply channelled a vast flow of fervent feeling which already existed into one enormous reservoir of partisan and religious ardour (or bigotry, according to how you view it). Men still preserved rusty old swords which their ancestors had drawn in the defence of Londonderry or had brandished at the Boyne. The Volunteers had marched to the tunes of *The Boyne Water*, *Lilliburlero* and other 'Orange' ballads. In Londonderry there

* As early as November 12th, 1688, in the West Country of England, an event occurred which could probably be regarded as the first manifestation of 'Orangeism'; there, a few days after he landed at Torbay on the Devon Coast, William of Orange—on his way to London and his coronation—attended a ceremony in Exeter Cathedral to mark 'the engagement of the Nobles, Knights and Gentlemen of Exeter to assist the Prince of Orange in the defence of the Protestant religion.' As a matter of interest, the official notepaper of the Grand Lodge of England carries the categorical statement that 'The Orange Order (now world-wide) was first formed in Exeter Cathedral in 1688'. I doubt if many of the rank and file Ulster Orangemen are aware of this piece of English Chauvinism; if they were, I don't believe they would march with their English brothers.

were already clubs dedicated to commemorating the closing of the City Gates by the Apprentice Boys and the relief of the siege. Even in Dublin, the statue of King William (the first of many relics of the British rule to be blown up when the Southern Irish first gained control of their own affairs) was the centre of an annual celebration, when the Lord Lieutenant and the Lord Mayor went in procession and the streets of the capital were decorated with Orange ribbons.

All over the country, there was at this stage among the Protestants a deep vein of Orange devotion which could be tapped as a protection not only against the Catholic peasants but also against the increasingly Jacobin-dominated and essentially working-class movement, the Society of United Irishmen, which by now most Ulster Protestants profoundly mistrusted and feared, although a hard core of Presbyterian Republicans still existed in Belfast.

2

The development of the Orange Boys into the Orange Order was a gradual process and in its early days the wealthier Protestant gentry, while fully aware that the muscles of the new movement might prove useful to them, were a little nervous both of its peasant-agrarian background and methods and of its almost primitive, tribal rituals. Hereward Senior gives this account of an initiation:

> The early meetings were secret with initiations and oaths administered on hilltops and behind hedges in the manner of any other agrarian society. Blacker described the first meetings of his Lodge held in the frame wall of a partially constructed house at the crossroads of Tanderagee and Lurgan, near the gate of Carrick. 'An assemblage of men, young and old, collected upon these occasions as far as could be seen by the light of a few candles—some seated on heaps of sods or rude blocks of wood; most of them armed with guns of every age and calibre . . . There was a stern solemnity in the reading of the scripture and administering the oath to the newly admitted brethren

> which was calculated to produce a deep impression and did so.' The original oath ran, 'I . . . do solemnly swear that I will, to the utmost of my power, support and defend the king and his heirs *as long as he or they support the Protestant ascendancy*'.*

The Orangemen broke the power of the Defenders. Disturbances continued in County Armagh and elsewhere throughout Ulster, and there was a widespread fear among Protestants that another rebellion was imminent. Protection, unity and the strength to fight back seemed now to lie in membership of the Orange Order, and the movement spread rapidly throughout the province.

The Defenders already knew that if caught, they could expect little mercy from the Protestant magistrates. And the magistrates, who were largely disposed to favour the Orange Boys, now had a local volunteer police force at their disposal in the Orange Order, 'though its methods might be a trifle rough, if ready enough' (again, I am quoting the Rev John Brown's official history).

He continues: 'There was what a correspondent of Lord Charlemont calls "a deadly and irreconcilable rancour in the minds of the lower people". The obvious thing to do was to disarm the Defenders, and if troops were not able to do it, others were quite prepared for the task. It seems that a determined effort was made to carry this out. Here was a situation which could be exploited by any who wanted revenge, plunder or violence, and the wilder Peep o' Day elements were still there. The winter of 1795–96 saw outrages both on Roman Catholics and Protestants—beatings, robberies, shootings and "wrecking" of houses. It was claimed that a large part of the population got the option of leaving Armagh for Hell or Connaught.

'There is no doubt that a good many Roman Catholics, Defenders or not, did leave. But it seems that not all of these were driven out, and it was always insisted in Armagh that some people "wrecked" their own houses to get compensation.

* The italics are mine.—T.G.

There is no evidence that Orangemen as such took part in outrages, though the Orange Society was accused of organizing them. Still it is not unlikely that individual Orangemen were involved in at least some of these acts of revenge or intimidation, which were at times condoned by others. The question remains whether the situation might not have been very much worse but for the discipline imposed on the members of the Orange Association; and the assistance they gave to the authorities.'

Others, naturally enough, put a very different interpretation on these events which were known as the 'Armagh Outrages'. A more common interpretation of them in the rest of Ireland is that as soon as the power of the Defenders had been broken, the Protestant Ulstermen set upon their Catholic neighbours with the express object of driving them from their homes. Slogans were as popular with the Orangemen then as they are now, and *Hell or Connaught* was scrawled on the walls and doors of many a Catholic homestead. Bands of armed men roamed the country terrorizing men, women and children, smashing furniture, breaking down fences and looting. The Rev John Brown is probably right when he says that many of the Catholics burned down their own homes before leaving, to get the compensation; certainly there was an act in existence which guaranteed compensation to people whose homes were destroyed in agrarian riots though it had been passed, ironically enough, to provide compensation for Protestant landlords whose homes were being destroyed at an earlier period by the Whiteboys elsewhere in Ireland. In general, Protestant raiders did not burn Catholic houses for the very good reason that they planned to occupy them themselves, as soon as they had intimidated the Catholics into leaving.

How many Catholics fled from Armagh during the outrages is not known for certain; according to one estimate, 4,000 refugees from Armagh fled to one county, Mayo, that winter; another estimate puts the figure at 1,400 families.

These disturbances irritated the landlords by causing rents to fall and they alarmed the more respectable members of the Order, but the movement continued to grow apace. Military lodges were formed in units of the Militia, and the movement spread to Dublin where it was viewed with some suspicion by the Dublin Castle authorities and the Irish Parliament; the latter in particular, having earlier taken advantage of the now disbanded Volunteers to press its own claims, did not want another militant, para-military organization to develop over which it could exercise no control.

3

The disturbances in Ulster continued, and took many forms: murder, arson, intimidation and discrimination. A millowner in Belfast was instructed to sack all Catholics in his employment and when he failed to do so his mill was burnt down. It is likely that the increasing ferocity of the outrages in Ulster was a direct result of events in Westminster and Dublin. Under pressure from Pitt, who realized—as the Orangemen have never done—that the Catholic Church would probably prove a steadying influence against the revolutionary movements which looked like developing in Ireland, the Irish Parliament had repealed most of the Penal Laws and had given Catholics the vote. Grattan and his friends in the Opposition, partly in a genuine spirit of 18th-century tolerance, and partly from a desire for political support, were also urging the Catholics they should be fully emancipated and allowed to hold seats in Parliament. The thought of this possibility would obviously strike terror into the hearts of the Ulster Protestants who would interpret it as the beginning of the end of Protestant Supremacy; for the Catholics outnumbered the Protestants in Ireland by three to one, and if they were given the vote and allowed to sit in Parliament they would soon be making the laws and running the country. There was, no doubt, a stiffening of attitudes among the already rigid Orangemen, who were not surprised to find this Liberal Opposition in Dublin decrying the persecution of Catholics in Ulster and quoting Lord Gosford, Governor of Armagh, who told a meeting of landlords, landowners and magistrates that a 'lawless banditti' were banishing innocent Catholics from Armagh 'with all the circumstances of ferocious cruelty'. He went on: 'The only crime which the wretched objects of this merciless persecution are charged with, is a crime of easy proof; it is simply a profession of the Roman Catholic faith. A lawless banditti have constituted themselves the judges of this new species of delinquency, and the sentence they pronounce is equally concise and terrible; it is nothing less than a confiscation of all property and immediate banishment.' The address was printed and distributed to influential people in Dublin. He did not use the word Orangemen but there is little doubt that he was referring to the Armagh outrages.

The Orangemen were under attack from other quarters, notably the United Irishmen who had steadily been becoming more militantly revolutionary in their views. By now they had become a secret society and had started to arm for rebellion. They were also drafting members of the now largely inactive Defenders into their organization. This confirmed the worst fear of most of the Ulster Protestants who had originally supported the idea of the United Irishmen. They now inclined to the view that the 'established order in Church and State', whatever the faults of the British Government, was a great deal safer than association with a revolutionary society which had no respect for Church, State, or—what was perhaps even more important in their eyes—property. It was at this stage that the more conservative elements among the Ulstermen began to join the Orange Order and in many instances took over the leadership of various of the Lodges. The prestige which these gentlemen gave to the Order helped it to spread and recruit members in areas which previously had fought shy of what looked like yet another agrarian army. By the summer of 1796, the Orange Order was becoming 'respectable'.

By the summer of 1796, too, the Order was exhibiting its strength openly, if not yet provocatively. The processions on the anniversary of the Boyne battle at Portadown, Lurgan and Waringstown featured flags depicting King William and King George III, and the Orangemen marched like the old Volunteers, in whose ranks many of them had served. The hostile *Dublin Evening Post* reported the occasion: 'The procession consisted of fourteen companies, each with ensigns and devices emblematic of the occasion, and formed a motley group of turncoats, Methodists, Seceders and High-Churchmen, at least double of the rest, with a multitude of boys and country trulls cheering up the lagging heroes.' There are people in the South today who would argue that this is not an inaccurate description of more recent parades, particularly in respect of the 'multitude of small boys' who seem to feature so prominently in all television coverage of sectarian displays in Northern Ireland.

The *Northern Star* reported: 'The gentlemen called Orange Boys, who had desolated the County of Armagh during the last year, paraded publicly in large numbers through the towns of Lurgan, Waringstown, and Portadown. This banditti ... parade in open day, under banners bearing the King's effigy and sanctioned by the magistrates. Irishmen! Is it not plain enough?'

The same issue carried an anonymous letter to the editor inquiring: 'Is it a truth that higher powers have hired men called Orange-men at five guineas per man and one shilling per day to disturb, destroy and harass harmless inhabitants, because they are Irishmen?'

Dublin Castle, too, still viewed the emergence of this new militant force with some apprehension. Cooke, the Under-Secretary, wrote to Pelham, the Secretary: 'The procession of the Orangemen to the Diamond on the 12th went off quietly. About 5,000 paraded without arms. Their banners, King George on one side, King William on the other. The Orangemen are beginning persecutions in the County of Down and the magistrates are not sufficiently active. This persecution works on Catholics in other places and naturally breathes revenge ... I fear the Militia will be tainted'.

The more reasonable Protestant settlers, in the South as well as in the North of Ireland, were in something of a quandary. They knew that the United Irish Movement was preparing for a rebellion, and using the Orange 'Armagh Outrages' as a means of attracting both Defenders and Catholic members of the Militia into their organization. Many of them didn't like the idea of encouraging the Orangemen but realized that they might have to rely on them for the preservation of their own lives and property. It was known that Wolfe Tone was in France and that a French fleet was assembling at Brest for an invasion, probably of Ireland.

Several attempts at compromise were made. A magistrate, Thomas Knox from Dungannon, proposed what came to be called 'The Dungannon Plan'—a new loyal association which would admit Orangemen into its ranks and thus control them more effectively. Cooke, the Under-Secretary, was against this idea and remained hostile to Orangeism. 'The irritating conduct of the Orangemen in keeping up persecution against the Catholics does infinite mischief,' he wrote in late July. 'It has been made the handle of seducing many of the Militia . . . All my information coincides in the increasing activity of the disaffected . . . and insurrection after harvest, aided by invasion.'

The point had now been reached, however, when it was necessary to accept the risk of allowing 'private' armies to exist to meet the danger of the threatened uprising and invasion with no army other than the Scottish fencibles—hastily recruited and inadequately trained, because at this time England was hard pressed for troops as she had been suffering a series of defeats in the Low Countries and on the French coast and had paid very dearly for a victory in the West Indies—and the highly unreliable and largely Catholic Militia. Accordingly it was decided to form a part-time volunteer 'Yeomanry' on the lines of the English Yeomanry. Camden, the Lord Lieutenant, wrote to Pelham: 'I do not like to resort to Yeomanry, Cavalry or Infantry . . . if I can help it . . . but I see no other recourse in the present times'.

Hereward Senior comments: 'By permitting the gentry to raise a force of part-time soldiers similar, in many respects, to the Volunteers, the government unintentionally provided the means of creating a national Orange movement. The Yeomanry could not be recruited without the co-operation of the lower class Protestants, and the Orange Lodges were to be both an agency for employing the energies of the Protestant peasants and a means of keeping them under some degree of gentry control.'

4

At the time of the July 12th parade in 1796, the strength of the Orange Order was probably only several thousand, organized into less than one hundred Lodges, and enjoying only very cautious and limited support from the Ulster gentry, landowners and magistrates. A year later it had grown into a strong popular movement which infiltrated the Yeomanry, many regiments of Militia in Ulster, and exercised considerable power, with the open support of the landowners and gentry; it had even been accepted as a potential ally by Dublin Castle.

All this came about as a result of the menace of the United Ireland movement. This movement, as we have seen, had been started in Belfast in the wake of the French revolution, among liberal Protestants, mostly Presbyterians, disaffected with Britain. The disbanding of the Volunteers had left it without an army and most of the original leaders—Wolfe Tone, Hamilton Rowan and Napper Tandy—were in exile. Now a new wave of republican leaders including Lord Edward Fitzgerald, brother of the Duke of Leinster, and Thomas Addis Emmet joined the movement in 1796 when it became clear to them that constitutional methods could no longer gain any further equality for Catholics or any additional parliamentary reforms.

In Ulster, in 1796, there were probably about 40,000 sworn United Irishmen, armed in some manner or other and answering to some form of authority under a central directory. The new leaders of the movement were nervous about the admission of so many former Defenders: in a letter, one of them wrote: 'They were composed almost entirely of Roman Catholics, and those of the lowest order, who, through a false confidence, were risking themselves and the attainment of redress by premature and unsystematic insurrection.' Both the United Irish leaders and the authorities knew that without an invasion by the French, or a large-scale defection on the part of the Militia, the peasants who formed the bulk of the United Irishmen in the North and South alike could not achieve anything more abiding or effective than sporadic outbreaks of violence which would make administration by the British difficult if not impossible, but could not offer any alternative administration.

The presence of the Orangemen in large numbers in both the Yeomanry and the Militia in Ulster was useful as an insurance against United Irish elements in these forces. On the other hand, the existence of the Orange Order also made recruiting for the United Irishmen a great deal easier, and there is no doubt that the propaganda value of the 'Armagh Outrages' was exploited to the full by United Irish agents, and the rumour was deliberately spread that it was the sworn aim and object of every Orangeman to exterminate, so far as it lay in his power, every single Catholic in Ireland.

In the autumn of 1796, while the Yeomanry was being raised, Orangeism was discussed in the Dublin Parliament and the right to suspend *habeas corpus* was requested and granted as a means of controlling internal disorders in Ulster. Grattan protested, pointing to the failure of the authorities to control the Armagh outrages through the existing legislation, and this spurred James Verner into the first defence of Orangeism in Parliament; he maintained that the outrages were exaggerated, that the Defenders had started the quarrel at the Diamond in the first place and that the Orangemen were all loyal members of the established church.

At this stage, things were remarkably quiet in Ireland, largely because the United Irishmen were holding themselves in readiness for the French invasion, which was expected at any moment.

It came, late in December; or rather, it didn't come, although it set out from France. The weather was bad, fog scattered the ships, General Hoche was separated from the remainder of his fleet and the entire force sailed back to France, taking Tone with them, without even attempting a landing. News that the French fleet was off the coast rallied most of the country to the Crown; even the Catholic Irish peasants of the South cheered the troops as they marched towards Bantry Bay.

Despite this, the immediate reaction at Westminster was a

decision to disarm and dragoon the Irish before the French could make another invasion attempt. And since the United Ireland movement had originated in Belfast, a start was made there. Throughout the winter of 1796–97, any United Irish leaders still in Belfast were arrested and the presses of their newspaper the *Northern Star* were raided and wrecked.

In March 1797 General Lake was given command in Belfast with powers which amounted to imposing martial law on the area. His task was to destroy the rank and file of the Republican United Ireland movement. This task was made considerably easier by the fact that the Militia regiments were now officered, and to a large extent manned, by members of the Orange Order. The Monaghan Militia had been stationed in Belfast since June 1796, however, and contained a fairly high proportion of United Irishmen. In May 1797, the regiment was paraded and the United Irishmen ordered to declare themselves. Seventy did so. Four of these were tried by court martial and executed as ringleaders; the remainder were pardoned.

In gratitude, or perhaps, in order to prove their loyalty, the Monaghan Militia began to treat the population of Belfast with excessive brutality. Many of them were Catholics and as Constantine Fitzgibbon puts it '. . . their new allegiance gave them the opportunity to indulge in hooliganism in their traditional fashion by bashing their hereditary enemy. The military and the Yeomanry rampaged through Belfast, shooting and burning . . . The almost leaderless United Irishmen responded with the only means at their disposal, murder and an occasional burning'.

The next event was the arrival in the province of Ulster of some regiments of Welsh fencibles with the absurd name of the Ancient Britons, who were sent to 'pacify' Newry which was suspected of being another stronghold of the United Irishmen. This they did with similar brutality. Hereward Senior quotes John Giffard, a Dublin Castle agent and journalist, who in June 1767 wrote: 'the Welsh burned a great number of houses, and the object of emulation between them and the Orange Yeomen seems to be, who shall do the most mischief to the wretches who may have seditious minds, but who are, at present, quiet and incapable of resistance'. In describing a search for arms, he wrote: 'I was directed by the smoke and flames of burning houses, and by the dead bodies of boys and old men slain by the Britons, though no opposition whatever had been given by them, and, as I shall answer Almighty God I believe a single gun was not fired, but by the Britons and the Yeomanry . . . From ten to twenty were killed outright; many wounded and eight houses burned'.

The Yeomanry in Dungannon were engaged in similar tactics; in a village called Tantaraghan a crowd of Yeomen—including some Orangemen—pulled down a Catholic chapel, stone by stone. In an attempt to stop things from getting out of hand, Dublin Castle ordered that the Yeomanry were not to take any action except under the instructions of officers; but this only worked in areas where the Orange gentry were in control. There were still some of the old Peep o' Day elements in the Orange Order, and where they were in the majority the *Hell or Connaught* notices started to appear again and a fresh wave of Catholic Ulster refugees opted for Connaught.

General Lake used public floggings, torture and drumhead courts martial to extract information about hidden supplies of guns and pikes, and his operations were successful in the sense that the Ulster Protestant republicans were soon effectively disarmed. On the other hand his methods, and the methods used by the Ancient Britons, the Yeomen of Dungannon and the Monaghan Militia turned many moderates into militants of one sort or another and enormously increased the power of the Orange Order. As Constantine Fitzgibbon puts it: 'Whipped, beaten and tortured by an increasingly Orange-dominated Militia and Yeomanry, they first surrendered their means of defence, their weapons and then enrolled in the Orange Order, not in order to undermine it from within but to become loyal Orangemen, free to hate Irish Catholics, Church of Ireland landowners, Englishmen and all other foreigners according to choice, but above all free to stop thinking about politics and get on with their own lives. It has been estimated that by the time the Rebellion of 1798 broke out, there were some two hundred thousand members of the Orange Order, all of them Protestants and most of them in Ulster. It would be scarcely an exaggeration to say that General Lake's bullies had whipped a great many of them into the Order'.

The effects of the trials and tortures and raids on the Catholics was quite simply to turn the moderates into potential United Irishmen, determined to support any rising against the British.

The United Irishmen in the South had decided to go it alone, without waiting for another French invasion, before they too were disarmed. In Dublin, as usual, details of the plans leaked out and many of the leaders were arrested on the eve of the day fixed for the rising, May 23rd, 1798. Despite this, in the south-east initially, and in other isolated areas all over the country later, the peasants, ill-clad, untrained, armed only with pitchforks and pikes and led in many cases by their priests—against the express instructions of the hierarchy—rose up against the British landlords and Anglo-Irish gentry.

In Ulster, a half-hearted attempt at a rebellion led by Henry Joy McCracken, a Belfast cotton manufacturer, and Henry Munro, a Lisburn linen draper, was made on June 7th; it was contained very simply and was all over, and the leaders executed, inside a fortnight.

In the South, General Lake, now Commander-in-Chief, introduced collective punishment to force the surrender of arms, using even more brutal and vicious tortures than he had used in the North and succeeded in driving many moderates into open rebellion. Within a few weeks over 30,000 people, Protestants and Catholics, and including many defenceless women and children, had been slaughtered, often with terrible cruelty. Half-hanging, flogging and the pitch-cap—a frightful form of torture in which pitch was rubbed into a man's hair and his head set alight—were among Lake's methods.

Convinced that every Protestant was an Orangeman and that it was the sworn aim of every Orangeman to exterminate all Catholics, the Jacobin-inspired United Ireland rebellion soon degenerated into another religious war, in which a whole succession of nightmare incidents occurred. At Dunshaughlin, the rebels killed a local Protestant schoolmaster and his gardener and mutilated their bodies, and put a third man into a cauldron of boiling pitch. In Kildare, the rebels piked to death an old Protestant gatekeeper, his 14-year-old daughter and a dog that had attempted to defend them. In the streets of sacked towns and villages drunken rebels piked the bodies of British horses screaming: 'Take that, Protestant!' In New Ross, thirty-five men—mainly Protestants but including a few Catholics who had refused to leave their masters—were shot on a lawn at Scullabogue and the barn in which their 100 women and children had been imprisoned was set on fire, and all were burned alive. In Wexford an 'Orange Plot' was discovered and a French Revolution-style tribunal set up which in the space of two hours condemned and executed ninety-seven prisoners; their backs and stomachs were ripped open with pikes and they were thrown into the River Slaney.

Garbled accounts of the atrocities reached the Orangemen of Ulster and strengthened them in their determination to preserve the Protestant Ascendancy forever against such savage Papish rebels.

In June Lord Castlereagh, who had replaced Pelham as Chief Secretary, referred to the rebellion as 'a religious Phrensy' in which 'The Priests lead the rebels to battle; on their march, they kneel down and pray, and show the most desperate resolution in their attack . . . They put such Protestants as are reported to be Orangemen to death, saving others on condition of their embracing the Catholic faith. It is a Jacobinal conspiracy throughout the kingdom, pursuing its object chiefly with Popish instruments; the hated bigotry of this sect being better suited to the purpose of the republican leaders than the cold, reasoning, disaffection of the Northern Protestants'.

Curiously enough, although you could never convince the Orangemen of this, and indeed Lord Castlereagh was equally biassed, the Catholic hierarchy, despite the behaviour of a few priests was as opposed to the '98 Rising as it has been to every attempt to overthrow the *status quo* in Ireland and elsewhere. A few days before the ill-fated rebellion burst on the country, a loyal address, signed by the entire staff of the Catholic seminary at Maynooth, four Catholic peers, and some 2,000 members of the Catholic gentry, was presented to the Lord Lieutenant. It ran as follows:

> We the undersigned, His Majesty's most loyal subjects, the Roman Catholics of Ireland, think it necessary at this moment publicly to declare our firm attachment to His Majesty's person, and to the constitution under which we have the happiness to live . . . We cannot avoid expressing to Your Excellency our regret at seeing, amid the general delusion, many, particularly of the lower order of our own religious persuasion, engaged in unlawful associations and practices.

The rebel forces were scattered and defeated with terrible reprisals. Father Roche, who had been the effective commander-in-chief at Vinegar Hill outside Wexford, rode into Wexford in the wake of the British forces to negotiate terms for his rebel troops. He was dragged off his horse, beaten about the face until he was barely recognizable and hanged after a court martial.

French help came in the end, but by the time it reached Ireland the rebellion was over. Three small naval expeditions arrived in August, September and October. The first landed and was defeated; the second, with the United Ireland leader Napper Tandy, reached Donegal and left again in haste after eight hours on Irish soil. The third, with Wolfe Tone on board, was defeated in Lough Swilly. Tone was captured and cut his throat in prison to avoid being hanged.

Throughout the country small bands of peasant rebels—the 'Croppies' of the ballad at the beginning of this chapter—were being remorselessly hunted down, and the Orangemen were exultant. The country was still safe in Protestant hands.

* * *

O the French are on the sea,
Says the Shan Van Vocht,
The French are on the sea,
Says the Shan Van Vocht.
O the French are in the bay,
They'll be here without delay,
And the Orange will decay,
Says the Shan Van Vocht.

O the French are in the bay,
They'll be here by break of day,
And the Orange will decay,
Says the Shan Van Vocht.

—Traditional Irish street ballad.

V

The United Kingdom of Great Britain and Ireland

In order to give a coherent picture of the events leading up to the disastrous Rising of 1798, I omitted certain events which had been happening both within the Orange Order and within the Parliaments of Dublin and London during this period and to which it is now necessary to revert.

Inside the Orange Order, the transformation of a small, secret, religious militant society into a mass nation-wide movement presented great problems of organization. The open support of the gentry and wealthy traders and their gradual assumption of control over the movement led to the creation of a central body designed to establish and maintain the leadership in their hands and, conversely, to exclude from positions of authority the newly converted ex-United Ireland Presbyterians—mainly working class—who had 'defected' to the Orange Order under Lake's oppressive measures in Belfast and who were not regarded as politically stable.

In 1797 a meeting at Armagh was attended by masters of the various Ulster Orange Lodges with James Sloan, who had been secretary of the movement since its inception in 1795, acting as chairman. A few days later, on May 29th, this declaration of their principles was published in the *Belfast News-Letter:*

> 1st. We associate together to defend ourselves and our properties, to preserve the peace of the country, to support our King and Constitution, and to maintain the Protestant ascendancy for which our ancestors fought and conquered; in short, to uphold the present system and establishment, at the risk of our lives, in opposition to the wicked schemes of rebels of all descriptions.

2nd. Our Association, being entirely composed of Protestants, has offered an opportunity to people who undeservedly assume the appellation of Protestants, to insinuate to the Roman Catholics of Ireland, that we are sworn to extirpate and destroy them, which infamous charge we thus openly deny and disavow. Our obligation binds us to second and protect the existing laws of the land; and so long as we remain under the influence of that obligation, loyal, well-behaved men may fear no injury of any sort from us.

3rd. We earnestly request that the several members of the administration in this country will not suffer themselves to be prejudiced against us by the unfounded calumnies of unprincipled traitors, of ambitious dispositions, and desperate circumstances, who detest us for no other cause than our unshaken loyalty; and who are using every exertion to increase their consequence and repair their shattered fortunes by plunging the kingdom into all the horrors of rebellion, anarchy and civil war. And we likewise request the nation at large to believe our most solemn assurance that there is no body of men more strongly bound to support, or more firmly attached to the Government of the Empire, than the Orangemen of Ireland.

4th. We further warmly invite gentlemen of property to reside in the country, in order that we may enrol ourselves as District Corps under them, and that as two guineas [the current Government allowance] is not a sufficient sum for clothing as a soldier, we entreat gentlemen to subscribe whatever they may think proper for that necessary purpose; many an honest fellow having no personal property to contend for, nor any other object than the laudable patriotic ties of our Association.

Signed (by Order)

Abraham Davidson, Secretary

Although there had been Lodges in Dublin—notably in Trinity College—for some time, the founding of a gentlemen's

Orange Lodge in Dublin could be regarded as the first step towards putting the movement on a national basis. Thomas Verner—son of the James Verner of Churchill, County Armagh, who, at the head of a party of militia, had turned back some Defenders at the River Blackwater, just before the battle of Diamond—was its first Master, but the real strength of the Lodge lay in its connections with Patrick Duigenan, members of the Beresford faction and other Dublin gentry who represented an informal 'Protestant party' opposed to the Catholic Relief Act of 1793. The whole idea of the Orange movement held a great appeal for them, but they had not dared to risk Government disapproval by forming Orange Lodges themselves until the influence of Grattan's supporters in the Yeomanry had reached such proportions that the Government feared it might be turned into another Volunteer force to be used to further Grattan's political aims. The existence of an influential Orange Lodge in Dublin would be an effective counter to this tendency, and so the Government no longer opposed it. Within a year its numbers included several prominent noblemen and it had become one of the most influential clubs in Dublin.

Shortly after the formation of this Loyal Lodge No. 176 in Dublin, a Grand Lodge of Ulster had been formed at Portadown on July 12th, 1797. James Sloan, Dan Winter, James Wilson and many of the early founders of the movement now stepped down and men like William Blacker (who as an undergraduate on vacation from Trinity College, Dublin, had been present at the Diamond); Thomas Verner, David Verner and Thomas Seaver of Armagh, Dr William Atkinson and William Hart of Antrim and John Crossle of Tyrone—all gentry or professional men—with Wolsey Atkinson as acting secretary, took over the organization of the movement.

The announcement of the formation of this Grand Lodge of Ulster was accompanied by a demonstration of strength and government support. General Lake granted permission for a series of parades, and rode out at the head of the Belfast Yeomanry to review 3,000 Orangemen parading at Lisburn and another 12,000 at Lurgan.

But even before the Ulster Grand Lodge had been formed a secret brotherhood had been set up within this already semi-secret order—I say semi-secret because, although its members joined in secret, swore secret oaths on being initiated, and had secret methods of recognizing one another, nevertheless they were so keen on marching and parading in public that membership of the Order could not be seriously regarded as, in any real sense, secret.

The members of this inner brotherhood, originally called Orange Marksmen—probably a reference to their prowess with muskets, though I have no evidence of this—took the name of Purplemen. Dispersed through the Orange Lodges now rapidly springing up all over the country and within the Militia and Yeomanry, their principal purpose was to see that the Order was not signing on too many dubious and unreliable recruits. This inner brotherhood also provided a means by which the gentry could control the unruly rank and file—what might be described as the Peep o' Day element—which still existed in the movement. Later, the Order of the Purple came to be conferred on any Orangeman with a long record of good behaviour in his Lodge, and is now almost automatic after six months' membership. Its members originally had a separate set of signs and passwords and were bound by a separate oath requiring a higher standard of behaviour. One special requirement of the Orange Marksman, according to Senior, was that he 'induct no man into the Order on the road or hillsides', a measure designed to stop the recruitment of disorderly elements by irregular methods.

After 1797, the Orange Lodges had two Orders—the Orange and the Purple. Later still, Black Lodges came into existence, but I shall deal with that development in due course. In general, the early Purplemen tended to be Lodge Masters (but not always) and usually—although again not always—members of the gentry. The outward sign of the Orangeman at this period was an Orange ribbon in his buttonhole or hat-band. Orange Marksmen or Purplemen could wear ribbons of orange, purple and blue—purple because it was the royal colour and blue because of King William's Blue Dutch Guards.

2

Not long before the outbreak of the Rebellion of 1798, the men in command of the Orange Order decided that it would be easier to control their rapidly escalating membership by organizing the movement on a national basis and moving the Grand Lodge from Portadown to Dublin. The Dublin Lodge was by now attracting members of the calibre of Sir Jonah Barrington, the writer and judge, and Major Sirr, who was the Castle's Chief Security Officer and who, in this capacity, was responsible for the arrest of the leaders of the 1798 rebellion.

A meeting was held in Dublin in March 1798 at which all the most important Lodges in Ireland were represented. At this meeting the framework for a national organization was drawn up. Grand Lodges which had been formed in many parts of the country were made subordinate to the Grand Lodge now to be established in Dublin. Counties were divided into Districts, each under a District Master chosen by the Lodges in the District, and each county was to have one Grand Lodge. The Grand Lodge of Ireland, in Dublin, would be formed by members elected by each County Grand Lodge. Grand Lodge elections would be held annually. Thomas Verner, the first Irish Grand Master—at whose elegant Georgian home in Dawson Street, Dublin, a set of resolutions embodying the above points was drawn up and a copy sent to every Orange Lodge in Ireland—had been associated with the movement from the beginning. He was the son of a Member of Parliament and a prominent Armagh landowner, James Verner, and brother-in-law of Lord Donegal.

The first official meeting of the Irish Grand Lodge was attended by the Marquis of Drogheda, Sir Richard Musgrave, later to become a historian of the rebellion, William Blacker, a Captain in the Armagh Militia, and nine NCOs wearing the uniform of the Armagh, Cavan and Fermanagh regiments of the Militia. The main business was to give official sanction to the decisions made at the earlier meeting and to assign to Harding Giffard the task of drawing up a set of rules which would apply to all Orange societies. The meeting was then adjourned until November.

While these meetings were taking place, the more influential Orangemen were, according to Hereward Senior, doing what they could to present the movement in a favourable light to the British Cabinet. 'The manner in which they gained the ear of the Duke of Portland is obscure,' he writes, 'but by March 20 he was persuaded of the Orangemen's usefulness and respectability. He wrote, "I heard yesterday that the Orange Association in Ulster has been joined by all the principal gentry and well-affected persons of property in that province, for the purpose of protecting themselves by an oath to defend the King and Constitution".'

Portland went on: 'Associations of any sort unless authorized by the Government are not generally to be countenanced, but, considering the circumstances of these times, and the necessity of counteracting the attempt of our domestic enemies, exertions of this kind may do more than all the military force you could apply towards the establishment of order. The example may produce the best effects in other parts of the Kingdom and may give you a disposable force to be carried to the South. The sense of danger and the proper spirit which has prompted this combination may dispose those who have entered it to allow your Excellency to methodize and bring them into the state of subordination which may enable you to employ their zeal to the best advantage.'

Lord Camden's reply to this was that he thought it unwise to give open encouragement to the Orangemen for fear of increasing the jealousy and fears of the Catholics, but by the same token he felt it was 'not expedient to suppress them' either.

This was the situation when the rebellion broke out, and we have seen the part played by the Orangemen in the Militia and the Yeomanry in that affair. The fact that a rebellion which had its beginnings in an attempt by Belfast Protestant radicals to challenge the authority of Dublin Castle ended in a religious war between Nationalist Catholics and Orangemen which looked, to the Protestants at any rate, very like a repetition of the 'Massacre of the Protestants' of 1641, drove a further wedge between the two communities which became greater rather than less, with the passage of time. Henceforth, Irish nationalism was based almost exclusively on Irish Catholicism and identified with it; and Orangeism and loyalty to the crown were taken as synonymous. 'In the course of the rebellion,' as Hereward Senior puts it, 'the Orangemen and the forces of the Crown had intermingled to such an extent that it became difficult to distinguish one from the other. As magistrates, Yeomanry and Militia officers were active Orangemen it was all but impossible for the public to discover to what extent the Government countenanced the activities of the Orangemen.'

Authorizations issued during the rebellion to bands of loyal Orangemen to entitle them to carry arms were used, after the rebellion, by minor Orange leaders to justify random searches for arms and even raids on Catholic homes. These activities were not approved or even countenanced by the central organization of the Orange Order, but as at the time of the 'Armagh Outrages' it was sometimes difficult to prevent the more unruly elements in the movement from pressing home their advantage after the collapse of the rebellion, and, as we have seen in the last chapter, the *Hell or Connaught* notices began to appear again on Catholic cottages.

The Grand Lodge in Dublin was particularly sensitive about these new 'outrages' and took immmediate action to disclaim responsibility for them. A second meeting of the Grand Lodge had been arranged for November 20th, 1798, but the officials of the Lodge were so nervous of criticism that on September 10th, at a meeting called to make plans for the November Grand Lodge meeting, the chairman, the Rev J. F. Knife, made a statement to the effect that the Orange Order was not an anti-Catholic body. The Orange Lodges, he said, were against sedition and had no quarrel with the Catholics on religious grounds. He disclaimed responsibility for any attacks on Catholics and pointed out that there was a clause in one of the Orange rules stating that '... no person do persecute or upbraid anyone on account of his religion'.

When the meeting of the Grand Lodge took place in

November further efforts were made to dissociate the movement from incidents involving religious intolerance. It was suggested that disorderly elements pretending to be Orangemen might be responsible for many of these incidents and there was implicit in the statements from the Grand Lodge a suggestion that membership of the Orange Order would not ensure immunity from justice, doubtless intended as a warning to the Peep o' Day elements which still existed in the Order. For the raids on Catholics in the North had been too widespread not to have included a proportion of Orangemen, whether they participated independently of their local Lodge Masters or with their connivance. But the Grand Lodge was in a quandary, wanting to discipline the members of the Order but not at the expense of undermining the anti-Catholic spirit which was the whole driving force behind it. There was, too, the danger of fragmenting the Orange Institution into a series of unconnected, uncontrolled and uncontrollable bands of the sort from which it had originally developed.

While there was undoubtedly an element of hypocrisy in the Grand Lodge's suggestion that impostors pretending to be Orangemen had perpetrated most of the outrages, it was also true that many bands of Protestant loyalists quite unconnected with the Orange Order either styled themselves Orangemen or were described as Orangemen by the Catholics they attacked. The name 'Black Lodges' was sometimes used to describe unauthorized Orange Lodges and there was the added complication that some of these 'Black Lodges' included members of other, official Orange Lodges who regarded the Black Lodges as in some way superior to the official Lodges. Harding Giffard, who had been commissioned to draw up the bye-laws for the Grand Lodge made a statement on this: '. . . many persons have introduced various orders into the Orange Society, which will very much tend to injure the regularity of the Institution; the Grand Lodge disavows any other orders but the Orange and Purple, and there can be none other regular, unless issuing from and approved of, by them'.

It was decided that the Grand Lodge would meet on the first Thursday of each month at seven o'clock and on the third

Thursday at three o'clock. Delegation of authority was to be from above, with the Master of each Lodge appointed by the Grand Lodge, while he in turn would appoint a deputy master, a treasurer and a secretary. At least ten or more members would have to be present to make voting legal. Meetings would open with a prayer, followed by a reading of the general rules. New members would then be proposed, reports of sub-committees read and considered, previously proposed members balloted for and accepted new members enrolled, and the meeting would close with another prayer. The procedure was one which was already followed in most Orange Lodges and was similar in many ways to normal Masonic practice.

After this meeting the Orange Order was firmly established on a national basis with a central leadership meeting regularly to control what had grown, in three short years, from an obscure agrarian Ulster Protestant society into the strongest single political force in Ireland and an organization unassailable in Ulster without the aid of troops brought in from outside the country.

3

Turning now to parliamentary matters during the years immediately before the 1798 Rebellion, there had been a growing feeling at Westminster and among some of the later Viceroys that a union between the Dublin and Westminster Parliaments might be the best solution to the Irish Question. There was a precedent: the successful union of the English and Scottish Parliaments nearly a century earlier.

In his final decision that Ireland could be more conveniently managed from Westminster, Pitt's motives were, it would seem, partly a desire to strengthen the defences of the British Isles as a unit for the coming struggle with Napoleon and partly irritation at the growing independence of the Irish Parliament, which had succeeded in gaining a considerable measure of free trade.

During the debates in the Irish Parliament on the Catholic Relief Act, it had become clear that once the Catholics were given full political rights it would be only a matter of time until the Protestants would find themselves a minority in the Irish Parliament. However, even this did not produce any enthusiasm for the idea of union within the Irish Parliament; and until it became law many members of the Orange Order were opposed to the whole idea of Union. As the Rev John Brown puts it: '. . . the great question in 1799 was what the Grand Orange Lodge and the Orangemen as a whole would think of Pitt's proposed Union. Division appeared. Thomas Verner, Grand Master of Ireland, representing his family and many of the Northern gentry, thought well of it. John C. Beresford, Grand Secretary, representing the great Beresford interest, was inclined to think ill of it. A large section of the Protestant Ascendancy, proud of their Parliament and still triumphant from their victory of 1798, thought very ill of it. It is likely that they expressed the opinion of very many members of the Orange body'.

This admission in the most recent official history of Orangeism makes ironic reading in relation to the almost fanatical steps to which today's Orangemen are prepared to go to maintain that Union; the very table on which the historic Act was signed is preserved at Stormont, where it is approached by Orangemen with something of the awe which overcomes a devout Catholic in the presence of the Host.

To the English statesmen at Westminster the question of union seemed inescapably bound up with that of Catholic Emancipation. They saw in it a means by which Catholics could be given a measure of the equality they were clamouring for without endangering the security of the Protestant minority in Ireland. Pitt even felt that he could now include in his arrangements for pushing the Act of Union through the Irish Parliament a promise to allow Catholics to sit in Parliament at Westminster since the Catholics in the Irish Party at Westminster would be inevitably outnumbered by Protestants in a House of Commons representing the whole of the British Isles. But in the event, King George III, who believed that to give the Catholics full freedom would constitute a violation of his coronation oath, refused to give his assent.

So the package deal which was offered to Ireland, and secured by about £1,260,000 in straight cash bribes, plus the creation of 28 new peerages and 26 promotions among the Irish peers, amounted to one Parliament for the whole of the British Isles, with 100 Irish Protestant members (later increased to 105) sitting in the House of Commons, plus four Protestant bishops and 24 Irish Protestant peers sitting in the House of Lords.

The citizens of Dublin—and in particular the professional classes and the wealthy merchants—were bitterly opposed to the Union as they did not wish to see their elegant capital relegated to the status of a provincial city. In general, the Catholic peasants were apathetic; they were more interested in potatoes than politics. Cooke, the Under-Secretary, who was one of the men charged with selling this package deal to the Irish Parliament, argued that Protestant Ireland was dependent on England for military protection; this infuriated the Orange Yeomanry and the gentry who had led them in 1798. They argued that it was almost entirely due to their efforts that the United Irish rebellion had been put down. Pamphlets were published, protest meetings were held and the talk went on and on; but the bribes achieved their purpose. Despite a threat of mass resignation from the Yeomanry and the breakaway of some Orange Lodges which defied the official policy of neutrality in political matters and declared that as Orangemen they considered the extinction of their separate Legislature to be 'the extinction of the Irish Nation', on February 6th, 1800, when a division took place on the Bill, the voting was 158 for Union and 115 against it.

The Royal Assent was given on August 1st, 1800, and the new Union Jack was unfurled over Dublin Castle, as Ireland became part of the United Kingdom of Great Britain and Ireland.

4

Once the Union had become an established fact a great deal of the opposition to it melted away, though a certain apathy descended on Dublin partly due to the drain of wealth and talent from Dublin to London and to the fact that many of the livelier and wealthier Anglo-Irish gentry now transferred their town houses from Fitzwilliam Square to Mayfair.

In Ulster, the Orangemen who had split on the Union issue were now united again and continued to gain in strength and to increase their control of the Yeomanry and the Militia. For a time after the Peace of Amiens it looked as if some of these irregular units might be disbanded, but when war with France broke out again in 1803 no regular British troops could be spared for Ireland, and the Yeomanry and Militia were again encouraged and even augmented. And when the Twelfth of July came round again ever-increasing armies of Orangemen in uniforms or wearing sashes and other para-military emblems marched behind their bands and their Lambeg drums through the streets of the Ulster towns and villages.

Although Irish legislation was now framed in Westminster, Dublin Castle remained the effective centre of British administration in Ireland, and the Parliament at Westminster, when it was not ignoring Ireland altogether, was legislating for it as if it were a typical British province. The provision of workhouses based on the English pattern, largely designed for urbanized industrial areas and utterly unsuited to the needs of a scattered peasant population, was one typical example of the sort of mistakes that were made.

In 1803 Dublin's apathy was briefly shaken by an attempt by Robert Emmet, a Cork Protestant, to revive the spirit of the United Ireland movement and stage a rebellion in the streets of Dublin. It turned out to be little more than a street riot in which only an old and well-intentioned judge was killed; Emmet was tried and publicly hanged. Thereafter, for half a century, Irish Nationalism confined itself to trying to find a solution to the Irish Question through constitutional means.

At this time, there were really a number of Irish questions only one of which concerned the bulk of the Irish Catholic peasants. Catholic emancipation meant very little to them unless it was accompanied by a relief from the tithes which they were obliged to pay to the established Protestant Church, which represented the religious faith of less than a quarter of the population. They were not interested in the vote as such as they were mostly too poor to qualify under the property clause which the franchise then still entailed. And they were not really interested in whether the country was administered from Dublin or London. What they were interested in was land: if they couldn't get their own lands back, at least they wanted some system of fair rents, some security of tenure and the right to sell their interest in their farms and profit from any improvements they made. It was quite clear that no mass support for any political movement could be expected from the Irish peasants unless it was clearly associated with some system of land reform.

In the meantime they looked after their interests in the only way they knew: by the revival of agrarian societies like the Whiteboys and the Defenders, under new names such as the Threshers and the Ribbonmen.

A contemporary Government report, quoted by Hereward Senior, stated:

> The peasants still retain the most rancorous antipathy against the Orangemen and every fresh act of outrage adds fuel to their passive and keen desire for revenge. Being made to believe that those outrages are committed on them under the authority and sanction of government, their antipathy against it and against the Orange party is exactly the same, for they conceive on this account the Government to be the real source of all this . . . suffering.
>
> They now have a general mistrust in every gentleman and they have been for a considerable time past organizing in many counties, although I cannot say to what ends. They admit no gentlemen into their secret, but choose leaders of their own body who had, upon former occasions, given satisfactory proof of their courage and resolution. Their object, as far as I can learn, is self-defence against the Orangemen . . . It's safer to be a rebel than to stay home as reprisals are indiscriminate.

Immediately after the Act of Union and the disastrous failure of Robert Emmet's Rising there was no political leadership available to organize the Catholic peasantry. The Catholic hierarchy and most of the Catholic middle-class merchants hoped that their co-operation in getting the Act of Union passed would persuade Pitt to grant full Catholic Emancipation, but a combination which included the King, the Orangemen and a large section of the Lords in England effectively blocked any further steps in this direction.

And the failure to follow up the Act of Union with some measure of Catholic Emancipation made it inevitable that sooner or later a political party *would* arise in Ireland which would utilize Catholicism as a source of political power. And, equally inevitable, that when that happened a further polarization would result between predominately Protestant Ulster and the remainder of the country, which would give the Orange movement yet another opportunity to exert its influence.

In the meantime, the Orange Order was still busy disclaiming the continuing acts of outrage and even, on occasion, putting notices in newspapers like the *Belfast News-Letter* announcing that it had tried and expelled certain members for unruly conduct and warning Orangemen who committed such crimes that they could expect no protection from the Orange Order.

Thomas Verner, the first Grand Master, and the man who was largely responsible for bringing the gentry into the Order, resigned in 1801, to be replaced by the Rt. Hon. George Ogle, an M.P. for Dublin at Westminster and a far more prominent man than Verner. As the Lodges grew older and more respectable they tended to attract more men in high places. At the same time Sir Richard Musgrave, the historian, was Grand Treasurer, and Patrick Duigenan had replaced J. C. Beresford as Grand Secretary. With the rebellion at an end and the country under the control of Westminster, the Grand Orange Lodges, for a period at any rate, changed in character and tended to turn into fraternal clubs which debated recent events in Ireland in terms of 'Popish Plots'. According to Senior, 'they justified their arguments by references to alleged actions of the Catholics in past centuries'. Their 'works abound in analogies between 1641 and 1798 and lurid stories of the Inquisition'.

But if the Grand Lodges turned into political debating societies the vast bulk of the ordinary members of the organization still much preferred marching and fighting. Attacks on Catholic homes continued and street fights and riots were commonplace occurrences, not only between Orangemen and Catholics but even between Orangemen and Masons; in Londonderry, a riot between Freemasons and Orangemen resulted in five deaths and Senior refers to rumours 'that at Saintfield money was offered for the head of an Orangeman'.

The Orange Marches, too, began to take on a new character in many parts of Ulster. On the Twelfth of July and on various other occasions throughout the year the Orangemen took to marching behind their banners and their bands and their Lambeg drums, choosing routes which ran through predominately Catholic villages or districts in the cities, carrying arms, shouting anti-Papish slogans and singing offensive songs. And when the insulted Catholics were sufficiently provoked to retaliate, as they invariably were, the Orangemen fired on them or attacked them with other weapons 'in self-defence'.

The Rev John Brown openly admits this in his contribution to the latest official historical appreciation of Orangeism and explains it as follows: 'Most Irish Protestants were deeply afraid of a repetition of the events of 1798 and of the years just before. They tended to consider Roman Catholicism and possible rebellion as almost identical terms. To keep things as they were in Church and State seemed the guarantee of safety. When attempts were made to secure Roman Catholic Emancipation, or when Threshers or Ribbonmen were more than usually active, the Irish Protestant reacted strongly . . . When reports of disorder, intimidation and "agrarian" crime came in from the South, the Northern Protestant refused to allow the slightest self-assertion "to the other side", lest the same should occur in his own neighbourhood. On the Twelfth of July and on other occasions, he marched with his lodge behind its flag and drums and fifes, wearing his regalia (cockade, ribbons, scarf or sash) and armed with his yeoman gun, to show his strength in the places where he thought it would do most good. Where you could "walk" you were dominant and the other things followed'.

* * *

King William called his officers, saying: 'Gentlemen, mind your station,
And let your valour here be shown before this Irish nation;
My brazen walls let no man break, and your subtle foes you'll scatter,
Be sure you show them good English play as you go over the water.

—From *The Boyne Water*,
a traditional Orange ballad.

VI

Orangeism In Trouble Over the Water

Long before the Battle of Diamond and the formation of the Orange Order there had been 'Orange' anti-Jacobite societies within the officers' messes of some British Army regiments. One of these I have already referred to: 'The Loyal Order of the Orange and Blew' which existed in the Fourth Foot, King William's Own. Initially it had no connection with Ireland other than the fact that the decisive battles in King William's British campaigns happened to be fought in Ireland.

But the fact that Scots and Welsh fencibles had seen service in Ireland, and English Militia regiments had been sent to Ireland during the 1798 rebellion and immediately after it, was probably the principal factor in the spread of Orangeism to England. The first recorded instance of an official Orange Lodge transferring to England was in 1798 when the Lancashire Militia took Orange warrant No. 220 back with them to Manchester. And when the regiment was disbanded the members of the Lodge continued to meet as a normal, civilian Orange Lodge. The following year the second battalion of the Manchester and Salford Volunteers returned home, bringing with them Orange warrant No. 1128, and numerous other British military units formed Orange Lodges among them the Welsh fencibles, known as the Ancient Britons, who had assisted Lake in 'pacifying' Newry. Before long there were Orange Lodges at Oldham, Bury, Stockport, Ashton-under-Lyne, Rochdale and Wigan, as well as in Manchester, which remained the principal Orange stronghold.

Membership of these clubs probably initially consisted of Irishmen who had served in these regiments and wished to keep up their associations when the regiments were disbanded or when they left the service. At the same time, once they became civilian clubs and civilians were free to join they would naturally attract Irish Protestants who had come to England looking for work. For this was the period of the industrial revolution and there were plenty of jobs in the new factories and mills that were springing up in the Manchester area.

A large number of Catholic Irish had already settled in Manchester and the other industrial conurbations then just beginning to form, and the Protestant workers who came to look for jobs in these areas—relatively few in numbers because the industrial revolution was at this time providing new jobs in Belfast and other Ulster cities as well—found themselves a minority within a minority and would naturally gravitate towards societies which had an Irish connection but were limited to Protestants, and where they would meet English and Scottish Protestants and establish their identity as different from the Catholic Irish immigrants who were regarded with some contempt by the English.

In this, of course, they were almost certainly misguided. One of the first shattering discoveries an Orangeman makes when he comes to live in England—and it was probably as true then, certainly among the ignorant working classes, as it is today among all classes—is that the English make no distinction whatever between the Protestant Ulsterman and the Catholic Republican; they are both regarded alike as Paddies.

As soon as the Orange Lodges in Britain were strong enough to do so they started marching, in the true Orange tradition, through predominantly Catholic areas. And inevitably, there were riots. The first of these occurred in Manchester on July 12th, 1807; the military were called out and a number of people were arrested. The Rev Ralph Nixon, an English clergyman to whose collegiate church the Orangemen had marched, wrote to one of the Manchester newspapers about the incident. 'Orange principles,' he said, 'are imperfectly known in England and those who attacked them are misled by an erroneous opinion that our views are hostile and directed against papists. Orangemen are zealously attached to the King and admire our matchless constitution.'

The Orangemen are forever talking about 'the constitution', a phrase which is meaningless in the context of the present Ulster sub-province inasmuch as the only constitution it possesses is the Government of Ireland Act of 1920 which includes a provision enabling Westminster to suspend or terminate its activities with or without its approval—the provision by which Stormont was prorogued in March 1972—and even more meaningless in the context of the United Kingdom as a whole, which has no written constitution. In fact, only the Irish Republic has a formal, written constitution.

Nevertheless the Manchester riots were regarded as the English Lodges' 'Battle of the Diamond' and were made an occasion for a reorganization and reinforcement of the whole movement. Lodges had been founded in London by this time and the Scots fencibles had imported two Lodges into Scotland.

Encouraged by this initial success, Nixon then set about trying to establish Orangeism as a nationwide movement in Britain. A visit to London convinced him that the headquarters of the movement would have to be the industrial North or Midlands; the London Lodges turned out to be disappointing both in the numbers and in the quality of their membership. Senior quotes an Irish Orangeman, C. E. Chetwoode, who went to London and found the only Lodge then functioning held fortnightly meetings 'attended by about twenty persons, mostly of the lower orders, at a public house in Clerkenwell called the Coach and Horses'.

Nixon had set up as his Headquarters a British Grand Lodge at the Star Hotel, Manchester, with a Colonel Taylor as Grand Master and Nixon himself as Grand Secretary. Irish warrants were cancelled and all Orange Lodges in Britain had to acquire new warrants from the British Grand Lodge; and the movement spread very rapidly in areas where there were large Irish populations. British workers, increasingly nervous that their living standards would be threatened by the mass immigration of Irish Catholics, realized that their fear and dislike of the Catholic Irish could find expression in the Orange Order.

There is some evidence that Nixon and Taylor and other Orange leaders in Britain tried to draw an analogy between the dispossessed and disaffected Irish peasantry and the neglected and restless industrial population of the North and Midlands in order to attract the interest and attention of the British ruling class to the Orange Order. And during the Luddite troubles of 1812 Orange magistrates swore in Orangemen as special constables in a very minor role in those disturbances.

Nixon and members of his Grand Lodge in Britain kept insisting that if a substantial number of Tories would form a London counterpart of the original Dublin Grand Lodge the British movement could become a nationwide political movement similar to the Irish one. The idea of an organization which could be used to oppose Catholic Emancipation undoubtedly appealed to ultra-Tory peers and to some of the noblemen and gentry, such as the Duke of York and the Duke of Cumberland, sons of George III.

In 1813, Lord Yarmouth, the Marquis of Hereford's son and a keen Orangeman, seems to have persuaded the Duke of York, who was Commander-in-Chief of the Army, to attend an Orange dinner, though it was described as a meeting of a 'Philanthropic Society', and towards the end of it the Duke appears to have joined the Order. This was raised in Parliament by the Whig Opposition, and whether or not the Duke of York had joined the Order (he was certainly a member of the Orange and Blew) the incident marked the beginning of an alliance between Orangeism and High Toryism from which the Unionist Party eventually developed.

The Whig objection to the Duke of York's association with the Order, according to Constantine Fitzgibbon's book, *Red Hand: The Ulster Colony*, was based on the fact that secret organizations had been abolished by an Act of Parliament of 1799. The British Orange Order reacted by altering its rules and ostensibly abolishing its 'secret' nature. An effort to tempt the Duke of Wellington into joining elicited the following reply:

> I confess I object to belonging to a society professing attachment to the throne and Constitution from which a large proportion of his Majesty's subjects are excluded . . . The principal objection which I have to belonging to this

> society is that its members are bound to each other by an oath of secrecy. If such an oath is legal, which I doubt, I can't swear it consistently with my oath of allegiance and the oath which I have taken as one of His Majesty's Privy Council.

But, according to Fitzgibbon, 'the Duke of York was less circumspect. In that same month he joined, or re-joined, the Order as Grand Master of the Orange Institution. There was once again a rumpus in Parliament and four months later he felt obliged to resign or re-resign from the Order. However, this fleeting brush with the Royalty had done the Order no harm, and no more had the attendant publicity. By then there were Orange Lodges in most of the great British industrial cities, as well as within many of the British regiments'.

He goes on: 'We have a glimpse of them in Liverpool in 1818, parading on July 12th with effigies of the Pope and the Cardinal which they intended to burn outside the main doors of a Roman Catholic Church, until forbidden by the Mayor to do so. In that same year the Manchester Orangemen supported the authorities during the period of social unrest and nascent trade unionism that culminated in the so-called Peterloo Massacre. A high proportion of the labourers flooding into the new city of Manchester, then little more than a vast and filthy shanty-town, were Irish. It is safe to assume that the support the Orangemen gave to the military was not another foreshadowing of future Unionist politics but was inspired by sectarian hatred transported across the Irish Sea'.

Fitzgibbon also makes the point that when the third decade of the 19th century opened there were at least five varieties of Orangemen united in their determination on one issue: to preserve the Protestant ascendancy over the Catholics in both islands. In England there was a small group of nobility and gentry, mainly High Tories. There were the Orangemen in the slum-cities created by the Industrial Revolution, whose members were either expatriate Irish Protestant labourers or English anti-Catholic workers. There were the Lodges within the British army, which then as now included a high proportion of Irishmen, Catholic and Protestant. And in Ireland, there were again two sorts of Orangemen. In the area that is now the Republic of Ireland, there were so few Protestants and those almost exclusively wealthy landowners or merchants and traders, that the Orangemen, he says, were like a corps of officers without any army. In the predominantly Protestant areas of Ulster the situation was the reverse: here, after the end of the Napoleonic War and the disbanding of the Yeomanry, the wealthy gentry and landowners had largely lost interest in the movement, which was by now mainly composed of working-class and peasant Protestants—an army, in effect, without officers.

Orange Lodges within the British Army came under official attack around 1809. An Orange warrant made out to Private Hall of the First West York Militia with a yellow ribbon attached to it by a wax seal stamped with a facsimile of King Billy crossing the Boyne reached the officer commanding the regiment and produced this reaction from the Home Secretary: '. . . His Majesty's Government considers such associations to be of the most dangerous tendency and that it is understood that oaths are administered . . . it is material that the Lt Colonel of the 1st West York Militia should be apprized that all such oaths are illegal'.

Nixon tried to avoid further trouble by altering the rules to make them more flexible and dropping the conditional oath by which Orangemen swore to defend King George III and his heirs and successors 'so long as he or they shall support the Protestant ascendancy' which meant, in effect, that they were free to withhold their allegiance if the King or his successors should ever do anything which, in the opinion of the Orange Order, endangered the Protestant ascendancy. This action very largely stymied a protest against Orangeism made by an M.P. called Wynn, because he based his case against the Order on the earlier version of the rules and in particular on the conditional oath. Nevertheless, the debate—in which the Prince of Wales and the Duke of York were mentioned as being connected with the movement—ended any possibility of open patronage by the Royal family, and, as a result, Orange Lodges were banned in a number of regiments.

But again in 1821 Sir John Newport raised Orangeism in Parliament and questioned the Duke of York's association with the Order. There is considerable confusion about the Duke's connection with the Order and even contemporary accounts contradict one another on matters of fact. But there seems to be little doubt that meetings of an organization which styled itself the Royal Orange Lodge were held in the 1820s at the residence of the Deputy Grand Master, Lord Kenyon, and that the Duke of York was Grand Master at this period. His letter of resignation, which followed Sir John Newport's parliamentary question, stated:

> The question put to the Marquis of Londonderry yesterday evening in the House of Commons by Sir John Newport and the answer given by his Lordship, place me under the necessity of making in writing that communication to your Lordship which I wished to have deferred until I had the pleasure of seeing you. Your Lordship is perfectly aware of the grounds and principles upon which I accepted the Grand Mastership of the Orange Lodge in England. I have within these few days learnt that the law officers of the Crown and other eminent lawyers are decidedly of the opinion that the Orange Associations under the Oath administered to their members, are illegal . . . Under that circumstance, and from the moment I satisfied myself of the existence of this objection, it became my duty to withdraw myself from an office and from an association of which I could no longer be a member without violating those laws which it has ever been my study to withhold and maintain.

Once again, the Orange Order met the challenge by altering its rules and regulations to keep within the law without dissolving the organization.

But for the moment, at any rate, the Order had lost face in Britain.

* * *

It is called the Orange Lily,
Its history Protestants love to tell.
Songs have been written about it,
In July it always looks so well.

They tie it on top of Orange Banners,
Wear it at the side of the hat,
King William himself planted it
In some unknown spot.

It's one of the nicest flowers
Protestants could ever grow.
From the City of Londonderry,
To Belfast's Sandy Row.

Wear it on your sash next Twelfth,
Wherever you may go.
You Protestant heroes of Ulster,
From Shankhill and sweet Sandy Row.

—S. Boyd, from *Orange-Loyalist Songs, 1971.*

VII

The Dog Days—and the New Menace

Although Irish nationalism had no effective leadership after the collapse of Emmet's Rising and the vast bulk of the Catholic peasantry were too poor and miserable to contemplate organizing themselves, agrarian unrest continued during the English war with France, when Ireland was held down by a garrison of about 25,000 men and for most of the time under the Insurrection Act, a measure similar to the present Special Powers Act in Northern Ireland.

The Orange movement continued to entrench itself during this period even in Dublin Castle circles, though the need to recruit Catholics for the British army made it impossible for the Castle to support Orangeism openly or whole-heartedly, and on occasion forced it into overt anti-Orange actions.

In 1805, when a number of Irish Catholic gentry and middle-class professional men formed a Catholic committee to petition the British Government for Catholic emancipation, John Giffard, a civil servant in the Customs department, used his influence to persuade the largely Orange-dominated Dublin Corporation to prepare a counter-petition; he was promptly sacked.

The Irish Orangemen at Westminster reacted to the Catholic petition in the House of Commons with more fervour than logic and gave Grattan the opportunity to establish himself as the leading advocate of the Catholic cause at Westminster. Dublin Castle made further attempts to appease Catholic opinion by removing some Orange magistrates and allowing the Insurrection Act to lapse. Since, however, these measures did not have any effect on what was rapidly becoming a new and more acute Irish Question, they were no more effective in ending the disturbances than the earlier, repressive measures had been.

There had been what is nowadays called 'a population explosion' in Ireland towards the end of the 18th and the beginning of the 19th centuries: the population increased from between four and five millions in 1800 to nearly seven millions in 1821 and by almost another million within the next ten years. Irish agriculture, primitive in the extreme and bursting at the seams to support the existing population—particularly in Connaught where so many of the Irish had been forced to settle and where nothing grew except potatoes and seaweed—could not hope to cope with all those extra mouths to be fed.

Furthermore, the end of the war with France aggravated the problem in two ways. First, the disbandment of British regiments no longer needed in peacetime resulted in the arrival back in their native land of thousands of Irish ex-soldiers all looking for work. And second, the end of the war brought about a change in the whole pattern of Irish agriculture. While England was at war with Napoleon there had been a constant demand for corn and other food, but when the war ended prices fell and the tenant farmers' return for their corn was not always adequate to cover the rents they paid, which in turn meant that the landlords' profits dropped away. In these circumstances it paid the landlords better to let off their land in larger packages for sheep and cattle ranching; and this in turn had two effects. First, it meant evicting the small tenant farmers who had to look for uncultivated land elsewhere which could be cleared of stones and planted with potatoes, and, second, since cattle ranching and sheep farming require little in the way of labour, it meant adding an army of farm labourers and evicted tenant farmers to the already massive ranks of the unemployed, and a drift to the only areas where there *were* jobs, the industrial North and Midlands of England—and Ulster.

For Ulster, unlike the rest of Ireland, was developing a new kind of prosperity in the wake of the Act of Union. The Industrial Revolution—which had by-passed Southern Ireland as it had few, if any, industries to develop—had changed the face of Ulster. New factories now replaced the old workshops and steam power was used for the mass production of goods. The cotton industry had been mechanized, a shipbuilding industry was started and the port facilities of Belfast developed, providing jobs for men as well as those which already existed for women in the cotton mills and the linen industry.

This new prosperity attracted workers into Belfast from the surrounding countryside and from even further afield, many of them Catholics, who tended to huddle together for self-protection in the ghetto areas in the narrow, soul-destroying, back-to-back streets of seedy houses which began to spring up to accommodate the factory workers; somebody has said that if Dublin degenerated into a slum, Belfast was designed as one.

Nevertheless, this new prosperity tended still further to emphasize the increasing difference between Ulster and the rest of Ireland, a difference smugly interpreted by Orangemen as the fruits of sober, loyal, Protestant industry as opposed to Fenian Catholic idleness and sloth, but it also brought the Orange/Catholic sectarianism from the countryside into the towns and cities. Now, on top of the fierce competition for farm-land, which already existed between Protestants and Catholics in Ulster, there was a new competition between them for jobs and houses in Belfast and the other developing towns and cities in the North.

Catholics all over Ireland had enjoyed freedom of worship for some time, and the Government had even endowed a seminary at Maynooth in County Kildare as early as 1795—though more to stop the practice of candidates for the priest-hood going abroad to study in France (where they were likely to pick up dangerously revolutionary ideas) than from any sincere desire to make it easier for Catholics to train their priests. But the Catholic peasants were still deeply aggrieved that they had to pay tithes to the established Protestant Church of Ireland which represented the religious faith of less than a quarter of the population. The time was ripe for a leader who would mould them together into a unified force; and now such a leader came along.

Daniel O'Connell, a highly successful lawyer from County Kerry, was a royalist, but also a strong nationalist. He was opposed to any attempt to solve the Irish Question by physical force, and was convinced that further reforms could only be won by constitutional means. In 1810 he supported what Senior called 'a half-hearted move of the Dublin Corporation for repeal [of the Act of Union] and announced he would "trample on emancipation if it interfered with repeal".' O'Connell was quick to realize that if he could stamp out agrarian violence among the Catholic peasantry and organize them into an orderly political movement the Orange Order would be deprived of a good deal of its usefulness to the Protestants and to Dublin Castle, and so he set about laying the foundations of a new political movement based on a policy of exerting influence on the Government by popular agitation. He started by setting up a Catholic committee, similar to that formed by Tone and Keogh, to consider the problem.

Almost immediately his committee ran into trouble with the Orange element at the Castle. With the aid of the Attorney-General, William Saurin, a prominent Orangeman, (a member of a French Huguenot family), Secretary Wellesley Pole proposed ordering the arrest of all persons actively or passively connected with the election of members or delegates to O'Connell's Catholic Committee.

Afraid that such an action might force the Government into taking similar action against the Orange Order, the Grand Lodge held a meeting in July 1810 and adopted a new set of rules, dropping some of the secret articles.

When Sir Robert Peel became Irish Secretary and virtual governor of Ireland in 1812, he championed the Orange cause to an extent that earned him the nickname of 'Orange Peel' from O'Connell's followers. But there is plenty of evidence that Peel had his private doubts about the wisdom of supporting the Orange Order, particularly at a time when Orangeism was coming under heavy attack in Great Britain, as we have seen. To Lord Liverpool, he wrote: 'We find it, I assure you, a most difficult task when anti-Catholicism (if I may call it so) and loyalty are so much united as they are in the Orangemen to appease one without discouraging the other'. And to the Viceroy: 'Supposing them to be perfectly legal, I must confess that I cannot look upon this, or any other political association in Ireland that is controlled by any other authority than that of the Government without jealousy . . . I admire the principles that the Orangemen maintain and avow. But when I find among their rules direct references to the "officers, non-commissioned officers, and privates of respective regiments", I cannot conceal from myself the possible danger of such an institution'.

On the same day—I am quoting Senior again—he wrote to Lord Whitworth: 'I suppose I shall be blamed by the one party for going too far in the vindication of the Orangemen, and by the other for not going far enough. The more I think about the subject, the more I am convinced that even the most loyal associations in Ireland for political purposes are dangerous engines. We may derive a useful lesson from the Volunteers'.

The end of the war in 1815, which added so much to the problems of the Catholic peasants, made Peel's job a lot easier. The disbanding of the Militia and an end to recruiting for the British Army meant that there was no longer any incentive to push further measures of Catholic emancipation through in order to appease potential cannon-fodder. O'Connell's Catholic Committee had lost a great deal of its initial momentum and Irish Protestants, who felt more secure now that the war with Catholic France was over, began to lose interest in Orangeism. The rules had been re-written again in 1814, and, following the lead of the British Lodges, the Irish Lodges had dropped the 'conditional' oath. In the Lodges there were internal disputes about the higher orders or inner circles which continued to develop under such names as Scarlet, Black and Arch-Purple orders.

But the movement in general lay dormant until it was shaken out of its apathy by the revival of O'Connell's Catholic Committee in a new and very much more vital form.

2

There were, of course, minor incidents. When George IV came to the throne the Castle indicated that displays of Orange emblems would not be welcomed at the Coronation celebrations, but they appeared nonetheless. In Newry a party of Yeomanry who ignored the order and paraded with orange lilies in their hats were given the alternative of removing the offending emblems or laying down their arms; they chose the latter course. In Dublin, the Lord Mayor incensed the Orangemen by requesting the citizens of Dublin to refrain from their traditional practice of 'dressing' the statue of King William on July 12th. They obeyed the order reluctantly, but the following year, when the Lord Mayor repeated the request, making it a precedent for a permanent ban rather than merely one designed to avoid trouble during Coronation Year, the Dublin Orangemen defied the Lord Mayor and the result was a clash with O'Connell's supporters.

Another blow to the Orange Order was the establishment of a new Irish constabulary, which would not only render the Orange-dominated Yeomanry obsolete but would replace it with an armed force composed, as far as possible, equally of Protestants and Catholics. Orangemen were not barred from joining the Irish Constabulary but the wearing of Orange badges and emblems was punished by instant dismissal. Stipendary magistrates independent of local politics—and consequently immune from Orange influence—were appointed, and one of the causes of the agrarian disturbances was removed when an arrangement was made by which the tithes were paid by the landlords and not collected from the tenants. Since the landlords immediately passed back the cost of the tithes to the tenants in the form of increased rents the tenants didn't really benefit at all; but they resented this arrangement far less than the direct collection of tithes by the authorities, and this, combined with O'Connell's unending diatribes against violence, began to have some effect. There was a marked decrease in indiscriminate violence, a situation which further weakened the case of the Orange Order by removing one of the original reasons for its existence.

On October 29th, 1822, an order was issued against dressing King Billy's statue in Dublin for a forthcoming Orange holiday on November 4th. Orangemen attempting to defy the ban were turned back by police and soldiers. As a protest, the Viceroy, Lord Wellesley—brother of the Duke of Wellington—was hissed at a gala performance of *She Stoops to Conquer*, there were shouts of 'No Popery' during the national anthem, and an orange stencilled 'No Popery' was flung into the viceregal box. This matter was raised at Westminster and the Orange Order came heavily under attack yet again. Lord Milton said that 'there were to be found in Ireland honourable men . . . so shackled by the oaths and obligations of the Orange Societies that they dared not act or decide according to the law of the land . . . What could be expected from a Government so divided . . . where a Lord O'Neill, the professed head of the Orange faction, held a high official position . . . Why was it that a Rt. Hon. Baronet (Sir George Hill) who was known to be a supporter of Orange principles, retained a high official appointment in Ireland?'

By 1823, the Orange Order was proceeding very cautiously indeed. The Grand Lodge in Dublin appealed to Orangemen everywhere to exercise restraint in their celebration of July 12th, as a result of which there were no parades in Dublin and only very orderly ones elsewhere, apart from Armagh, where as usual there were countless clashes and one man was killed.

On July 19th, 1823, the Unlawful Oaths Bill was passed, making it illegal for the Orange Order to administer an oath on any person becoming a member of an Orange Lodge, and in effect the Order had to be dissolved and reconstituted.

Under the new system, based on the British one, the Lodge administered no oath directly but satisfied itself that each new member had previously sworn an oath of allegiance before a qualified magistrate. But there were doubts as to whether even this was legal under the new act, and there were lengthy debates about how the Orange Order could keep within the law without, so to speak, changing its spots. In the spring of 1824, the Grand Lodge went so far to avoid trouble as to ban all celebrations of July 12th. This ban shocked and dismayed the rank and file of the Orange Order but was obeyed in most places. The Grand Lodge, not for the first time, was in a deep quandary; they knew that by banning the marches on July 12th they were undermining the morale of the rank and file of the movement, but equally they knew that marching always led to violence and any further violence might result in a complete ban on the movement in any form.

In 1825 a bill banning unlawful associations—largely directed at O'Connell who had, by now, revived his Catholic Association in an entirely new and explosively powerful form—compelled the Orangemen once more to dissolve their organization.

The Grand Lodge held a final meeting in Dublin on March 18, 1825, with Colonel Pratt in the chair. Hereward Senior writes: 'A statement was drawn up and sent to all Lodges which read "At no period was the institution in a more flourishing condition or more highly respectable in the numbers added to its ranks. Notwithstanding this, the Parliament of the United Kingdom have considered it necessary that all political societies should be dissolved. Of course, our society is included. It therefore becomes our duty to remind you that any Lodge meeting after this day becomes a breach of the law." The Grand Lodge of Ireland was at an end, and so was a phase of Orange History'.

Orange forces were at a low ebb indeed. What the movement needed now was a powerful stimulus from an outside source, an attack, real or imagined, on the very root and branch of the Protestant ascendancy. This stimulus was now provided by Dan O'Connell's new mass movement of the Irish Catholics to secure complete political emancipation and full civil rights.

3

The problem behind organizing the Irish peasants into an effective political force was principally a financial one; there were not enough rich Catholics in Ireland—and most of the rich Catholics were Castle Catholics and as little interested in the plight of the peasants as their Protestant counterparts—to finance a political party; and the peasants, suffering from the first of a long, intermittent series of failures of the potato crop, had nothing to contribute. So, at least, it had always been assumed until O'Connell had a brainwave. He set up his new Catholic Association in May 1823 with the aim of gaining not only political emancipation for Catholics but other civil rights as well, fixed the membership fee at one penny a week—a sum which even the poorest peasant could normally find—and arranged that these fees would be collected every Sunday, after Mass, by the Roman Catholic clergy. By the end of the year, £1,000 a week was being collected in the churches, and if the far more generous subscriptions from some of the Catholic merchants and gentry are included, plus the Catholic clergy who were exempted from fees, O'Connell's movement soon had a membership of well over 250,000, with an adequate fighting fund.

O'Connell travelled the country from end to end, addressing vast gatherings with all the skill and oratory of a highly successful barrister. As a barrister, he also knew how to keep on the right side of the law. When Dublin Castle, alarmed at the ever-increasing crowds which flocked to O'Connell's rallies, proscribed his Association he simply dissolved it and continued its activities under another name, the Liberal Clubs. In the 1826 General Election his movement began to contest seats in Westminster, putting up Protestant candidates who were pledged to the cause of Catholic Emancipation. Then in 1828, O'Connell himself contested a by-election in County Clare and won such a resounding victory over his opponent Mr Vesey Fitzgerald—one of the most popular landlords in the country, a champion of Catholic Emancipation and a Cabinet Minister to boot—that Westminster had no alternative but to agree to full Catholic Emancipation; the bill became law in the spring of 1829. What the Orangemen had long dreaded had now happened; Catholics were free at last to take seats in Westminster and play a part in framing the laws of the land.

And as soon as he had taken his seat in Parliament, O'Connell began to fight for the repeal of the Act of Union; for he was convinced that until the Irish Parliament was revived there would be little chance of removing the remaining grievances of the Irish peasants. He realized, as Irish M.P.s sitting at

Westminster increasingly realized from then onwards, that unless the Irish happened to hold the balance of power between the Whigs and the Tories at any given moment the Westminster Parliament was not interested in wasting time discussing any Irish Question.

This development further increased the alarm of the Orangemen everywhere in Ireland, but particularly in Ulster; a revival of the old Dublin-based Irish Parliament, with Catholics free to vote and to take seats in that Parliament, meant only one thing—a Catholic-dominated Parliament controlled from Rome, and an end to the Protestant ascendancy. They decided to double their efforts to resist this, by whatever means.

In point of fact, of course, Catholic Emancipation meant very little to the Catholic peasant in terms of voting, much less in terms of contesting Parliamentary elections. When the Emancipation Act was passed, the 'property' clause which would already have ruled out most Irish Catholic peasants, was altered raising the limits of the property qualification from a rateable valuation of £2 to one of £10; this was a deliberate policy designed to nullify the effects of emancipation and ensure that Catholics would not be elected in sufficiently large numbers to form a Catholic party in Parliament. At the same time O'Connell's Catholic Association was again proscribed and the Lord Lieutenant given special powers to prevent it arising again under a new guise.

But on the rank and file of the Orange Order such subtleties were lost; to them it all added up to the simple fact that the 'Constitution' and the privileges they enjoyed, as a matter of right, under that illusory Constitution, as loyal Protestants, were once more in danger.

This was all the stimulus that was needed. From this moment on, the Orange Order re-emerged in a new and even more militant form.

* * *

The Protestant boys are loyal and true,
Stout-hearted in battle, and stout-handed, too:
The Protestant Boys are true to the last,
And faithful and peaceful when danger has passed.
And oh they bear
And proudly wear
The colours that floated o'er many a fray,
Where cannons were flashing,
And sabres were clashing,
The Protestant Boys still carried the day.

—From *The Protestant Boys*,
a traditional Orange Ballad.

VIII

Catholic Emancipation—the Orange Backlash

In a last-minute attempt to avert Catholic Emancipation the Orange Lodges had borrowed a leaf from O'Connell's book and continued to fight the good fight using different names.

Sir Harcourt Lees, a clergyman of the established church and a staunch Orangeman, attempted to reorganize the Orange Lodges in the guise of benevolent societies. The Loyal and Benevolent Institution of Ireland was founded in 1825 with the Earl of Aldborough as Grand Master, but without the support of such originators of the movement as Verner, Blacker and Archdall. The declaration of the new society stated that it was formed of persons desirous of supporting the principles and practices of the Christian religion, to support and relieve distressed members of the Institution and to offer assistance to other such religious and charitable purposes. The declaration went on: 'We associate ourselves in honour of King William III, Prince of Orange, whose name we bear, and whose immortal memory we hold in reverence'.

The declaration also made the point that the organization was an exclusively Christian one, 'detesting every species of intolerance and excluding persons not well-known to be incapable of upbraiding people on account of their religious practices'. One object of the society was to support what was known as the 'new reformation'—a belated effort by Evangelists and other militant Protestants to spread their faith among the Catholics in Ireland, a project in which the Orangemen had previously shown little interest, probably for the reason that the Orangeman didn't believe that a converted Papist was any more to be trusted than an unconverted one. No secret signs, passwords or initiation ceremonies were permitted. Although it never secured much of a following, this benevolent society continued to exist until it was assimilated into the reconstituted Orange Order.

At this period, the Orangemen were convinced that they had behind them the great mass of public feeling in Britain. Cobbett wrote in 1823 that 'the Orangemen have for allies all the unconquerable prejudice of ninety-nine hundredths of the people of England, as well as an imposing array of Protestant peers headed by the Duke of York and the Duke of Cumberland.'

As an alternative to Sir Harcourt Lees's Loyal and Benevolent Orange Institution, other Orange Lodges, both in Ireland and England, continued their activities, calling themselves the Brunswick Clubs, just as O'Connell had changed his Catholic Association into the Liberal Clubs.

In England, the office of Grand Master had been left vacant since the resignation of the Duke of York. Now the Duke of Cumberland became Grand Master, an event which gave great heart to Orangemen throughout the British Isles as the Duke was known to be a fervent Protestant.

The Duke of Cumberland was toasted at the founding banquet of the Brunswick Clubs, but not in his capacity of Orange Grand Master, and although there were the usual Orange toasts there were no oaths, signs or passwords and none of the atmosphere of mystery which surrounded the old Orange Order. The principal objective of the Brunswick Clubs appears to have been to persuade the British Government of the dangers inherent in Catholic Emancipation. Most Orangemen favoured straight intimidation by marching and, if necessary, fighting, and the Brunswick Clubs were a poor substitute for the old Orange Order; nevertheless within a few months virtually all the male members of the Protestant working class had joined the movement which, like O'Connell's Catholic movement, had a nominal subscription.

O'Connell, although opposed to violence as a means of securing political aims, had created a semi-military arm of his own movement known as the 'Liberators', ostensibly to protect

Catholic tenants from landlord reprisals. He now decided to show up the new Brunswick Clubs for what they really were, perhaps in the hope of getting the movement suppressed, by ordering a Belfast anti-Orange journalist, John Lawless, to lead a mass of Liberators and other supporters into Belfast, there to organize meetings of the Catholic minority and preach in favour of Emancipation.

As O'Connell's forces approached Ulster the Orangemen turned out in thousands, carrying their arms, Yeomen out of uniform, well-trained and well-disciplined. Despite rumours that he had tens of thousands of men, Lawless did not get very far. At Ballybay, two of his supporters were killed and a party of Orange Yeoman under an innkeeper called Sam Gray prevented them from entering the town. A few days later, when he attempted to enter Armagh, the Orangemen again turned out with their muskets while the military commander, General Thornton, stood by, powerless to intervene. O'Connell now called off the march and ordered Lawless to return, but the damage had been done. All the old fears of mass attacks by Catholic peasants were revived in Ulster and the nobility and gentry, who had been fighting shy of the Orange movement because of the legality question, now came openly out in support of it again. And when, as we have seen, O'Connell secured first a seat in Westminster, then full Catholic Emancipation, and finally started to work for the repeal of the Act of Union, the Orangemen started to march again.

The lapse of the act of 1825 had enabled the Orangemen to reconstitute the Grand Lodge of Ireland and in the autumn of 1828 Eustace Chetwoode, the British Grand Secretary, visited Ireland and gave the new English signs and passwords to Irish Orangemen as an initial step towards a formal revival of the Irish movement. He then went on a tour of the North where he visited the old Orange strongholds, and arranged for a revival of traditional Orangeism, bringing back men like the Verners, Blacker and others who had shown no interest in the Benevolent Society or the Brunswick Clubs. In November, Chetwoode returned to Dublin to reform the Grand Lodge, with the difference that it was now linked with the British Grand Lodge;

the Duke of Cumberland, already Grand Master of the British Grand Lodge, now became known as Imperial Grand Master.

The leadership of the Irish Grand Lodge was divided among three Deputy Grand Masters: the Earl of Enniskillen to represent the aristocracy; Colonel William Verner to represent the gentry of Armagh; and Robert Hedges Eyre of Cork to look after the interests of the Orangemen in the South. A new development was the fact that fifteen of the twenty-five members of the Grand Committee of the new Irish Grand Lodge were clergymen of the established Church of Ireland. This was probably not greatly to the liking of the rank and file of the Orange Order who by now were mainly Presbyterians and it had the effect of establishing more firmly than ever, in the minds of Catholics, the idea that all Protestants were Orangemen.

The Orangemen's success against Lawless's march and their anger at the passing of the Catholic Emancipation Act made it certain that there would be displays of Orange strength on July 12th, 1828, despite the Party Processions Act and all the efforts of the Castle authorities and the nobility and gentry to restrain the Lodges. In any event many of the Orange gentry, particularly men like the Verners and the Blackers in the border counties, though prepared to go through the motions of discouraging parades, were convinced of the necessity of tolerating them.

In May, the Duke of Cumberland wrote to the Earl of Enniskillen:

> Caution and vigilance are at the present crisis specially requisite for the prosperity and safety of our cause, particularly in respect of our public processions which, I think, ought by all means to be avoided . . . as leading, or at least, being interpreted to lead, to an infraction of the law, and a breach of the public peace which . . . would probably be followed up by some legislative measure ruinous to the Orange Institution. I assure you, I feel an intense anxiety on this subject.

A committee representing the Irish Grand Lodge and including Enniskillen and Verner chose to issue a vaguely worded statement which could easily have been interpreted as an encouragement to go out and march, despite the official warning. The statement said: 'Of the recommendations contained in the letter of our illustrious Grand Master, the Committee do not conceive it necessary to say very much. They merely declare their opinion, that the utmost vigilance and caution are required to prevent the strength of Protestant Ireland from being broken and dispersed'.

In the event, over twenty Orange processions were held. About 50,000 Orangemen marched in defiance of the Party Processions Act, with or without the consent of their Masters. Disorders and riots were reported in Armagh, Newry, Belfast and Strabane, where there were casualties, including some deaths. In one of the clashes at Glenoe, County Tyrone, there was what amounted to a pitched battle between Orangemen and Ribbonmen in which two Orangemen and twenty Ribbonmen were reportedly killed. (The disproportionately heavy casualties among the Catholics in all these engagements could have two possible explanations: one is that most of the written accounts are based on Orange sources and it is in the nature of all fighting men to exaggerate the enemy's losses and minimize their own; the other is that the Orangemen, almost all ex-Yeomen, were both better armed and better disciplined. The truth probably lies somewhere between the two.)

In Fermanagh, Ribbonmen attacked a party of Orangemen who had been attending a banquet and killed three of them; later—or possibly earlier, for accounts of the event vary considerably—a party of drunken Orangemen charged the Catholic 'enemy' with fixed bayonets and, again, there were some casualties.

A few days later the Viceroy issued a proclamation condemning processions. Peel was inclined to hold the Duke of Cumberland responsible, as Grand Master, but Wellington, the Prime Minister, advised him against taking any action. 'I entertain no doubt that the Duke of Cumberland is doing all the mischief in Ireland he can. The difficulty will be to prove a case of which we can take notice.'

What looked like a case on which they might act arose on the following July 12th when an Orange procession, halted by a party of policemen who read to them the Viceroy's proclamation against processions, produced a warrant signed by the Duke of Cumberland and argued that the Duke, the king's brother, was more important than the Viceroy, who was merely one of his servants.

The Government's attitude to July 12th processions had been made very clear well in advance of the 1829 anniversary. The proclamation prohibiting all processions was posted on churches and public buildings, but the Orangemen marched again, in roughly the same numbers as the previous year, and once again there were riots and disturbances. One incident in Maghera, Co. Londonderry, is worth describing in detail. Anticipating trouble, a company of the 64th Regiment was stationed at Maghera. Towards the evening these troops intervened in an armed encounter during which several Catholic houses had been burned down, and they disarmed and arrested about twenty-six Orangemen. On the following day, when the Orangemen came up before the court, the courtroom was rushed by a mob of other Orangemen and the prisoners rescued: and the magistrates instructed the police not to intervene.

In November 1830, an informal concert was held in the village of Maghery, County Armagh—Verner country. The musicians appear to have been Orangemen and the audience mixed. The concert started innocently enough, but at some stage the Orangemen began to play sectarian, anti-Papish songs. This infuriated the Catholics in the audience who set upon them and smashed their drums. The Orangemen left the hall, and returned with reinforcements. Colonel Verner attempted to halt them, but failed, and the village of Maghery was sacked. And, although he had attempted to stop the Orangemen from marching into the village, and must have known them all, since they were his tenants, Verner sympathized with them to the extent that he claimed he was unable to identify a single offender in court, so that all efforts to prosecute them broke down. This was typical of incidents which occurred all over Northern Ireland in the years immediately following Catholic Emancipation.

But worse was to come.

2

If it is possible to pinpoint in time and place one man who created sectarian hatred in Belfast it is a certain Dr Henry Cooke, who imported anti-Catholicism from his native Derry in the early 1820s. Constantine Fitzgibbon says that while Cooke was not an Orangeman his aim 'was no less than the creation of an anti-Catholic bloc, to include all Protestants of every denomination and every class, a monolithic grouping based on religious bigotry among the masses and on class interest among the richer classes, with the purpose of ensuring perpetual domination by the Protestants, in all Ireland if possible, but certainly in Ulster'.

The time was right for such a movement. The first Reform Bill of 1832 had not achieved much, but the wealthy landowners knew it would be followed by others which would eventually whittle away the privileges of their class, as would O'Connell's Repeal Movement, if it ever got anywhere.

At Hillsborough, County Down, Dr Henry Cooke held a mass demonstration attended by 60,000 Protestants, mainly Orangemen, which is described in detail in R. M. Sibbett's *Orangeism in Ireland and Throughout the Empire*. It is interesting if only in view of the sentiments expressed by some of the speakers. The Marquis of Downshire said that he felt called upon to come forward and state that there were limits beyond which concession should not go. He considered himself bound to make that declaration when he saw measures advocated and when he heard the advocates of those measures state that the minds of the people would not be satisfied till they were carried, the ultimate effect of which he did in his heart believe would be the separation of Ireland from England, the destruction of all kinds of property, and finally of the Protestant religion in Ireland.

The Marquis of Londonderry asked with what object had the Legislative Union been established? It was to give the Roman

Catholics the rights to which it had been deemed they were entitled; it was to enable them to receive the boon of Emancipation. It had been thought that if they could succeed in connecting themselves with Great Britain there would be no danger in permitting the Roman Catholic people—the immense body of their fellow-countrymen—to partake of those rights to which all were deemed to be equally entitled. But had their Roman Catholic brethren made any adequate return for the boon conferred on them? Had they been tranquil and content; had they ceased from agitation? No. He was sorry, deeply sorry, to say they had not. They had raised a cry of 'Repeal of the Union' from one end of the country to the other.

Lord Castlereagh complained that the Protestant Yeomanry had been banished, and the means of preserving the peace of the country and their lives had been taken from their hands. When they looked to the unprotected state of the Protestant magistracy and the growing violence of the effects and exertions of a powerful party, could they wonder that the Protestant peasant, returning to his home at night, frequently found that that home had been burned or his property destroyed. Could they wonder that any clergyman of their faith could hardly with safety be a dweller in the country? But it was not by emigration alone that their Protestant population was reduced. Let them look to the burnings, the murders and the slaughters that were committed.

Dr Cooke announced the bans of a marriage between the Church of Ireland and the Presbyterian Churches. 'Who forbids the bans?' he asked. 'None. Then I trust our Union, for these holy purposes, is indissoluble and that the God who has bound us in Christian affection, and by the ties of a common faith, will never allow the recollections of the past, or the temptations of the present, to sever those whom He has united'.

Dr Cooke also referred to the Orange movement: 'The members of the Orange Society do not encourage sectarianism. Their organization was begun and continues to promote Protestantism and every evangelical form of that faith can command its sympathy and assistance. The strong bond of union among Orangemen exists in the fact that their society is "exclusively Protestant".'

3

Through the 1830s, although attempts were made by the Government, the Grand Lodge and even by some local Lodge Masters to restrain them, the Orangemen continued to march, and O'Connell continued to protest in Parliament about their behaviour. In 1832, when a bill forbidding processions by law was again under consideration, the Duke of Cumberland wrote an open letter to the Lodges: 'With regret, therefore, but with a full conviction of the wisdom of my advice, I call on you, one and all, to make the sacrifice of declining this year to attend the Orange processions on the glorious 12th'. The county Grand Masters of Ulster decided that it would be inexpedient to circulate the Duke's address as 'he had written it under the impression that Parliament was about to declare processions illegal'. So the Orangemen marched again, and although there was relatively little violence the anti-procession measure was made law in August of that year. A deputation of Orangemen paraded to Colonel Blacker, who had been a member of the movement since 1795 but who was also a magistrate, to protest against this Act; as a magistrate, he was obliged to order them to disperse, but he indicated his true feelings in the matter by having the ladies of the household stand behind him wearing Orange lilies. This compromise was acceptable to the Orange Order but not to Dublin Castle, and Blacker ceased to be a magistrate. His neighbour, Colonel William Verner, who also had associations with the Orange movement almost from its inception, intervened on Blacker's behalf, and when he got nowhere resigned his own commission as a magistrate.

'. . . the rank and file believed it essential to walk and felt that the Grand Lodge was showing weakness in advising them to refrain,' writes the Rev John Brown. 'The largely upper-class Grand Lodge looked on the Institution as a means of countering "inroads on the Constitution", repeal, and attacks on the Church of Ireland. Ordinary Orangemen joined in Lodge and walked defiantly in procession as an assertion of old rights and to keep Papists in their places. They did not realize what capital would be made at Westminster out of the hot skirmish near Gulladuff, outside Maghera, when houses were burned there and the "nest cleared out" on the Twelfth Day of 1830. No one thought any sin was committed by burning John Hancock, an unpopular magistrate in Armagh, in effigy. But it occupied the attention of the Select Committee of Parliament, set up in 1835 by the Whig Government (now in power after the English and Irish Reform Acts had changed things) under pressure from O'Connell and the Radicals. Dan hoped through this to break the power of the Orange Institution in Ireland.'

It is quite clear from the tone of the above that the Orangeman felt then, as he does now, entitled to behave exactly as he pleased in his own corner of the land without interference from any quarter, including the forces of law and order; and it is equally clear from what followed at Westminster—both in the immediate aftermath of these events and far more recently—that the English, when circumstances have forced them to give any thought to the matter, have had precious little time for the Orangeman and his tiresome 'loyalty to the Constitution'.

* * *

The illustrious House of Hanover,
And Protestant succession,
To these I do allegiance swear—
While they can keep possession:
For in my faith and Loyalty
I never more will falter,
And George my lawful King shall be—
Until the times do alter.
And this is law, I will maintain,
Until my dying day, Sir,
That whatsoever king shall reign,
I'll be the Vicar of Bray, Sir.

—From *The Vicar of Bray*,
a traditional English ballad.

IX

Orangeism in Trouble in England Again

The inability of any combination of prohibitions and exhortations on the part of the Government, the police, the Grand Masters of the Lodges, or the gentry to prevent the ordinary Orangemen from marching, put Orange peers and Orange M.P.s in a very difficult position, which they attempted to alleviate by trying to swing the Orange Order against what was the big political question of the day—parliamentary reform.

The first Reform Bill, which came before the Commons in 1831, had listed over 150 'pocket boroughs' which were to be abolished and replaced by new constituencies for the unrepresented areas of London, the industrial North and Midlands. The Whig leader, Earl Grey, had studied the pattern of insurrections and revolutions on the Continent, and although he was himself a landowner who far preferred to be on his country estates than at Westminster, he was also convinced that unless something was done to give some political power to the prosperous middle classes who had been influenced by French revolutionary ideas, he might have to come to terms with the far more dangerous discontented working men and farm labourers; poverty in the villages and on the farms had already led to rioting in south-east England and even while the Reform Bill was being framed over 400 farm workers were deported for rioting.

However to the Tories—and to the gentry in the Orange movement—the Reform Bill looked like the first step on the road to revolution, to rule by the people, on the French pattern. They believed government meant the rule of the propertied, landed classes, in what in their view were the best interests of the community.

The Orange Order was by no means united behind its leaders in opposing the Reform Bill. The rank and file had no great interest in politics, and some of the leading Orangemen were believers in parliamentary reform; nevertheless, John Hitton was expelled in June and Major Brownrigg in September 1832 for supporting the Bill. Two clergymen were expelled from the Grand Lodge and it was ordered that district Lodges in Dublin remove from the list of officers of the Grand Lodge any person supporting the Reform Bill or anyone who voted for a Reform candidate at the last election. The Orange opposition to the Reform Bill may have been a contributory factor to the two subsequent parliamentary inquiries into the activities of the Orange Order.

In the years immediately before the Reform Bill came before the Commons, Orangeism in Britain was at a low ebb, demoralized perhaps by the Order's failure to prevent Catholic Emancipation. Cumberland, Kenyon and the Orange peers, in an effort to pull the movement together and give it a fresh impetus, used the offices of an ex-solider, William Blennerhasset Fairman, who had been a Captain in the Royal Irish Infantry and a Lieutenant-Colonel in the 4th Ceylon Foot. He had been a member of the Orange Order from 1814. In 1830 he had written to the Duke of Cumberland telling him that the Duke of Wellington was plotting to make himself Regent to Princess Victoria, then about ten years old and likely soon to come to the throne as King George IV was dying and his brother, William IV-to-be, was sixty-four. When he received no reply to the letter Fairman managed to arrange an interview with the Duke of Cumberland during which he appears to have suggested the reorganization of the Orange Lodges along more militant lines to protect the country from Wellington's Cromwellian ambitions.

By 1831, Fairman had become joint Deputy Grand Secretary (with Chetwoode) and in 1832 Chetwoode was removed from office and Fairman became Deputy Grand Secretary. He then went on a tour of the Midlands, the North and Scotland, carrying an itinerant warrant which empowered him to found Lodges wherever he could. The object of the tour appears to have been to use opposition to the Reform Bill to rally members of the nobility, gentry and Tory-minded middle classes to the British Orange Movement. In testing out potential Orangemen on their attitude to reform he did so as personal representative of the Duke of Cumberland, asking whether they would be prepared to rally to the Duke 'if any row took place'. According to Hereward Senior 'there are passages in Fairman's correspondence which suggest preparations for civil war. To Lord Londonderry he declared, "We have the military with us as far as they are likely to avow their principles and sentiments" . . . Fairman's quixotic letters, like his conversations with local Orangemen, were probably the means of sounding the peers out on the question of a coup d'état'.

In February 1833, Fairman returned to London briefly and then departed on a similar tour of Scotland, where he stayed with the Duke of Gordon, Deputy Grand Master of the Order in Scotland, where there were now forty-five Lodges, and where, in certain areas, there were frequent riots between Orangemen and immigrant Irish Catholics. Fairman used the prestige of the Duke's name to form a gentleman's Lodge known as the Royal Gordon Lodge.

From Scotland he travelled to Yorkshire, where he founded the Royal Cumberland Lodge at Barnsley. In 1834 he made various attempts to interest the recently-formed Carlton Club in the Orange Order. One circular he sent them read 'This society (The Orange Order) is useful for purposes of intercourse between the higher and lower orders . . . for correspondence with bodies or individuals, and is capable of being rendered eminently available in elections, whenever it is desirable to return representatives whose principles are the protection of the Protestant Establishment'. According to Senior, the circular also mentioned that the Orange Lodges were useful for presenting petitions and loyal addresses and 'hinted that they would be happy to supply physical force against Radicals if the occasion should arise'.

The Carlton Club showed no interest in Fairman's proposition, and his expensive series of tours brought relatively few new influential members. Orangeism had far less to offer in England than in Ireland. As nearly all Lodges met in inns and taverns of one sort or another, innkeepers always played an important role in the organization and it is possible that the Orange Order was in a position to enable members to get licences to run public houses. But British Orangemen could not expect the immunity from the law enjoyed by Irish Orangemen in the heyday of the movement when magistrates, particularly in Ulster, openly displayed Orange emblems and consistently acquitted Orangemen brought before them. Also outside the industrial slums, the appeal of the Order as a 'defensive' unit against immigrant Irish Catholic workers had no parallel in the countryside since they all gravitated to the cities and towns.

By the autumn of 1834 Fairman seems to have been losing face, but so many rumours had been circulating about his activities and about the activities of the Order as a whole that the Radicals at Westminster began to demand a parliamentary investigation. In 1835 these demands were granted and a Select Committee was appointed to inquire into the whole question of the Orange Order, its sphere of influence, its aims and objects, even its rituals and oaths. The Committee initially was composed of twenty-seven members including eight Orangemen, and twelve members hostile to the Movement. They interviewed dozens of witnesses, studied reams of letters and documents, and then submitted four monster reports, consisting of three volumes with a total of 4,500 pages. The first three reports dealt exclusively with Orangeism in Ireland and did not carry any final summary or general conclusions; they were presented to Parliament on July 20th and August 6th, 1835. The final report, which dealt with Orangeism in England, was presented on September 7th and is worth quoting in detail because it contains what amounts to the committee's summary of its findings on the effects and influence of the Orange Order as a whole.

The reports on Ireland established 'beyond doubt,' Senior says, 'what had been general knowledge in Ireland since 1795—

that is that the Orangemen controlled the Irish Yeomanry, had Lodges in the army, enjoyed a certain immunity from justice in Ulster and were frequently engaged in civil disturbances'.

The Committee began its summing up with the general finding 'of an organized institution, pervading Great Britain and her Colonies to an extent never contemplated as possible... and highly injurious to the discipline of H.M.'s Army'. It referred to the way in which the Order had become a source of patronage in almost every walk of life, from 'the procuring of licences for public houses' to 'pensions in the artillery' and indicated the magnitude of its numbers in Great Britain, some 40,000 in London alone, who 'in any emergency... might be immediately assembled by the Grand Lodge', and particularly its inclusion of all ranks of society 'from the nearest to the throne [a reference, of course, to the King's brother, the Duke of Cumberland, Imperial Grand Master of both the British and Irish Grand Lodges] to the poorest peasant'.

The Committee referred to the way in which the movement had penetrated the Army, not only in Britain and Ireland but also in the Colonies, particularly Australia, in open defiance of military orders, and stressed the fact that where necessary such defiance was officially encouraged by the Order.

Hostility to the Government, especially the reforming Government of the Whig Party, was charged against the Order. The Committee cited evidence that the Order was armed to a substantial degree or at any rate had access to considerable supplies of arms and ammunition, quoting a boast in a letter from the Deputy Grand Master in which he stated: 'We shall speedily have such a moral and physical force, I trust, as will strike with terror and sore dismay the foes of our country'.

The Committee gave instances of the Order's use of armed force, or the threat of it, during election times, notably in Ireland 'by the interference of large bodies of armed Orangemen', and quoted from its circular to the Carlton Club Conservatives which began: 'The day has passed when a debate and a vote in either House (of Parliament) could settle even for a time a vital question. To restore that day a portion of the community must be bound in union for the support of the institutions of the country'—and went on to point out that this 'union' could be achieved only through the Orange Order.

The report then quoted a further paragraph from this circular to the Carlton Club, which ran as follows:

> [The Orange Order] is not an occult society; it is not one of concealments and is not bound by oaths. [This statement was found by the committee to be quite misleading.] It is governed by a Grand Master, the first Prince of the Blood, who with the aid of noblemen and gentlemen eminent for loyalty, wisdom and sound discretion, will be able, when the Institution shall become more extensively ramified, to muster in every part of the Empire no small portion of all that is sound in the community and thus present in every quarter a phalanx too strong to be overpowered by the destructives, which will give a moral as well as a known physical strength to the government of the King, and will be able to set at defiance the tyrannous power that has so madly been called into existence. [This is, of course, a reference to the reform of Parliament.]

The report then drew attention to the fact that 'the power of calling out the members of all the Orange Lodges in Ireland rests with the Grand Master and his Deputy on the application of twelve members of the Grand Committee [and that] the same person is Grand Master of Great Britain and of Ireland, having the same powers, which are stated to be uncontrolled and arbitrary, of bringing together large bodies of armed and unarmed men to make a demonstration of physical force which might prove highly dangerous'.

The Committee reached the following general conclusion: 'The obvious tendency and effect of the Orange Institution is to keep up an exclusive association in civil and military society, exciting one portion of the people against the other; to increase the rancour and anxiety too often and unfortunately existing between persons of different religious persuasions—to make the Protestant the enemy of the Catholic and the Catholic the enemy of the Protestant—by processions on particular days attended with the insignia of the Society, to incite to breaches of the peace and to bloodshed—to raise up other secret societies among the Catholics in their own defence and for their own protection against the insults of the Orangemen—to interrupt the course of justice; and to interfere with the discipline of the Army, thus rendering its services injurious instead of useful when required on occasions when Catholics and Protestants may be parties.

'All these evils have been proved by the evidence before the House in regard to Ireland where the system has long existed on an extended scale, rendered more prejudicial to the best interests of society by the patronage and protection of so many wealthy members high in office and rank taking an active part in the proceedings of these Lodges, though in Great Britain in a more limited way.

'The Orange Lodges have also interfered in political subjects of the day and made Orangeism a means of supporting the views of a political party to maintain, as they avow, the Protestant ascendancy. The Orange Lodges have addressed His Majesty and individuals on special occasions of a political nature, have patronized and supported by subscriptions, votes of thanks, etc., parts of the public press which advocated their opinions and views in politics, have interfered in the course of justice by subscriptions to defend and protect parties of Orangemen, and to prosecute the magistrates for interfering with them (as in the case of Liverpool in 1819 when the Mayor of Liverpool interrupted an Orange procession on the 12th of July of that year) and have also interfered with the elective franchise by expelling members of their body, as at Rochdale in 1835, for voting for the Liberal candidate.'

The report then gave at length some of the many instances recorded in the minute books and branch circulars of the Institution of such activities, and examples of other inquiries into the effects of the operations of the Orangemen all over the country. Typical of the latter is this excerpt from a report on Scotland where Mr Cosmo Innes, a Deputy Judge Advocate, had been deputed by the Law Officers of the Crown to inquire into the nature, extent and causes of the Riots that had taken place in July of the previous year (1834): 'on authority on which your Committee place confidence that the existence of the Orange Lodges, their meetings, processions and proceedings have roused opposition on the part of Catholics to protect themselves from the insults offered by the Orangemen and that secret societies have been formed for that purpose by which members can be called forth at any time when occasion shall require their meeting to protect themselves against the insults of the Orangemen or to be revenged upon them . . . The opinion of Mr Innes, after all the information he has become officially possessed of, is that it will not be possible to restore the West of Scotland to tranquillity, and to prevent breaches of the peace occurring occasionally, unless measures are taken to put down the Orange Lodges and Ribandmen [an alternative spelling of Ribbonmen, the principal Catholic successors to the Defenders] and every other secret society.

'Whether the existence of the Orange Lodges has produced the Riband Lodges, or the Riband Lodges has produced the Orange, appears to be of little consequence. It is notorious that the Orange Lodges exist, under the patronage of men high in rank in England, Ireland and Scotland, and the countenance given, in consequence of all the orders of the Orange Institution being issued by and under the authority of such men as HRH the Duke of Cumberland as Imperial Grand Master, and of His Grace the Duke of Gordon as Deputy Grand Master of Scotland, will be found to have a greater effect upon the poor and ignorant, of which the Orangemen there chiefly consist, than might be expected . . . the mischievous effects of Orange Lodges shown, though on a small scale in Scotland, may be expected wherever such a system is upheld and protected by men of high rank . . . a reference to the evidence before the House of the working of Orangeism in Ireland on the broadest scale and after many years continuance will completely bear out that opinion.' [Mr Cosmo Innes obviously prepared his report between the time that the parliamentary committee submitted its reports on Ireland and the final one on Britain.]

As a proof of the sectarian effects of the existence of the Orange Order in Scotland, Mr Innes cites one example where a Lodge of pitmen expelled from their working party all the

Catholics with whom they had previously lived and worked in peace and harmony.

The report then turned to the question of finding 'a corrective to those evils which disturb both civil and military society so much and threaten the most serious consequences to the community of the United Kingdom if allowed to continue' and gave its opinion that it should be sufficient to enforce effectively the existing laws against secret and other illegal associations 'bound together . . . by a religious sanction with secret signs and passwords by which the fraternity may be known to each other in every part of the world' but added a few specific recommendations such as 'the immediate removal from office of all public servants who shall continue or become members of any Orange Lodge or any other association bound together in a similar manner'.

In conclusion, the report noted the large number of Orangemen in Ireland (some 220,000) 'and these chiefly with arms in their possession', and referred to those in Britain and the colonies in the following terms: 'A great political body thus organized in the ranks of the Army, and in every part of the British Empire, is a formidable power at any time and in any circumstances, but when your Committee look to the political tendencies of the measures of the Orange Societies in England and Ireland, and particularly to the language contained in addresses to the public and in the correspondence to Grand Officers of the Institution, and consider the possible use that might be made of such an organized power, its suppression becomes in their opinion imperatively necessary.'

The Government could not afford to ignore a report couched in such forceful terms; the very fact that the Duke of Cumberland, a Field-Marshal, was Imperial Grand Master of a semi-secret society with Lodges in many regiments holding warrants signed by him was in itself enough to force the Government to take action. Hume, who had been chairman of the Committee, tabled resolutions declaring the Orange Order illegal and emphasizing the danger, which had been stressed in the report, of having Lodges in the Army. The debate on these resolutions was postponed in the hope that the Duke of Cumberland would resign. He did not do so, but wrote to the Committee explaining that he was ignorant of the existence of Lodges within the Army, as the warrants he had signed were signed in batches and he was not always aware of their ultimate destination. Hume moved his resolutions again on August 11th, but modified somewhat so that the Duke of Cumberland was not specifically accused of deliberately signing Army warrants and a week later the Orange Grand Lodge cancelled all military warrants.

At this stage in the proceedings, Lieutenant-Colonel William B. Fairman came back into the limelight. On August 19th, Hume reported that Fairman, who had been called on to give evidence before the Committee, had failed to produce a letter-book dealing with the military Lodges. When he persisted in refusing, this counted as contempt of Parliament but when an order was sent out for his arrest he could not be found.

By September 1835 all the reports on Orangeism in Ireland and Great Britain and the Colonies had been considered, but the Duke of Cumberland had still made no move to resign as Grand Master or to urge the dissolution of the Order. In October, Hume and Sir William Molesworth produced evidence of what they described as a new and dangerous conspiracy. Haywood, the District Master of Sheffield, who had been expelled from the Order as a trouble-maker, accused Fairman of sounding out Orangemen as early as 1832 as to their possible attitude in the event of a *coup d'état.*

To quote *Orangeism: a New Historical Appreciation*: 'Then there came forward one Haywood (or Hayward), an expelled Orangeman of Sheffield, who wrote to the paper [there is no indication of which paper was meant] to say that Fairman had been ordered when on his tours "to sound the Orangemen if they would be willing to support the deposition of William IV on account of having sanctioned the reform of Parliament, and assist the Duke of Cumberland, who would then be called to the throne". Fairman, at that time in hiding because the famous letter-book had not been produced and he was in contempt of a Parliamentary Committee, managed to bring an action against this man. Haywood died from a burst blood vessel before the case came on . . . if there had been a conspiracy, of which there is no real evidence, it existed in Fairman's ingenious and peculiar mind. No one of any consequence believed that Cumberland had plotted to supersede Victoria . . . for probably a good deal less than 10,000 Orangemen in Great Britain, without any preparation that has ever been reported, with the aid of a few soldiers scattered over the country and held under severe discipline, to start a rebellion to put the Duke of Cumberland on the throne, would have been a remarkably futile undertaking. Brother Nucella's scheme of 1832 for establishing an Orange Lodge in Rome looks, beside this, the height of practical wisdom'.

Hereward Senior is even more circumspect in his estimate of the number of fighting men the Orange Order could have rallied in support of such a projected *coup*. 'One Orange witness', he writes, 'when questioned closely, doubted that more than 2,000 London Orangemen could be assembled in one place, and it is questionable whether even 500 could be assembled.' Nevertheless, he makes the point that the Orange conspiracy has been credited by reputable historians. Halévy wrote: 'Incredible though it may seem, there can be little doubt that their leader, the Duke of Cumberland, the King's brother, believed it possible to set aside by a military *coup* his little niece, the Princess Victoria, who was a devoted Whig, and seize the succession of William IV'.

Senior reckons that in 1830 there were thirty-one military warrants under the British Grand Lodge. There is no evidence of a marked increase in the years immediately following 1830. Military Lodges consisted usually of a sergeant and a dozen or so men who met, like civilian Orangemen, in inns and taverns. This would give a total of military Orangemen of about 500 in Britain as a nucleus of a revolutionary army, scattered in groups of between five and thirty in different military units in a well-disciplined army led by the Duke of Wellington's officers. 'Not even Colonel Despard or Robert Emmet would have attempted a *coup d'état* with such a scattered and unreliable band,' Senior comments.

Letters purporting to give evidence of this Orange conspiracy were published in the April 1836 issue of the *London and Westminster Review*. These may have been stolen, or, as Senior suggests, sold by Fairman to the newspaper or to Hume.

But even before that, in February 1836, Hume had again pressed in Parliament for the dismissal of all Orangemen from civil and military office, and when the royal reply made it clear that measures would be taken against the Orangemen, the Duke of Cumberland decided to dissolve the British Lodges.

On April 14th, 1836, after much controversy, the Grand Lodge of Ireland resolved by 79 votes to 59 that 'the end for which the Orange Association was originally framed—namely, the promotion of the interests of the Protestant population of Ireland—will no longer be served by the further continuance of that Institution; and that in conformity with the expressed will of the Sovereign, the Orange Association at the rising of this Grand Lodge ought to be and is hereby dissolved.'

Another chapter in the history of the Orange Order was at an end.

* * *

'Twas on the twelfth day of July, in the year of forty-nine,
Ten hundred of our Orangemen together did combine,
In memory of King William, on that bright and glorious day,
To march around Lord Rodin's park and right over Dolly's Brae.

And as we walked along the road not fearing any harm,
Our guns all over our shoulders, and our broadswords in our hands,
Until two priests came up to us and to Mr Speers did say,
'Come turn your men the other road, and don't cross Dolly's Brae'.

Then out bespeaks our Orangeman, 'Indeed, we won't delay,
You have your men all gathered and in a manger lay;
Begone, begone, you Papist dogs, we'll conquer or we'll die,
And we'll let you see we're not afraid to cross over Dolly's Brae.'

And when we came to Dolly's Brae they were lined on every side,
Praying for the Virgin Mary to be their holy guide;
We loosed our guns upon them and gave them no time to pray;
And the tune we played was 'The Protestant Boys' right over Dolly's Brae.

The Priest he came, his hands he wrung, saying, 'My brave boys, you're dead,
Some holy water I'll prepare to sprinkle on your head';
The Pope of Rome he did disown, his heart was grieveful sore,
And the Orange cry as we passed by, was Dolly's Brae no more.

There was a damsel among them all, and one we shall adore,
For she wove the Orange around her head and cried 'Dolly's Brae no more'.
And if they ever come back again they'll be ten times as sore,
And we'll christen this King William's Bridge, and cry 'Dolly's Brae no more.'

—From *Dolly's Brae*, a traditional Orange Ballad.

X

The Great Famine—and its Aftermath

The parliamentary inquiry into the affairs of the Orange Order and the dissolution of the Grand Lodges of Great Britain and Ireland did not meet with much approval among the ordinary Orangemen in Ireland, particularly in Ulster. It was the view of most of the District and some of the County Lodges that if the Grand Lodge wished to dissolve itself that was its own business, but it had no power to dissolve the Institution as a whole. Most of the Lodges continued to meet as if nothing had happened and went on marching and taking whatever other action they deemed advisable to support 'the cause' in the existing circumstances.

In Belfast, on July 12th, 1835, the Orange celebrations had ended in a riot. The military were called out, including the cavalry, and some of the rioters were treated for sabre wounds. One man and one woman were shot dead. This was the first bad outbreak of sectarian violence in the city, but as Irish Catholic peasants continued to pour in, looking for work, it clearly was going to set the pattern for the years ahead. In 1784, when the first Catholic Church in Belfast, St Mary's, Chapel Lane, was consecrated, the Catholic population of Belfast was only eight per cent of the total; by 1835 it had risen to very nearly one-third.

However, despite this and other obvious dangers in continuing to march, the Orange Order in Ireland set about reorganizing itself. The lead was taken by Armagh, where the Order had originated; the County Armagh Grand Lodge declared at a meeting on June 13th, 1836, 'that the business of the Institution in this country be entrusted, as in its early days, to the Grand Lodge of the same [Armagh] until the Grand Lodge of Ireland resumes its function' and elected Lieutenant-Colonel William Blacker as Grand Master. In November it assumed the functions of the Grand Lodge of Ireland and a year later the Grand Lodge of Ireland was reconstituted in Dublin with Lord Roden as Grand Master. But the Dublin Grand Lodge was not capable, so soon after voting for its own dissolution, of controlling the movement, and the District and County Lodges in Ulster tended to go very much their own way.

This was the period when the potato crops, particularly in the west and south-west of Ireland, began to fail and the state of the peasantry reached an alarmingly distressing level. The huge increase in population, inefficient agricultural methods, the endless division and sub-division of land, careless absentee landlords, corrupt and cruel agents, lack of educational facilities, and the hopeless squalor of grinding poverty had all combined to turn vast areas of beautiful countryside into an over-populated rural slum. O'Connell attributed all these ills to the Union with Britain and redoubled his efforts to secure the repeal of the Act of Union. For a time he even contemplated another march on Ulster to preach his message in Belfast and the other Ulster cities, but decided against it. Instead, he organized a series of repeal meetings in the South which soon were attracting enormous crowds.

In 1843 the Government banned a monster rally which he had planned at Clontarf, on the site of Brian Boru's victory over the Danes, and called out the troops to enforce the ban. O'Connell, law-abiding as ever and opposed to violence in any form, cancelled the meeting and was arrested. On his release after a successful appeal to the Lords about three months later, he seems to have lost heart and thereafter largely dropped out of politics, leaving the fight for the repeal of the Act of Union—soon to re-emerge under the far more telling title, 'Home Rule'—to younger men.

In 1847, broken-hearted at his failure and by the tragedy of the Great Famine, O'Connell died on his way to Rome on a pilgrimage.

2

At first glance there may not appear to be much connection between the Great Famine—which principally affected the poorer Catholic peasants in Connaught and the south-west of Ireland—and the Orange Movement, but Ireland is so small that anything which happens in any part of it palpably affects the remainder, and the mass emigration of Irish Catholic peasants to America during and after the Great Famine certainly contributed to the pressure that America was later to exert on the British Government to offer the Irish a measure of Home Rule, which again had deep and lasting repercussions within the Orange Movement. So it is germane.

Many people in England today find it difficult to understand how the failure of one—now relatively unimportant—crop could possibly have caused such a widespread and disastrous famine as overtook Ireland in the three years 1847–49. Only this year I heard an Englishman remark that any nation daft enough to concentrate on one single crop deserved to die of famine. I asked if he had ever driven through Connemara; he hadn't. I don't think anybody who has seen those miserable one-room thatched cottages could make such a statement. Set among fields littered with boulders and rocks and criss-crossed everywhere with a crazy-paving pattern of loose stone walls—built partly to prevent the fierce winds of the Atlantic from tearing away the thin coating of poor soil that covers the underlying rock which breaks through, in places, like the backbone of a whale breaking the surface of the ocean and partly to get the stones up off the earth and stack them somewhere out of the way—those cottages in this barren, savagely beautiful wilderness make the story of the Great Irish Famine completely credible. With no tools other than a spade, and no fertiliser other than seaweed collected on the shore, this land could not be used to grow any crop more demanding in its requirements than the potato.

And eaten in the quantities in which they were consumed by the Irish peasant in the good years—one estimate of the average daily consumption by a healthy male puts it at 14 lbs—

they provided an adequate if unbalanced diet, which combined with milk, produced a hardy, healthy race of people. On feast days and holy days the milch cow was bled a bit to add a touch of flavour to the unvarying diet, and potatoes have the added advantage that they can be used to produce alcohol similar to American 'moonshine' and known as potheen (pronounced potcheen). It is raw, sour in flavour and among the most unpleasant drinks imaginable. I have sampled what I was assured by a Connemara policeman—and policemen are in a good position to judge since a constant supply of the stuff is the price of their continued connivance in its illegal manufacture—that this was a veritable Chateau Mouton Rothschild among potheens, though he didn't phrase it exactly that way. However, it has one undeniably attractive property: it makes you drunk. So with potatoes enough to eat, potheen to get drunk on, and turf to keep them warm—turf, or peat, grows all over Connemara; it is easy to dig and, given a good 'drying' year, burns merrily, exuding a fragrant aroma, a lot of smoke and a small quantity of gentle heat—the Irish peasants had a way of life that was tolerable enough, if not exciting. Until the potato crop failed. It failed partially in a number of years early in the 19th century, and completely and disastrously in 1845. When that happened, the Irish starved to death in hundreds of thousands in their hovels, in the fields, by the roadside, or cleared out, battened down in the holds of coffin ships, to make a new start in America.

Outside of Connaught, potatoes were not the only crop which would grow and a curious feature of the famine was that throughout this entire period, while Catholic Irish peasants were starving to death in thousands, Irish food was being exported to England. The Irish grew corn; but they couldn't afford to buy it. Still less could they afford to buy meat. Some well-meaning but disastrously ill-managed attempts were made to provide maize and other cheap food for the starving Irish, but this was the period of *laissez-faire* and no scheme which threatened the sacrosanct policy of private enterprise was countenanced. Consequently, instead of using the vast army of unemployed and starving farm labourers on useful projects such as land drainage or railway building, they were set to digging holes and filling them in again, or erecting the high walls around the estates of the gentry which to this day obscure the view in so many parts of Ireland. Since no man who held land was allowed to do any relief work unless he gave up his holding, and starving men couldn't pay their rents anyway, evictions continued right through the Famine years.

During the five years from 1845 to 1850 the population dropped by about two million mainly in the poorer, Gaelic-speaking Catholic areas. Ulster was relatively unaffected by the Famine, except to the extent that it brought a new wave of starving peasants and farm labourers swarming into Belfast and other Ulster cities looking for work, some of them suffering from disease—there was a typhus epidemic in Belfast in 1847 and one of Asiatic cholera in 1848—and to the extent that it added to the Ulster Protestant conviction that wherever you have Roman Catholicism you have poverty, unrest, disease and discontent.

In the middle of all this ghastly confusion of mismanagement, ineptitude and lack of communication, a small group of Irish patriots under William Smith O'Brien attempted yet another rebellion. Once again information leaked out in advance; John Mitchell, one of the few Ulster Protestants in the movement, was captured and sentenced to deportation. If the rebellion had any effect in the North it was to strengthen the Orange Movement as a safeguard against this sort of nonsense. In the South, where William Smith O'Brien had been hoping for another peasant uprising on the 1798 pattern at the very least, his efforts were doomed because the Irish peasants were too cowed and miserable to fight, though he did stage a siege on a party of Irish constabulary at Ballingarry, which managed to hold out until reinforcements arrived. O'Brien was sentenced to death but this was commuted to transportation for life.

The pattern of emigration set up by the Famine years continued long after the Famine; indeed for the best part of a century from 1847 emigration to America was a permanent part of the pattern of Irish life.

In his book, *A Nation of Immigrants*, the late President John F.

Kennedy wrote: 'The Irish were the vanguard of the great waves of immigrants to arrive during the 19th century. By 1850, after the potato famine, they had replaced England as the chief source of new settlers, making up 44 per cent of the foreign-born in the United States. In the century between 1820 and 1920, 4½ million people left Ireland to come to the United States.'

And since those who emigrated were almost all Irish Catholic peasants from the South, this mass emigration had the effect of altering the religious ratio. The Protestant population remained steady around the million mark, as it has ever since, while the Catholic population was about halved. If there had been no Famine, and no mass-emigration, the population of Ireland might well have reached 10 or 11 millions by 1860, roughly a third of the population of the British Isles, of which only about 10 per cent would have been Protestant. As it happened, the mass emigration of Catholics meant that by the end of the 19th century, Protestants numbered over a third of the entire population, and between 60 and 80 per cent of the population of the most Protestant counties of Ulster.

The problem was at its most acute in Belfast, where, after the Famine, about a third of the population was Catholic, living in Catholic ghettoes cut off from one another and very vulnerable to attack by Orangemen. There were sectarian riots in Belfast in 1835, 1843, 1857, 1864, 1872, 1880, 1884, 1886 and 1894; and these were serious riots, in which many lives were lost and large numbers of people injured, to say nothing of damage to property. There was trouble of one sort or another every July 12th and on most other occasions when the Orangemen chose to march; but in those days such routine disturbances were rarely recorded.

3

Returning now to the Orange Order and its 'constitutional' problems in the wake of the British commission of inquiry, the Grand Lodge in Dublin remained largely ineffective, and a Grand Lodge of Ulster was formed in February 1844, with

Lodges in Derry, North and mid-Antrim, Fermanagh and South Donegal. The expiry of the Party Processions Act allowed Orangemen to come out openly the next year—not that they had ever stopped marching—and in 1845, the size and composition of the processions demonstrated the latent strength of Orangeism. Many of the men who had voted for dissolution and had been holding aloof from the movement now began openly to associate themselves with it again.

On August 27th, 1845, a meeting in the town hall at Enniskillen decided to set up a committee to redraft the rules yet again; the British Orange Order had long since reorganized itself along modified lines which kept it within the letter of the law. At Enniskillen, the committee took counsel's opinion and drew up a scheme which retained the name of the Orange Order but, to comply with the law, dropped the idea of an oath-bound society.

In 1846 the Orange processions were bigger and more numerous than ever and there was a demand from many of the District Lodges for a full revival of the movement in its original form, but a number of the men at the top were still nervous because of the hostile tone of the parliamentary commission's conclusions, and some of them were even against the use of the name Orange. On the other hand, the Whigs were now out of office and Peel and his new Conservatives were thought to be less critical of the Orangemen. So in August 1846 the Grand Orange Lodge of Ireland was again reconstituted in Enniskillen town hall, with the Earl of Enniskillen—who, it will be remembered, was one of the Deputy Grand Masters under the Duke of Cumberland—as Grand Master.

During William Smith O'Brien's ill-fated attempt at a rebellion in 1848, Orangemen were given an opportunity to demonstrate their loyalty and were issued with arms and licences entitling them to carry arms. As it turned out, the arms were not needed, because there was no rebellion to put down. However, there seems to be little doubt that many of the Orangemen held on to their arms and they had occasion to use them the following year in the affair known and celebrated in Orange folklore as Dolly's Brae.

There were clashes earlier in the year between parties of Ribbonmen and Orangemen in which some lives were lost. Then Lord Roden—now acting as Deputy Grand Master—decided to mobilize his men for the coming July 12th. According to another version of the popular Orange ballad, he

> '*sent an invitation to Rathfriland Orange corps,*
> *To come and spend the day with him at sylvan Tollymore;*
> *The Orangemen they did obey their noble chief's command;*
> *So over Dolly's Brae they marched, a loyal, stalwart band.*'

It had become a tradition and a point of honour with the local Orangemen to show their determination and strength by marching over a hill known as Dolly's Brae, near Magheramayo in County Down, using the old road through Catholic territory, where it was equally traditional for large masses of Ribbonmen to congregate to attempt to prevent them.

Escorted by troops and police, with two priests helping to restrain the Ribbonmen, they set off. According to the Rev John Brown 'On the return journey a squib went off and two shots were fired. Military and police witnesses swore that these came from the hill where the Ribbonmen had stayed all day. A volley was fired at soldiers, police and Orangemen. They cleared the hill under fire, and two Lodges planted their flags at the top. Lives were lost, and houses burned, and Orangemen were said to have acted savagely. A special committee of the Grand Lodge later queried the accuracy of some of the report made by a Commissioner on the affair, but the results were that Lord Roden, Mr William Beers, Grand Master of County Down, and Mr Francis Beers, his brother, were dismissed from the commission of the peace. It was William Beers who, at a dinner in Downpatrick on the 19th of July, 1849, seems to have first used the expression "Dolly's Brae no more" when he announced that its new name must be "King William's Hill".

'Prosecutions against both Orangemen and Ribbonmen were finally given up by the Crown. But the affair caused a renewal of the Party Processions Act in 1850. It had possibly some effect already by giving the impression that the new Orangeism was going to be violent and scaring off men who might otherwise have joined—much was made of it in Parliament by members who had followed O'Connell. Inside the Institution the Party Processions Act caused trouble. The ordinary Orangeman considered that his loyalty had been thrown in his face by the Government; that he had been humiliated by the Queen's Ministers before murderous rebels. When the intensely respectable Grand Lodge accepted the situation, and insisted so far as it could that the law must be obeyed, many Orangemen showed bitter resentment. Only a few lodges in Armagh and Tyrone showed this by threatenening to burn their flags and warrants, and only very few actually did so. But on occasion the old spirit manifested itself in disregard of the law and the Grand Lodge'.

I have quoted this account of the affair of Dolly's Brae at length because it tells far more about the attitude of the case-hardened Orangeman now, as then, than any official, hostile report of the event. The calm acceptance, in what amounts to a throw-away sentence—'Lives were lost, and houses burned, and Orangemen were said to have acted savagely'—of what amounted to another effort to intimidate the Catholics into clearing out of the area, like an earlier reference I have quoted to 'clearing out the nest', tells far more about the outlook of the Orangemen than all the thousands of words of criticism which have been written about them. There is a note of almost jubilant support for the diehards who refused to recognize either the laws of the land or the instructions of their Grand Masters in that final sentence: 'But on occasion *the old spirit* manifested itself in disregard of the law and the Grand Lodge'.

The Orangemen fervently believed that as Loyalists it was their right and their duty to harass the Catholics whenever they could be provoked into displays of rebellious violence brought on by insults, defiant marches through their territory, and other displays of Protestant force and solidarity; and when the Government made laws to prevent them from doing so, and these laws were upheld by the Grand Lodges, the Orangemen felt that they had been deserted.

This is exactly what William Craig and the Orangemen in today's Vanguard and the Ulster Defence Association movement feel; and, as I write, it remains to be seen whether they will carry on the ancient tradition of defying law and Lodge alike to ensure the maintenance of the Protestant ascendancy 'in their own time and in their own way'.

* * *

Scarlet Church of all uncleanness,
Sink thou to the deep abyss,
To the orgies of obsceneness,
Where the hell-bound furies hiss;
Where thy father Satan's eye
May hail thee, blood-stained Papacy!

Harlot! Cease thy midnight rambles
Prowling for the life of saints,
Henceforth sit in hellish shambles
Where the scent of murder taints
Every gale that passeth by—
Ogre, ghoul of Papacy!

—From an ancient Orange ditty quoted in the *Contemporary Review* for August, 1896.

XI

Roaring Hanna and the Demagogues

For twenty years following the Famine, although the Orangemen continued to march and, as we have seen, riots were a regular feature of life in Belfast and the other growing industrial areas in Ulster as well as in the North and Midlands of England and in Glasgow, the Orange Order was not deeply involved in political events either in Ireland or at Westminster.

One reason for this is that during the years following the famine Ireland's political efforts were almost entirely concentrated on what became known as the Land War—the fight to get a better deal for the Irish tenants and peasant proprietors. But in Ulster, partly as a result of the 'Ulster Custom' under which tenants had both security of tenure and freedom to dispose of their tenancies at a profit, and partly for other reasons, there was relatively little agrarian trouble during this period.

The collection of tithes had never caused as much resentment in Ulster as it had throughout the rest of the country. For one thing, many of the settlers were Church of Ireland and felt the money was going to support their own ministers. The Presbyterians resented the payment of tithes initially, but when Pitt offered a direct State payment to Presbyterian ministers loyal to the British connection this removed their resentment. The Catholics in the border counties bitterly resented paying tithes of course, and the fact that Orange-dominated Yeomanry had sometimes been used to enforce their collection convinced Ulster Catholics that the Government was behind the Orange Order. However, as we have seen, the alteration of the system by which the tithes were collected removed this source of agrarian strife.

The whole pattern of agriculture in Ireland changed yet again in the years following the Famine. To provide cheaper bread for the ever-growing industrial areas the Westminster Government had decided to repeal the Corn Acts and had removed restrictions on imported corn, which meant that Ireland could not compete with countries like Canada and the United States, and the small farmer who had formerly paid his rent by tillage had to emigrate or at any rate spend part of the year working in England or Scotland. The growing demand for beef led to further increases in ranching, which again meant putting many small farmers off their land and out of work. The Encumbered Estates Act of 1849, which allowed for compulsory sale of estates so heavily mortgaged that they could no longer show a profit, further altered the pattern of Irish agriculture by introducing a whole new generation of landlords, many of them without any ties with Ireland, who tried to run their new estates so as to extract the maximum profit from them without any regard for the rights of the tenants. This led to the Land War, which was conducted in Ireland by means of the boycott—a very powerful instrument, similar in many ways to excommunication, by which a landlord or agent who evicted a tenant for refusing to pay an unfair rent was 'boycotted' by everyone in the neighbourhood; nobody would work for him, or serve him, or look after his animals or buy his farm produce or even bury his dead, and if another tenant took the land from which the original one had been evicted he in turn would be boycotted.

At Westminster the Land War was conducted by the Irish parliamentary party now under Charles Stewart Parnell, a Protestant landowner, by obstructing the business of the House in every possible way to draw attention to the Irish grievances. This combination of tactics caused a certain amount of ill-will but it worked and by the 1870s a whole series of Land Acts were passed which for all practical purposes removed the land from the English landed gentry and absentee landlords in Ireland and allowed the Irish to buy it back, on favourable terms, through Government loans. Not all of it, of course; the great aristocratic families with seats in the House of Lords and considerable influence in Westminster retained their estates.

The North of Ireland was not affected in anything like the same way by these changes. The traditional 'Ulster custom' and the fact that the Scots settlers were more industrious and more advanced in their farming methods meant that there were far fewer encumbered estates in the North and consequently the big estates were not broken up, except again in the border areas of the west and south, where there were large Catholic populations. Although some Orange Lodges sent help to boycotted landlords, in general the Orangemen were unconcerned with Parnell's struggle to get a better deal for the Irish peasant, though they should have seen in the Land Acts, and in Gladstone's disestablishment of the Church of Ireland in 1869, a portent of things to come: for it was clear that by now the Protestants in the South of Ireland had outlived their usefulness to Britain, and Britain was preparing to abandon them as part of the price of appeasing the Irish Catholic majority. And although the Orangemen didn't realize it until Gladstone's first Home Rule bill was introduced in 1886, it should have been clear to them even then that they were now out on a limb. But loyalty to the Crown was such a strong feature of the Orangeman's make-up that it didn't occur to him that the Crown might not always show the same loyalty in return.

'In north-eastern Ulster', writes Fitzgibbon, 'the Presbyterian farmers worked hard, prospered in good times and survived in bad, put on their best suits and black dresses for church on Sundays, the boys joining the local Orange Lodge as they reached men's estate, marching on summer days with sashes and drums to celebrate their ancient, tribal victories over the old Irish, convinced by their own clean-living, non-swearing, hard-working and industrious rectitude that they were the master race, the *Herrenvolk*, because they were the Lord's Anointed. His strong arm would protect them from their enemies, and as they oiled their muskets and made sure that they kept their powder dry they knew they were not acting selfishly but as His agents, to ensure that His will be done.'

2

During the period between the end of the Famine and the introduction of the first Home Rule Bill, the Grand Lodge seems to have lost touch with the rank and file of the organization. Indeed, the Rev John Brown admits as much: '... the Grand Lodge had too much of a landlord and a Church of Ireland flavour for these men at the time ...'

In these circumstances, leadership came from another quarter: the churchmen. Fiery preachers like the Rev Hugh Hanna (known as 'Roaring Hanna'), the Rev Thomas Wellesley Roe and the Rev Dr Thomas Drew followed Dr Henry Cooke's example and kept the fires of sectarianism fiercely burning by their attacks on Popery.

A typical sample, taken from a sermon by the Rev Thomas Drew on July 12th, 1857, to a congregation of about 2,000, included such sentiments as the following: '... The Sermon on the Mount is an everlasting rebuke to all intolerance ... Of old time, lords of high degree, with their own hands, strained on the rack the limbs of delicate Protestant women, prelates dabbled in the gore of their hapless victims. The cells of the Pope's prisons were paved with the calcined bones of men and cemented with human gore and human hair ... The Word of God makes all plain; puts to eternal shame the practices of the persecutors, and stigmatizes the arrogant pretences of Popes and the outrageous dogma of their bloodstained religion'.

This same Drew was the author of a number of Orange songs and pamphlets including *Twenty Reasons for Being an Orangeman*, one of which reads as follows: 'I learn by the doctrines, history and daily practices of the Church of Rome that the lives of Protestants are endangered, the laws of England set at nought, and the Crown of England subordinated to the dictates of an Italian bishop'. When sentiments of this kind were expressed, as they often were, in the open, in public places where Catholics could also congregate to hear themselves insulted in such terms, it is not surprising that rioting frequently resulted.

Andrew Boyd's *Holy War in Belfast* contains some detailed accounts of riots in Belfast and elsewhere occasioned and encouraged by these firebrand preachers. Typical of these disturbances are the events of Sunday, September 6th, 1857, described in Boyd's book. On the previous Saturday, word reached *The Ulsterman* that the Rev Dr Thomas Drew was to preach on the steps of the Customs House the following afternoon. *The Ulsterman* immediately printed posters and leaflets urging Catholics to assemble there. Drew, however, had decided not to preach, in deference to Bishop Knox's request to Church of Ireland clergy in his Diocese to desist from such provocative actions. Roaring Hanna, being a Presbyterian, was not under any obligation to respect the Bishop's wishes, so he stepped in to replace Drew.

The crowd which turned up at the Customs House was disappointed because Hanna had switched his plans and was preaching instead outside the Seamen's Church in Corporation Square. The entire Town Police Force of Belfast and large numbers of the Royal Irish Constabulary were stationed in Corporation Square, between Hanna's Orange audience and the Catholics around the Customs House. Despite a warning from a former Mayor of Belfast that the crowds were in a dangerously excitable mood, Hanna began to make a short sermon. During the sermon, the Catholic crowds, having discovered where the meeting was taking place, began to converge on Corporation Square through various side-streets. Hanna's supporters, following a pre-arranged plan, obtained from the harbour constable the key of a storeyard, armed themselves with sharp-edged staves, iron crowbars, oars, marlin spikes, ship's blocks and tackle from the store, and fell on the Catholic crowds, who replied with the only weapons they could lay their hands on—paving stones. Hanna decided to end the meeting. Raising his voice above the turmoil he appealed to the mob: 'Please go home now, my good people. We have asserted our right to preach the Gospel in public, but let your conduct for the rest of the day be worthy of Christians. Don't linger in the streets; afford no opportunity for tumult and disorder. I believe the good work we have been engaged in today will be pregnant with a mighty influence. God bless you, one and all'.

Having delivered himself of this benison, Roaring Hanna stepped delicately into his waiting carriage and drove home, undoubtedly aware that his supporters had no intention whatever of following his advice and departing in peace, but would continue the good work of bashing the Papishes late into the evening. The hussars were called out and many people received dreadful wounds.

A few days later, Roaring Hanna published a letter to the Protestants of Belfast: 'Men and Brethren,' he wrote, 'Your blood-bought and cherished rights have been imperilled by the audacious and savage outrages of a Roman mob . . . But you were not to be bullied or cajoled out of your rights. They are not to be surrendered, and they are to be strenuously maintained. That you have unmistakably shown on the past Sabbath. Then you arose, calm but powerful, as the thunder reposing in the cloud . . . A few more Sabbaths like the last will achieve a permanent good'.

Some idea of the confusion which existed in the upper echelons of the Orange Order can be gained from the Rev John Brown's official history of this period: 'The Orange Institution had enough to think about. There were the Belfast riots; for the growth of a great industrial city created new problems and it seemed that Protestant open-air services whether conducted by the Rev Mr Roe of the Church of Ireland Parochial Mission, or the Presbyterian Rev Hugh Hanna, were no more acceptable to a certain element than Orange demonstrations, and one thing led to another. There was the growing conviction of the Orangemen that the Party Processions Act and the Party Emblems Act of 1860 were not being fairly enforced as between Orangemen, and Ribbonmen, and other groups. It was a sore point, and became sorer. The Laws and Ordinances and Ritual had to be brought up to date. The Grand Lodge had its somewhat meagre finances to husband, and had to try to secure a suitable headquarters, as well as run a Sabbath School in Dublin for some years, and make an attempt to organize a benevolent fund.

'One of its most delicate tasks was to oppose the Anti-Processions and Party Emblems Acts, and restrain the more excitable Orangemen at the same time. One William Johnston, of Ballykilbeg, son-in-law of Dr Drew, prominent in County Down, leader of the Royal Black Institution, had already caused some difficulty. The embodiment of Orangeism to the rank and file, eloquent, ceaselessly campaigning for the cause on platform and in Press, he had caused embarrassment to a Grand Lodge desperately anxious to be right with the law. He had helped to reorganize the Black Institution, which preserved the old degrees, and in its rules mentioned the Orange Institution in such a way as to alarm Lord Enniskillen and others. Perhaps Enniskillen was apt to be easily alarmed since his escape from death with a trainload of excursionists who were derailed at Trillick some years before, presumably by Ribbonmen. But the Black Rules were revised, and the difficulty removed.'

It is clear from the above extract that despite earlier attempts to limit the Orange Lodges to two Orders, the Orange and the Purple, the Black Institution had persisted and was still regarded as being in some way more deeply traditional and more reputable than the others.

3

In 1864 a most violent and long-drawn-out series of riots occurred in Belfast, arising out of an event in Dublin.

On August 8th of that year, the Lord Mayor of Dublin laid the foundation stone for the statue of Dan O'Connell, the Liberator, which still adorns O'Connell Street, known in those days as Sackville Street. The Irish Nationalists celebrated the occasion and a trainload of Irish Catholic Nationalists from Belfast travelled to Dublin for the day. There had been a great deal of advance publicity, both about the Dublin celebration, and about the Belfast contingent's excursion to take part in it, and none of it was much to the liking of the Orangemen. O'Connell, to them, was the man responsible for Catholic Emancipation—and that could result in a revival of the old Dublin Parliament, which would now be dominated by

Catholics, and would end Protestant Ascendancy for all time. In fact this possibility had in the meantime been advanced by a considerable increase of the franchise.

Accordingly, the Orangemen made an enormous effigy of O'Connell which—in the manner of the London apprentice boys of the 17th century—they stuffed with fireworks and other highly inflammable substances—and lay in wait for the arrival back in Belfast of the Nationalist excursion. The Royal Irish Constabulary prevented them from mobbing the Catholics as they got off the train.

For a whole day they carried this great effigy of the dead Catholic leader around Belfast, trying to penetrate the Catholic areas in order to set fire to it in a place where it would be likely to cause the strongest reaction, but they were constantly foiled by the police and the military. In the end, they set fire to it on the banks of the Lagan and tipped it into the river, an insult which produced the expected Catholic reaction and led to several days of severe rioting during which lives were lost and a great deal of property destroyed.

The event was probably most significant in the fact that it was the first time that Dublin and the Catholic Ulster Nationalists were linked in the Orange mind and probably marked the point when the ordinary rank and file Orangeman ceased to think of Dublin as the Protestant capital of a country still largely dominated and controlled by the Ascendancy and began to think of it as a city where the Papishes were in the majority and might one day gain control of things.

By now, too, a new dread word had entered the Orange hagiology: Fenianism. The Fenian movement—known also, and later exclusively, as the Irish Republican Brotherhood—was founded in Paris in 1858 by two survivors of William Smith O'Brien's abortive rising of ten years earlier and it set about trying to achieve its aims by infiltrating other organizations—sporting, political, even cultural. It also acquired great strength amongst the large Irish minority groups in England and above all in America, where the organization was known as Clan-na-Gael (the clan of the Gaels).

By 1865 James Stephens and others had in the Fenian

Brotherhood the nucleus of a powerful secret society whose aim it was to stage an armed rebellion at the earliest opportunity. As usual, information leaked to the authorities and in that year many of the leading Fenians were arrested and sentenced to long terms of imprisonment in British jails. Stephens himself escaped and attempted a rising in 1867 which was suppressed within twenty-four hours.

Unlike the previous Irish revolutionary movements, the Fenians carried the struggle to England. In an attempt to rescue two Fenian prisoners from a Manchester jail, a policeman was shot dead and three Fenians—Allen, Larkin and O'Brien, thereafter known as the 'Manchester Martyrs'—were executed for their part in the rescue attempt. Elsewhere in England, the Fenians carried out similar raids and arranged indiscriminate dynamite explosions, sometimes involving the loss of innocent lives. From that moment the word Fenianism was inextricably coupled in the Orange mind with that of the Catholics, the Nationalists and ultimately, the Southern Irish. When Gladstone almost immediately announced his intention to embark on a programme designed to pacify Ireland many people felt—as they felt in March, 1972, when Heath's 'political initiative' was finally revealed—that violence had succeeded after years of peaceful opposition and civil disobedience of one sort or another had failed.

The Orange reaction was immediate and predictable. William Johnston of Ballykilbeg, the man responsible for reorganizing the Black Institution within the Order, decided to ignore the Party Processions Act and the Party Emblems Act and offer a display of Orange strength against the growing menace of Fenianism. He led a mass march of Orangemen from Newtownards to Bangor on July 12th, 1867, stood trial at the Assizes and was sentenced to twelve months in Downpatrick Jail where he spent much of the time penning Loyal Orange Ballads, including one about his own exploits:

Shall Ulster furl the flag we bore
So proudly on to Bangor?
The watchword of the brave and free
Will still be 'No Surrender'.

On his release from jail, he succeeded in getting himself returned as an Independent Orange candidate for South Belfast, went to Westminster and set about organizing the repeal of the detested Acts.

In the late 'sixties and early 'seventies, Orangeism was rapidly expanding throughout Ulster and particularly in the city of Belfast. The Fenian Rising had shocked many Protestants out of the lethargy into which they had lapsed during the Land War. The disestablishment of the Church of Ireland, and the end of the state payment to the Presbyterian clergy had caused Irish Protestants once again to feel insecure. For the first time Presbyterian ministers began to join the Lodges in large numbers and the repeal of the Party Processions Act gave the movement new heart.

The first Grand Orange Conference was held in the Belfast Orange Hall on July 18th, 1866, in response to a suggestion from Canada, where Orangeism was now strong and where, according to the Rev John Brown, 'Brother Sir John MacDonald got the notion of the Confederation of Canada from the organization of the Grand Orange Lodge of British America'.

But it was the election of 1885, which put Gladstone in power—an election in which the Home Rule Party headed by Parnell secured almost all the Irish seats outside Ulster and held the balance of power in the House of Commons—which welded the Orange Order together again and brought the Grand Lodge back in line with the rank and file. On December 27th, 1885, the Earl of Erne and the Earl of Enniskillen issued a communiqué from the Grand Lodge to Orangemen everywhere: 'We therefore appeal to those, who though hitherto differing from us, now realize the imminent peril which in common confronts us all to stand shoulder to shoulder with us in defence of the Union, and to advance the cause of loyalty, liberty and religion.'

The Rev John Brown adds this comment: 'As Orangemen pondered these words, and wondered what Mr Gladstone might do in the new situation, they might well have repeated the lines written by William Blacker, who had carried bullets to the Diamond in 1795, and in the troublous 'thirties had echoed the advice of Oliver Cromwell:

The thunder clouds are driving
Athwart the lurid sky,
But 'Put your trust in God, my boys
And keep your powder dry'.

* * *

We know the war prepared
On every peaceful home,
We know the hells declared
For such as serve not Rome—
The terror, threats and dread
In market, hearth and field—
We know when all is said,
We perish if we yield.

Believe, we dare not boast,
Believe, we do not fear—
We stand to pay the cost
In all that men hold dear.
What answer from the North?
One Law, one Land, one Throne.
If England drives us forth
We shall not fall alone.

—From *Ulster 1912*, by Rudyard Kipling.

XII

Ulster Will Fight . . . and Ulster Will Be Right

The idea of introducing a Home Rule Bill came to Gladstone, it is said, as he cruised the Norwegian fiords on board Sir Thomas Brassey's yacht *Sunbeam* and mused on the apparent content of the people of Norway who were citizens of Sweden at this period but enjoyed what amounted to a system of Home Rule by which they managed their own purely domestic affairs. His decision may have been genuinely motivated by a desire to improve the state of affairs in Ireland, but it is also likely that he was thinking of Parnell's eighty-six Home Rulers at Westminster, who had caused the fall of his previous Government by switching their allegiance to Lord Salisbury's Conservative Party.

There was, however, no real need for the Orange Order to feel any alarm at this stage. For one thing, the House of Lords still had the power to veto any measure passed by the Commons and could be counted on to throw out the Home Rule Bill, if it were passed by the Commons.

It was another politician—and whatever one thinks about Gladstone's motives there is not much doubt that Lord Randolph Churchill was cynically playing the party game—who involved the Orange Order directly in militant action against the threat of Home Rule long before there was any real danger of it being introduced. Early in 1886 he decided that if Gladstone was going to support Home Rule 'the Orange card would be the one to play'. He travelled to Ulster and launched a campaign which amounted to an incitement to the Orangemen to resist Home Rule in arms if necessary. It was during this campaign that the famous slogan 'Ulster will fight and Ulster will be right' was evolved, and although the Conservative Party had carried the additional label 'and Unionist' since Disraeli's day, it was only now that the 'Unionist' element in that title and party became crucial.

In Belfast and several of the other cities Randolph Churchill made rabble-rousing speeches as demagogic in their own way as those of Roaring Hanna and the firebrand preachers. He must have known the effect that these speeches would have. Constantine Fitzgibbon takes the charitable view that Churchill, who was to die less than nine years later, at the age of forty-six, from general paralysis of the insane, was already partially out of his mind when he made this disastrous visit to Ulster; maybe, but other politicians before and since have done equally irresponsible things from the narrowest of political motives and with total disregard for the human suffering which must inevitably ensue. In Belfast, the result of Churchill's visit was three days of the fiercest rioting the city had ever known.

In addition to his general war cry, 'Ulster will fight and Ulster will be right'—which might be held to apply to all Unionist Ulstermen—Churchill issued a specific challenge to the Orange Order. At a meeting arranged by the Order in the Ulster Hall in February 1886, he said: 'Now may be the time to show whether all those ceremonies and forms which are practised in Orange Lodges are really living symbols or idle meaningless ceremonies'.

But the Orange Order needed no such battle-cry. It had already been aroused from its torpor by the threat of Home Rule. In the third essay on the Order in *Orangeism: A New Historical Appreciation*, the Rev S. E. Long writes: 'The Orange Order . . . had been very much a labouring and poorer artisan class Protestant movement. It had not gained the support, in size, of the gentry, the clergy, the business and professional men and the farmers until the pressure of a Bill, popularly understood to be aimed at giving over the country to a Dublin government and the control of the Roman Catholic Church, was mooted. This made Protestant people of unionist loyalties turn to the Order as a likely instrument for maintaining the British connection and preserving the Protestant religion.

There was a huge fear because the terms of the Bill appeared to give power to the proposed Irish Parliament to grant money to religious bodies and for the erection of chapels.

'Lord Cushendun had noted a tendency prior to 1886 for Lodge meetings and anniversary celebrations "to become little better than occasions for conviviality wholly inconsistent with the irreproachable formularies of the Order". The introduction of Gladstone's Home Rule Bill gave the Order a membership which was to transform it completely to make it a highly respectable and exceedingly powerful religious political organization.'

And later, in the same essay, amplifying the Orange objections to the Home Rule Bill, he adds: 'The objections to Home Rule had crystallised into a granite-like determination that on religious and economic grounds Roman Catholic influenced control would be impossible. The errors and heresies of Romanism made nonsense of Christian doctrine and ethics. It was argued that the inadequacies of Roman Catholic politicians would impoverish the country, as it had pauperised Eastern Canada, the very poor neighbour of Protestant-inspired Western Canada'.

An interesting point here is the assumption that Rome was behind the initial agitation for Home Rule. In point of fact at this stage, Rome was every bit as strongly opposed to Home Rule as the Orange Order, though for a very different reason. So long as the Union was maintained, the Roman Church could count on a solid bloc of eighty-odd Catholic votes at Westminster in addition to those of the few English Catholics in Parliament. Later, in view of the intensity of feeling among Irish Catholics, the Church supported Irish independence, though it never condoned revolution.

On April 8th, 1886, Gladstone introduced his Bill, which would have set up an Irish parliament and executive in Dublin with powers of legislation and control over the whole country except in relation to the Crown, peace and war, the defence forces, foreign and colonial relations, customs and excise, trade and navigation, the post office, coinage and legal tender. To safeguard the minority there was to be an upper house, including 28 elective Irish peers, which would not, however, sit separately although they could vote separately if they wished to do so. Irish representation at Westminster would have been abolished.

After sixteen days of debate in the Commons, the Bill was defeated in June, 1886 by 30 votes and Gladstone dissolved Parliament. The defeat of the bill was greeted in Ulster with delirious rejoicing (and rioting, needless to say) and the Orangemen lit bonfires on the hills around Belfast. It is hard to find figures for the casualties that occurred during the sporadic riots which went on well into September of that year. One reason may be that then, as now, the rioters often carried away their dead and wounded to avoid trouble with the police; another may be that since many of the injuries were in fact inflicted by Orange elements within the police forces, it is probably not unfair to assume that they were not always meticulous in recording injuries which were incurred during riots.

The Orange Order emerged from the victory revitalized and convinced that it now had the solid backing of the Conservative and Unionist Party in Britain for anything it might decide to do to protect the 'Constitution'. The Ulster Unionist Party was entirely dominated and controlled by the Orange Order, though sixteen of the thirty-three Ulster members of the Parliament which defeated the Home Rule Bill were in fact Home Rulers, and even as early as this the idea of partition had been mooted: Churchill had referred in his speeches to the possibility that Ireland should in fact be regarded as two nations rather than one.

If the bitterness of the Ulster Protestants dates back to the events of 1641 and 1798, their unshakeable conviction that they have a moral and legal right to run things in 'their' part of the country was sown during Randolph Churchill's visit to Ulster early in 1886.

2

The menace of Home Rule disappeared with the return to power of Lord Salisbury and his Conservatives, but the fact that it had been discussed, and might be raised again when the

Liberals next gained power made the Orangemen determined that there would be no let up in their preparations to defeat it if and when it reared its ugly head again.

This happened five years later when the Liberals were returned with a majority. The Orange Order strengthened its ranks by forming an alliance with the newly formed Unionist Clubs, founded by Lord Templeton.

A convention was held in Belfast in June 1892 to demonstrate the determination of the Ulster people to resist Home Rule. In a temporary building designed to hold 13,000, more than 21,000 managed to get in, and another 3,000 had to be excluded because there wasn't an inch of spare space left. The meeting was opened with prayers by the Primate and the Moderator, and the speakers included Mr Thomas Andrews, father of J. M. Andrews, a future Stormont Prime Minister and Grand Master of the Orange Order, and the second Duke of Abercorn, who was in the chair. It was Abercorn who got the crowd chanting: 'We will not have Home Rule'.

Around the same time, Major Fred Crawford, an Orangeman and an ex-Artillery officer, founded a secret society called 'Young Ulster' which had one single declared aim: to resist Home Rule. Nor was there much doubt about the way in which the Young Ulster movement intended to resist it; for a condition of membership was the possession of a revolver or a cavalry Winchester carbine with one hundred rounds of ammunition.

The second Home Rule Bill was introduced in February 1893, debated at no fewer than 85 sittings of the Commons and finally passed its third reading on September 1st by a margin of 34 votes. In the Lords it was thrown out on its second reading by a massive majority of 419 to 41. The jubilation in Belfast was enormous. Bonfires were lighted on the hills again. While the debate was in progress, the Orangemen had organized various displays of solidarity both in Britain and in Ireland, including a four-hour march past in Belfast in April, taken by A. J. Balfour, representing Lord Salisbury, leader of the Conservative and Unionist party. At the Linen Hall, a copy of the Home Rule Bill was ceremoniously burned.

The Liberals remained firmly committed to the idea of Home Rule, but they were also politicians, and when they next came into power in 1906, it was with a big enough majority to manage without the Irish vote, and although Home Rule remained a part of the Liberal platform, no effort was made to introduce another Home Rule Bill. It was not until the elections of 1910, which once more put the Liberals in power but with such a reduced majority that they were again dependent on the Irish vote, that Home Rule again became a vital—indeed an explosive—issue.

In the meantime, the Orange Order was having some internal troubles. During the celebrations of July 12th, 1902, at Castlereagh, the County Grand Master of Belfast, Colonel Edward Saunderson, was heckled by Thomas Sloan, an Orangeman. His complaint was that Saunderson, an M.P., had voted against the inspection of Roman Catholic convent laundries. According to the Orange Order, Sloan was in error. He was charged with unbecoming conduct and brought before the Belfast County Lodge's disciplinary committee. When he was expelled from the Order by the Grand Lodge in June, 1903, Sloan replied by founding his own Independent Orange Order.

The Independent Orange Order held its own demonstrations and during one of them, in 1905 at Magheramorne, made a declaration which sounded as if this breakaway Orange movement had now turned its back on the Unionist idea and looked with favour on Home Rule. It even entered into a brief alliance with the Belfast Labour Party and the Ancient Order of Hibernians. The idea was to bring Catholic and Protestant workers together for the good of the country—an approach to a solution of Ulster's problems more recently preached by Miss Bernadette Devlin among others. The official Orange comment on the idea is given by the Rev S. E. Long: 'It did not prove a worthwhile experiment except perhaps to show that Orange and Green on a Labour canvas was pigment which proved soluble in the religious wash'. For a time, under its Grand Master Robert Lindsay Crawford, the author of the Magheramorne manifesto which offered 'the right hand of friendship to... our countrymen', and under Thomas Sloan, who held an Independent seat at Westminster, the Independent Orange Order was a movement of some influence. But in the 1910 elections Sloan lost his seat, and when it was clear that the Home Rule was going to become a live issue again—with the difference that in the meantime legislation had been introduced by which the Lords could no longer veto a Bill passed by the Commons but merely delay it for up to two years—the ranks of the Orange Order closed again, and the Independent Orange Order vanished into oblivion.

3

Gladstone had retired in 1894 and Campbell Bannerman was quickly succeeded as Premier by Asquith, who, the Orangemen very well knew, was busy drawing up a third Home Rule Bill. Also, relations between the Prime Minister and the Irish Nationalist Party at Westminster, now led by John Redmond, were very good. Redmond was willing to give the Ulstermen almost any safeguards they might require, short of exclusion from the Home Rule Bill—for although the question of some form of partition came up again and again Redmond knew that he could not survive if he accepted partition as a prerequisite condition. The Ulster Unionists did not want Home Rule in any shape or form, either for a partitioned-off Ulster or for the whole country, and were convinced that if they could put up a sufficiently determined resistance the Government would drop the idea altogether. It is one of the many ironies of Irish history that the Orangemen of Ulster were prepared in 1910 to take up arms against the British Army to resist Home Rule; what they wanted was to *retain* complete integration with the United Kingdom and direct rule from Westminster. Yet Home Rule is exactly what they got; and when Heath's political initiative was announced in 1972, Craig and his Vanguard Movement—Orangemen, most of them—threatened to take up arms to retain Home Rule and *resist* full integration with the United Kingdom and direct rule from Westminster.

But that is jumping ahead. In February 1910, Sir Edward

Carson accepted an invitation to lead the Ulster Unionists in the House of Commons. A Dubliner with no roots in Ulster, he was a successful barrister and politician and a forceful orator.

In 1911, the year before the Bill was introduced, Carson held at Craigavon a review of members of the Ulster Unionist Clubs and Orange Lodges and announced Ulster's programme to an audience of over 100,000 people. They would not merely defy Home Rule from Dublin but would prepare an alternative provisional government which would be ready 'the morning Home Rule passes, to become responsible for the government of the Protestant Province of Ulster'. By January 1912, Carson was recruiting and drilling his own private army, the Ulster Volunteers, dominated by the Orange Order and pledged to resist Home Rule by force.

Closely involved with Carson in the formation of the Ulster Volunteers was Major Fred Crawford, the ex-Royal Artillery officer who had already formed 'Young Ulster' and an adventurer who was never happier than when he was risking his life. Another of Carson's associates was James Craig, of the Unionist Council, a former captain in the Irish Rifles, a massive man with a face of granite who later became one of Northern Ireland's Prime Ministers.

The secretary of the Grand Lodge of Ulster, a lawyer called Colonel H. Wallace had, with the assistance of another lawyer, J. H. Campbell, K.C. (later Lord Glenavy) found a loophole in the law by which this private army could be legalized. Any two Justices of the Peace might authorize 'military activity' by amateur soldiers within the area of their jurisdiction, provided that such men were dedicated to the preservation of the 'Constitution' and provided that they marched under patriotic slogans. Naturally there was no problem about finding Justices prepared to authorize such military activity on the part of Orangemen, since they were almost all Orangemen themselves.

A small Liberal Home Rule Group invited Winston Churchill, then a Liberal and Home Ruler—'Whatever Ulster's rights may be,' he had once said, 'she cannot stand in the way of the rest of Ireland. Half a province cannot impose a permanent veto on the nation'—to attend a meeting to be held in the Ulster Hall, Belfast, in February 1912. Other speakers were to include John Redmond, leader of the Irish Nationalist party at Westminster, James Dillon, another Nationalist M.P., and Joe Devlin of Belfast. The Orangemen took especial exception to the venue chosen, as it was here that Winston Churchill's father had given Unionism its fighting slogan and what looked to the Orangemen like their *imprimatur* for resistance to Home Rule in arms. They engaged the hall for a Unionist Meeting the evening before, making it clear that they would have to be ejected by force before the Liberal meeting could take place. The Liberals changed the venue of their meeting to a marquee at Celtic Park in the Falls Road area. According to the Rev S. E. Long, they had tried to book the Opera House but its director refused a knighthood and considerable financial reward rather than give them permission to hold their meeting there.

'When the meeting was held', writes Long, 'Unionist and Orange leaders patrolled the city streets discouraging truculent crowds from violence. Carson remained in the city, in case he was needed. The precautions on the Orange side did not prevent the mishandling of Churchill's car. The man [Churchill] might have been lynched but the crowd had compassion on his wife who was with him and he was saved for her sake'. Other accounts of the events of the evening do not present the Orangemen and Unionists in such a purely peace-keeping role.

The Unionist answer to the Liberal meeting was a mass rally at Balmoral on Easter Tuesday. The chairman was Archbishop Crozier and the principal speaker was Bonar Law, son of Ulster Presbyterian parents, who said: 'Ireland is not a nation, but two peoples, separated by a deeper gulf than that dividing Ireland from Great Britain.' Carson was on the platform with him, and the audience probably numbered 200,000. Carson said: 'I know that force has been used to compel retention to government against the will of the people. But a precedent has yet to be created to drive out by force loyal and contented citizens from a community to which by birth they belong . . .

Assume for the sake of argument—what I do not believe—that the people of this country would condone the coercion of their kith and kin, what would be the effect upon the Army? Many officers would resign; no army could stand such a strain . . .'

Many Liberals saw in this speech an incitement to the Army to mutiny rather than allow themselves to be used to force the people of Ulster to accept Home Rule. Shortly after the rally, a £1,000,000 fund was set up to compensate wounded Ulster Volunteers and the bereaved dependants of Volunteers killed in action.

In all these events the Orange Order was inextricably bound up, as the Rev S. E. Long admits. 'The leaders and the led were for the most part members of the Institution or sympathetic to it,' he says. 'In July 1913, 150,000 Orangemen and Loyalists met at Craigavon. In September the Provisional Government of Ulster was formed.' Craig headed this Provisional Government.

On September 28th, 1912, designated as 'Ulster Day', a Solemn League and Covenant was signed by 447,000 of the 500,000 adult Protestants in the province. So strongly did some of the Ulstermen feel about the situation that they signed the document with their own blood. Based on the old Scottish Covenant of the 17th century, it informed the world that:

> Being convinced in our conscience that Home Rule would be disastrous to the material well-being of Ulster as well as the whole of Ireland, subversive of our civil and religious freedom, destructive of our citizenship, and perilous to the unity of the Empire, we, whose names are underwritten, men of Ulster, loyal subjects of His Gracious Majesty King George V, humbly relying on God whom our fathers in days of stress and trial confidently trusted, do hereby pledge ourselves in solemn Covenant throughout this our time of threatened calamity to stand by one another in defending for ourselves and our children our cherished position of equal citizenship in the United Kingdom, and in using all means which may be found necessary to defeat the present conspiracy to set up a

> Home Rule Parliament in Ireland. And in the event of such a Parliament being forced on us, we solemnly and mutually pledge ourselves to refuse to recognize its authority.

Thousands of Ulster people supported the declaration, but the British Government could not believe that loyal Ulstermen would oppose the British army, even when Carson, with typical efficiency, landed 40,000 rifles and several million rounds of ammunition*—purchased in Germany by Major Fred Crawford—at Larne, Bangor and Donaghadee, County Antrim, while the customs police and military were arguing with the Ulster Volunteers and the captain of a decoy ship in Belfast harbour as to whether the hatches could legally be opened before daylight. Carson's private army, now 110,000 strong and openly parading and drilling with arms illegally imported from Germany, was clearly a menace to peace in the country but Asquith was reluctant to act because he knew that there was a considerable body of public opinion behind the Ulstermen, and he was by no means sure that the Army could be trusted. Already, in the British Army camp at the Curragh in County Kildare, in what is now the Republic, 58 of the 70 officers under General Hubert Gough had mutinied and threatened to resign their commissions rather than be involved in any operations to force Ulster to accept Home Rule.

In Britain, Lord Milner collected two million signatures to a British Covenant supporting 'any action that may be effective to prevent it [the Home Rule Bill] being put into operation, and more particularly to prevent the armed forces of the Crown being used to deprive the people of Ulster of their rights as citizens of the United Kingdom'.

Lord Milner closed his Covenant lists at the end of July, 1914. War broke out on August 4th, the Home Rule Bill was rushed through Parliament, with the proviso that it should not come into effect until after the war, and James Craig

* This is one of the standard official estimates which vary between 30,000 and 50,000 rifles; it seems probable from more recent research that the total was a good deal lower.

offered the Ulster Volunteers for service in the British Army. They became the 36th (Ulster) Regiment and distinguished themselves in the opening hours of the great battle of the Somme, in which they lost 2,500 of the 9,000 men who had gone into the attack, marching through a hail of machine-gun fire as calmly and as jauntily as if they were 'walking' the streets of Belfast on a typical July 12th Orange procession.

That year (1916) the traditional July 12th parade of the Orangemen was cancelled and in the streets of Belfast thousands stood for five minutes in silence, in pouring rain. It is not surprising that they felt little sympathy with the Southern Irish Catholics; only a few months earlier the Sinn Fein Easter Week Rising in Dublin had altered the whole pattern of Irish politics yet again and irreversibly widened the already unbridgeable gulf between the two communities.

* * *

We put them down in Twenty-Two, we'll put them down again
For in our little Province, Sinn Fein will never reign.
For we are members of the Crown and there we mean to stay,
Where we can have our Loyalty and just go where we may.

A Parliament in Dublin will never rule us here,
For we will fight with all our might, to keep our Province clear
Of vagabonds and murderers who dare not face the light,
And always do the dirty work, in the darkness of the night.

Now you Protestants of Ulster, pay attention to me,
Don't go down to Dublin town to spend your £ s d,
Spend it here in Ulster, and it will help Sinn Fein to see,
The Loyalty for which we stand, to the Crown of Liberty.

—Verses from an Ulster street ballad, printed in
McKeague's *Orange-Loyalist Songs, 1971.*

XIII
The Troubled Times: 1916–23

This is in no sense a history of Ireland as such but it is impossible to understand attitudes and events in Northern Ireland during the last fifty years without dealing, however briefly, with some of the principal events in Southern Ireland during 'the troubled times'.

The IRB, active as ever behind the scenes, realized that the formation of the Ulster Volunteers to resist Home Rule opened the way for a similar private army in the South to fight, if necessary, *for* Home Rule. But already, even before that, a small private army had been founded in Dublin by James Connolly, the Labour leader, not initially to fight for Irish freedom but simply to protect Irish workers from police attacks. The year 1913 had been a year of great labour unrest in Dublin, with repeated baton charges, and Connolly's Irish Citizen Army was a small, well-drilled and well-disciplined force, initially armed with hurley sticks (stout ashplants used for a Gaelic forerunner of the game of hockey) dedicated to protecting Irish workers.

In the same year the IRB, operating in and through various other societies, assembled a collection of people likely to be favourably disposed towards such a project to discuss the setting up of an Irish Volunteer force similar to the Ulster Volunteers. Among those present were Professor Eoin (John) MacNeill, vice-president of the Gaelic League, and Arthur Griffith, a political journalist who had been expounding a new doctrine of separatism based on Hungarian passive resistance to Austria. His movement was known as Sinn Fein (pronounced Shinn Fayne, it means 'ourselves', though with an emphatic overtone, like *nous-mêmes* in French) and the movement eventually became the political arm of the secret IRB, just as the Unionist

Party in Ulster became the political arm of the semi-secret Orange Order.

The Volunteer movement spread like wildfire; drill halls were opened all over the country and the separate elements which had been working in their own way towards Irish independence now had a focal point on which to concentrate their frustrated energies. Before long there were 15,000 Irish Volunteers drilling in the villages, the hills and the fields; one of the first recruits was Eamon de Valera, a young mathematics teacher. In June 1914, John Redmond, leader of the Nationalist Party at Westminster, began to grow nervous at the mushroom growth of the Volunteer movement and tried to gain control of it; the IRB allowed him to nominate twenty-five members of his own choosing to act on the Volunteer's provisional committee, but this was purely a gesture. The real control of the militant section of the movement remained in the hands of the IRB.

There is probably no better example of the contrast between the Ulsterman and the Southern Irishman than the way in which they went about arming their respective Volunteer Forces. Whereas Carson used a decoy ship and then landed some 40,000 modern, efficient rifles and several million rounds of ammunition from another ship at a different place, at dead of night and without any fuss at all, the Southern Irish landed a derisory 1,500 out-of-date, second-hand German Mauser rifles and some 50,000 rounds of ammunition from a yacht at Howth, outside Dublin, in broad daylight and carried them openly, almost defiantly, to the city. They were intercepted by a party of policemen and military, there was a scuffle during which a few shots were fired, and nineteen of the guns were confiscated before the Volunteers broke ranks and escaped over the fields with their guns. On their way back through the city the British soldiers were jeered and stoned, and at Bachelor's Walk they halted and fired into the crowd, killing two men and a woman and injuring 32, an ugly and ill-timed incident which made the Southern Irish feel that there was one law for Ulster and another for the rest of the country.

When war broke out, Redmond followed Carson's example

and offered his Volunteers to the British Government either as a replacement for the British garrison in Ireland to free the garrison troops for service in France or for active service overseas. About 140,000 Irish Volunteers, Redmond's supporters, styling themselves the National Volunteers, left the organization almost in a body and joined the British Army, though unlike the Ulster Volunteers they were not allowed to form a separate regiment. The remainder, between 10,000 and 12,000 men, remained faithful to the original provisional committee. They believed that Ireland should at the very least remain neutral. Sir Roger Casement, an Irishman who had been knighted for his work for the British Foreign Office and who had been involved in the gun-running at Howth, said: 'Ireland has no blood to give to any land or cause, save Ireland'.

The IRB inner council took the ancient attitude that England's difficulty was Ireland's opportunity and began to make plans for an armed insurrection at the earliest possible moment. Casement went first to America, to raise support, and then to Germany, where he tried to talk the Germans into supplying 200,000 rifles for a projected rising planned for Easter 1916. He was offered 20,000 obsolete Russian rifles which were sent to Ireland in a vessel called the *Aud* with the Norwegian flag painted on her side. Casement himself travelled to Ireland in a German submarine. As usual, everything went wrong. There was nobody to meet the *Aud*, so she put to sea again, was challenged by a British warship and scuttled herself, arms and all. Casement was arrested almost as soon as he set foot on Irish soil (a German sleeper ticket still in his pocket) and he was on his way to trial for treason in London before the day fixed for the Rising.

In the Volunteer headquarters things were equally confused. The Inner Circle of the IRB had not taken Professor Eoin MacNeill into their confidence. Nor had they told James Connolly about their plans; he had long since graduated from defending workers from police attacks and had been training his Citizen Army in house-to-house fighting and was openly referring to such exercises as 'Attack on Dublin Castle' or 'Capture of the Magazine Fort'. The fear in Connolly's case was that he might stage a premature rising. He was kidnapped, disappeared for a few days, and re-emerged in the full confidence of the IRB inner council. Eoin MacNeill was regarded as too moderate, too cautious, and when, on hearing of the scuttling of the *Aud* and that no help would be coming from Germany, he put a notice in the Sunday newspapers cancelling the nationwide 'manoeuvres' that were to have been the cloak for the Rising, Pearse promptly countermanded his orders and went ahead with his own plans for a Rising anyway, though on a much smaller scale and limited to the Dublin area. Pearse's thinking was that a 'blood sacrifice' was needed to shake the Irish people out of their lethargy.*

The story of Easter Week 1916 is well-known. On Easter Monday, small parties of rebels occupied the General Post Office and various key positions around the city and held out until the Saturday, by which time the centre of Dublin had been reduced to rubble. As they were marched through the shattered streets to the jails and cattle-boats (for transportation to England) the rebels were jeered and spat on by the Dublin people. During the week about 60 Irish Volunteers, 130 British military and police and 260 civilians had been killed and a total of about 3,000 people injured. Most Dubliners regarded the whole thing as a stupid exhibition which, if it proved anything, proved that the Irish were not ready yet for self-government, and those women who had sons and husbands away fighting in Flanders were particularly bitter in their condemnation of the Sinn Feiners.

But the British authorities changed all this when they began to take the ringleaders out in twos and threes to execute them, over a period of about a week. Sean MacDermott, crippled with infantile paralysis, limped out to face the firing squad; James Connolly was so badly wounded that he had to be propped up in a chair to be shot. By the time fifteen executions had taken place public opinion began to swing sharply against General Maxwell, the British Supremo. 'The executions are becoming

* Patrick Pearce, a schoolmaster and writer, once wrote of the Orange Order: 'The Orangeman is ridiculous insofar as he believes incredible things. He is estimable insofar as he is willing and able to fight in defence of what he believes.'

an atrocity', the *Manchester Guardian* warned, and there were protests from George Bernard Shaw ('I cannot regard as a traitor any Irishman taken in a fight for Irish Independence against the British Government which was a fair fight in everything except the enormous odds my fellow countrymen had to face') and from the Bishop of Limerick among many others. Eamon de Valera, the last of the Battalion Commandants to surrender, had his death sentence commuted to one of life imprisonment—probably his American birth was a factor in this decision—and Ireland, in effect, was put under martial law. Public meetings were banned and raids on the civilian population became a regular feature of Irish life.

2

The execution of the rebel leaders and the imposition of martial law changed the whole situation in Southern Ireland, and even moderates who would have been more than satisfied with the sort of Home Rule envisaged by Gladstone and Asquith—which would have been perfectly acceptable to John Redmond—were now demanding a far wider measure of freedom from British rule. Demands for the release of the 2,500-odd political prisoners—some interned in prison camps, some imprisoned in British jails—now began to be voiced not only in Dublin but in the United States. The American pressure, plus the fact that the men were proving a problem to handle, led to their gradual release, in small groups, until by Christmas 1916 only a handful, including de Valera, were still in prison.

During the rising, Michael Collins—a member of the Inner Circle of the IRB—had emerged as a potential leader; now, with Arthur Griffith, he planned a new political strategy. Whenever a by-election occurred they put up a Sinn Fein candidate who would abstain from attending Westminster. When they had succeeded in getting a 'quorum' of Sinn Fein members elected, they planned to set up their own provisional government in Dublin and do everything possible to make British administration unworkable. Their first candidates were successful; support for Redmond's old Parliamentary

Nationalist Party was rapidly dying. One of Sinn Fein's earliest candidates was de Valera; he was nominated while still in jail.

It was clear at Westminster that Home Rule as envisaged in 1913 would now have to be scrapped and something would have to take its place which would offer the Southern Irish a greater measure of independence and the Ulster Loyalists a greater measure of protection. Lloyd George, who had succeeded Asquith as Premier, made his first stab at a solution to the Irish Question. He released all the remaining prisoners, including de Valera, and set about trying to arrange a convention representing all shades of political opinion in Ireland, north and south, to see whether some solution to the North could be reached. As the terms of reference of the convention excluded Ireland's freedom to declare itself a republic, and because Sinn Fein was convinced that Lloyd George had only called the convention so that when it broke up in disorder, as inevitably it would, he could then turn to America and point out that the Irish could not agree among themselves as to what sort of Government they wanted, they decided to boycott the convention. As a result, it achieved nothing.

Recruiting in Southern Ireland had failed completely after the Rising, and early in 1918 the British, sorely pressed for men, made yet another grave error by enacting a Bill to extend conscription to Ireland. The only result of this was to alienate those sections of the Southern Irish population previously prepared to work with Westminster; even Redmond and his Parliamentary Nationalist Party now followed Sinn Fein's lead and boycotted Westminster. The Bishops, in session at Maynooth, issued a pronouncement against conscription. The Trades Union Congress called the first general strike in Europe; it lasted for a day. The British replied by discovering an imaginary 'German plot' and re-arresting most of the Republican leaders, but Collins and a few of the ringleaders—who had by now built up a highly effective counter-intelligence network throughout the British army, police and civil service in Ireland—were warned in advance, and escaped the net. De Valera was imprisoned in Lincoln Jail.

Throughout this entire period talks had been going on between Lloyd George and men like James Craig and Edward Carson to try to reach some conclusion on the area which might eventually be partitioned off, if partition proved the only acceptable solution. Asquith had already offered to exclude the six counties of Antrim, Armagh, Down, Tyrone, Fermanagh and Londonderry, plus the two county boroughs of Belfast and Londonderry, from the operation of the old Home Rule Bill for a period of six years, but Carson had turned this proposition down flatly; he said he did not want a sentence 'with a stay of execution of six years'. And it was around these six counties that Lloyd George now began to form his plans for a 'Better Government of Ireland' Act as it was originally called. The Unionists did not want the whole area of Ulster, because this would have given them an unmanageable total of Catholics; nor did they want only the predominantly Protestant counties—Antrim, Armagh, Down and Londonderry—because they felt this area was too small to be economically viable. So the Six Counties which began to emerge as the 'acceptable' compromise included Fermanagh and Tyrone,* which are both predominantly Catholic, as well as Derry City where the population is 54 per cent Catholic, although in the county as a whole the Protestants have a slight majority. This compromise gave the Protestants a comfortable two-thirds majority over the Catholics and it was on this basis that Lloyd George began to work out his second stab at a solution to the Irish Question: two parliaments, one in Dublin and one in Belfast, with power over all purely internal matters (powers very similar to those which Stormont held until it was prorogued) with an over-

* In a despairing reference to the negotiations—made in the House of Commons in February 1922—Winston Churchill said: 'Then came the Great War. Every institution almost in the world was strained. Great Empires have been overturned. The whole map of Europe has been changed. The position of countries has been violently altered. The modes of thought of men, the whole outlook on affairs, the grouping of parties, all have encountered violent and tremendous changes in the deluge of the world. But as the deluge subsides and the waters fall short we see the dreary steeples of Fermanagh and Tyrone emerging once again. The integrity of their quarrel is one of the very few institutions that has been unaltered in the cataclysm which has swept the world'.

riding Council to decide on matters affecting both parliaments and a provision which would enable the border to be redrawn within a few years after examination by a commission, plus another provision which would allow the two parliaments to merge into one if both should desire to do so.

The threat of conscription disappeared with the Armistice in November 1918, and before Lloyd George could put his 'Better Government of Ireland' Bill before the House, a general election was due in December—the so-called 'khaki' election, which was to allow the Tommies their say in the government of the country.

Collins and Griffith decided to put forward as many Sinn Fein candidates as possible for the 105 Irish seats at Westminster, despite the fact that Sinn Fein was banned as an illegal organization. Collins himself was on the run and 47 of the candidates were in English jails. Despite these handicaps, Sinn Fein fought 80 of the 105 seats and won 73 of them. Redmond's Nationalist Parliamentary Party, which had previously held 80 seats was reduced to seven. Griffith and Collins had their 'quorum' and an unmistakeable mandate from the Irish people to set up a separate provisional government in Ireland.

All 105 men who had been elected to the Westminster seats—Ulster Unionists, Independents and the remnants of Redmond's party as well as the victorious Sinn Fein members—were invited to a meeting in Dublin in January 1919. Only Sinn Fein members turned up, and only 27 of these; the rest were in jail, in exile, or on the run. Collins was in England 'springing' de Valera from Lincoln Jail. At the second session of the Irish Parliament (known as Dail Eireann), de Valera was elected President. 'There is in Ireland, at this moment, only one lawful authority,' he declared, 'and that authority is the elected Government of the Irish Republic.'

The breach with Ulster was complete and, in Orange eyes, irrevocable. And Ireland's troubles were only beginning.

3

As soon as Dail Eireann was set up, two other things happened. De Valera left for a tour of the United States to raise both funds and American moral support for Ireland's fight for freedom, and the IRA under Michael Collins, began a series of raids on post offices, banks, police stations, military barracks and other British installations. Originally these raids were carried out partly to raise funds to run the new Government of the country, partly to get arms for the IRA and partly to undermine the British administration; later, other motives entered the picture. There were atrocities on both sides; men were murdered in front of their wives and families, others died on hunger strike in British jails, dead men were found in the ditch with notes pinned to their trench-coats saying: 'Spies and traitors, beware', a curfew was imposed and the entire civilian population was confined indoors from ten o'clock or even earlier in some places, while the police and military roamed the country, raiding houses for arms, looting and ravaging. The Black and Tans and the Auxiliaries, two volunteer forces recruited in England from misfits unable to settle down in post-war Britain, were enlisted to assist the RIC in maintaining order; the British were reluctant to use the military because it would have meant admitting that a state of war existed between the British Army and the IRA.

Throughout the period, the British continued to make martyrs by executing prisoners—a typical example was Kevin Barry, aged 18, whose revolver had jammed and who had not fired a single shot in the engagement in which he was captured—and the climax came on Bloody Sunday, November 21st, 1920, when in an effort to liquidate the British Secret Service in Dublin, Collins sent members of his execution squad around to their lodgings and hotels. Fourteen men were murdered that morning, in their beds, in front of their wives, or wherever they happened to be, shortly after nine o'clock. In the afternoon, the British forces retaliated by firing on the crowd at a football match in Dublin, killing fourteen people and wounding sixty.

It was clear that this couldn't go on, and early in 1921 various peace feelers were made—Lord Derby, General Smuts, and Arthur Cope, Under Secretary, were among the people who made guarded approaches to Mr de Valera, but he held his hand and waited for an official move.

In May 1921, Lloyd George's 'Government of Ireland' Act came into force and in June, King George V went to Ulster to open the new Northern Ireland Parliament which came into existence under the Act. Ironically Northern Ireland, so bitterly opposed to Home Rule, was the only part of Ireland to get it. The King appealed to Irishmen to 'forgive and forget' and a few days later de Valera had a letter from Lloyd George inviting him to London to explore the possibility of a settlement. A truce came into force on July 11th and the following day de Valera crossed to London.

Despite the fact that the Border was now a *fait accompli* and was not under discussion at this stage—the machinery was there for its removal or alteration later, if both Parliaments agreed—the talks bogged down on this, and on the Oath of Allegiance, and de Valera returned with an offer from Lloyd George which was thrown out by the Dail on August 16th, without a single dissentient voice, despite the threats of the terrible repercussions which would ensue if the terms were not accepted.

In October a delegation, without de Valera this time, left for England with a draft treaty which had been drawn up by the Irish cabinet. De Valera argued that his absence could always be advanced by the delegates as a good reason for not allowing themselves to be stampeded into making any hasty decisions in London—though this is exactly what did happen, with tragic consequences. On December 5th 1921, Michael Collins and the other delegates signed a Treaty which accepted both the Oath of Allegiance and the Partition of Ireland, as a stepping stone, Collins argued, to further concessions later.

On their return to Dublin the Dail and the IRA both split on the issue, and de Valera resigned as President, to be succeeded by Arthur Griffith. At an election held in June 1921, de Valera's anti-Treaty candidates won only 36 seats out of the total of 128. More than two-thirds of the people had clearly indicated that they were tired of the troubles and were prepared to accept the Treaty pro tem, for want of something better. But not de Valera; he had already made ominous remarks such as 'There are rights which a minority may justly uphold, even by arms, against a majority'.

And to the Orangemen of Ulster, whose own Parliament at Stormont was just beginning to function, the Civil War which now flared up in Southern Ireland merely confirmed them in their worst fears. They read of the atrocities now being committed on former comrades-in-arms, even on brothers and cousins, and of the executions—seventy-seven during the winter and spring of 1922–23; the British reprisals after Easter week had been trivial by comparison—and they redoubled their efforts to protect their own corner of Ireland from the enemy within and without.

4

By concentrating on events in Southern Ireland in an effort to give a coherent if abbreviated account of the troubles, I may have given the impression that all was calm and peaceful in Ulster during this period. Nothing could be further from the truth. And the truth is not easy to pin down. Throughout the entire period of the troubles, there had been continuous shooting, rioting and burning in Belfast and all the other Ulster towns.

Republican writers in general interpret these events as continued attempts by the Orangemen to rid themselves of the 'enemy in their midst' and represent the intervention by IRA men from the South as an effort to protect the Catholic minority from the depredations of the vicious Orange Unionists. Right up to the moment when the Civil War broke out, Collins himself was playing a double game; he felt that by signing the Treaty he had let down 'his own people' in Ulster, and was surreptitiously supplying Rory O'Connor and the breakaway, anti-Treaty IRA Irregulars with arms and ammunition to help to protect the Catholics in Ulster from Protestant pogroms.

Viewed from the other side of the border the picture looked somewhat different. '. . . the fire in Ulster today is small, however, compared with the one the Ulstermen had to face and subdue when their Government was founded in 1921—and for a near-desperate year or so afterwards—as the men of the Irish Republican Army flung themselves on the infant state and strove to kill it,' writes Patrick Riddell in *Fire Over*

Ulster. 'The flames that had lighted Dublin and the other Southern Irish Cities and towns were seen then in Belfast, the same language of machine-gun, rifle and grenade was heard in its streets and from its rooftops, there was the same ruthless and cowardly and horrible killing. The Ulstermen had been in no way provocative, they had not attacked their fellow-Irishmen of the South, they had merely asked to be let alone, to be allowed to run their minute corner of Ireland in peace and to the best of their ability. They had a Parliament House to design and build, an electoral system to bring into being, a police force to reorganize and re-name, a code of law to frame and institute, a Law Courts to erect for the housing of judges and the legal administration. They had no experience in such fields, they had to learn. They were walking slowly, tentatively, sometimes mistakenly, but always determinedly. They were very busy with their own affairs, very busy indeed, they had neither the time nor the wish to interfere with others. Others, however, had both the time and the wish to interfere with them. Thousands of well-armed Irish Republican Army men infiltrated secretly into Ulster, coalesced with those already there, found concealment with resident sympathizers and prepared to strike.'

He goes on: 'They were years of horror, a time of martial law, when soldiers of the British Army and the men of the Royal Ulster Constabulary fought and died in the struggle to save the Province from being ruined by men ruthlessly resolved to wreck it, however much misery they might bring to their fellow Irish in doing so. There were between eight and nine thousand Irish Republican Army men in Ulster, armed with revolvers, rifles and grenades, and possessed of supplies of materials for incendiarism, hidden in the cellars and buried in the backyards of the houses of the local Nationalist sympathisers. . . . the Irish Republican Army men operated in civilian clothes, as they had done against the British forces in Dublin and elsewhere in Southern Ireland. This made them inconspicuous and thus able to stroll up behind an unsuspecting and armed man in a central and busy city street . . . shoot him in the back and escape in the immediately gathering crowds . . . The men of the Irish Republican Army argued that they were outnumbered and that, as they lacked and had always lacked the equipment and armament that could be employed against them—armoured cars, wire-netted fast motor tenders, light artillery and mortars—they could not possibly wage open warfare with an equal chance of winning and were consequently compelled to adopt guerilla tactics. This was true enough in the fight against the English forces in Southern Ireland and against the Ulstermen of the Ulster countryside the argument had a reasonable and acceptable basis. Guerilla fighting has been used by many elements in many struggles and, provided it is conducted with observance of recognized rule, there is no substantial objection to it. Deliberate terrorism against innocent civilians in the public thoroughfares of a city, however, and indiscriminate firing into thickly peopled shopping and housing areas with no concern for whomsoever might be killed or wounded—the very crime for which the Black and Tans had been blamed by the outraged Irish—cannot possibly be justified in the name of patriotism or in the name of anything, if those who would justify it especially claim to be faithful to a Christian Church'.

I have quoted Patrick Riddell's view at length on this point because it is not one you often hear south of the border, and it is valid within its limitations; also, it gives a fair indication of how the Unionist Ulstermen felt about the continued outbreaks of violence in their new state. The fact that one-third of the people in that state did not want any part of it, but were being forced into it willy-nilly, is another matter, and explains their failure or their refusal to co-operate with the authorities; but it is so very easy for somebody brought up in what is now the Republic to ignore Riddell's view of events that it seems to me necessary to give it a fair amount of attention.

Constantine Fitzgibbon puts the other point of view: 'It was their [the IRA "Irregulars"] intention to "liberate" the six counties which contained half a million Catholics and twice that number of Protestants, thus ensuring a perpetual Unionist-Orange domination in the area, soon to be reinforced by skilful gerrymandering of the electoral boundaries, both for election to Westminster and Stormont as well as of the municipal districts. This was accompanied by particularly savage attacks, especially in Belfast and above all in the shipyards there, on the Catholic minority, which can be not unfairly described as a pogrom. It was against this state of affairs that elements of the IRA rebelled'.

During the period, 232 people were killed in Belfast, including two Unionist M.P.s, and nearly 1,000 injured.

5

Despite continued outbreaks of violence north and south of the border, the Government of the Irish Free State under William Cosgrave—Griffith had died during the Civil War, and Collins had been killed in an ambush—and the Northern Ireland Government under William Craig settled down to make the best of a bad lot and salvage what they could from the wreckage left behind after an insurrection followed by a war of independence followed by a civil war. They were both suffering under enormous disadvantages; neither Government had an effective Opposition since de Valera refused to recognize the Free State Parliament and abstained from attending the Dail as he had previously abstained from attending Westminster, while in Northern Ireland the Nationalists also boycotted the new Parliament. The Boundary Commission, which Collins and Griffith had sincerely believed would re-adjust the Border more equitably, met in 1924 but in the face of stubborn, intransigent Ulster determination, Cosgrave caved in and agreed to leave the Border as it was. Craig had warned the British that if the Commission recommended any change in the Border he would resign as Prime Minister and place himself at the head of an Ulster Volunteer Force which would maintain the Protestant Ascendancy in Ulster against all comers. 'Not an inch' was added to the long litany of Ulster war-cries.

Owing to the exhaustion of the Free State in the decade following the end of the Civil War, the new state of Northern Ireland had a chance to 'put its house in order' and prepare to defend itself against what it still believed to be a Popish plot to take over Ireland.

It is worth digressing here, perhaps, to make the point that both north and south of the border there is a fundamental misunderstanding of the relationship between religion and politics. Ever since the Free State was set up in 1922, the Northern Ireland Parliament has been watching it closely, studying its measures and concluding from the fact that some of these measures are, in broad general terms, Catholic in outlook, the Free State (and latterly the Republican Government) is controlled from Rome. Equally, the Southern politicians, observing that many of the measures passed by the Stormont Parliament seem to favour the Protestant majority, assume that this is because Unionist policy is dictated by the Orange Order. The plain truth, of course, is that most of the members of the Free State (and latterly the Republican) Government happen to be born Catholics and consequently tend to think like Catholics and to produce laws with what might be described as a Catholic bias, without any influence at all from Rome; and equally, the vast majority of the Unionist politicians happen to be staunch Protestants and in many cases Orangemen, and consequently think and act like staunch Protestants and Orangemen, not because they have received express secret orders from the Grand Lodge.

In their 'siege' mentality, to which I have referred earlier, the Orangemen saw three enemies: the Pope, in Rome; the Catholics in their midst; and the Republican Forces to the south of the Border. The measures which they took to combat these enemies included the enlistment of several armed police forces. First there was the Royal Ulster Constabulary—a natural development of the Royal Irish Constabulary—and here it is only fair to mention that Craig initially reserved one-third of the places in this force for Catholic Ulstermen and it is not his fault if they refused to join; equally, it is understandable that not many of the Catholic Nationalists in Ulster would want to join an armed police force which in their view, represented an alien occupying force which had no business to be in 'their' country.

The RUC was supported by the Special Constabulary, a force of over 50,000 men formed initially by Sir Henry Wilson in 1920 and handed over to Northern Ireland when it came into existence a year later. There were three branches in the Special Constabulary. The A Specials, like the Black and Tans, were all ex-soldiers, including unemployed ex-officers from England. The B Specials were part-time police, available for patrol work on one or two nights a week and unpaid except for an allowance of £10 a year for wear and tear of their clothes. They were armed and were allowed to keep their arms in their homes. The B Specials remained a part of the Northern Ireland Security Forces until disbanded under pressure from Westminster in 1970. And finally there were the C Specials, 20,000 strong, mainly older men who turned out in major emergencies or when the As and Bs had to be called away for other duties. They received no payment, but were allowed to have arms and ammunition without licence.

The B Specials, almost exclusively Orangemen, constituted what amounted to the armed branch of the Orange Order, and their primary purpose was to guard the Border against attacks by the IRA, and the state against attacks from the enemy within.

These attacks came in waves over the years between 1923 and 1968, when the present disturbances started. In 1935, twelve people were killed and ninety-eight injured in riots which followed shots fired during an Orange procession in Belfast. In 1939, the IRA mounted a terror campaign, mainly directed against England, in which there were bomb explosions in many English cities injuring innocent bystanders, but Ulster did not escape; four RUC men and two B Specials were killed and twenty RUC men and two B Specials wounded. In 1948, the IRA carried out a series of raids against military installations in Ulster, with the aim of stealing arms and ammunition. In November 1955—and these dates are taken at random, because there were sporadic outbreaks of violence throughout the entire period—a police station in Fermanagh was attacked with bombs and machine guns, and in a series of raids between 1956 and 1962, six RUC men were killed, twenty-one wounded and eleven B Specials wounded.

The A and C Specials ceased to function in 1924 and it was left to the B-men of the Ulster Special Constabulary to work with the RUC in maintaining law and order. The Orange Order has never made any secret that the force in effect represents its military arm; in *Orangeism: A New Historical Appreciation*, the Rev S. E. Long writes: 'The membership of the Force has always been predominantly Orange, continuing evidence of the determination of the Order to safeguard the country against attacks from the enemy within and without'. The Rev John Brown, another of the Orange Order's official historians was a Commandant of the B Specials until the disbandment of the force.

The Orangemen do not make any bones about the reason for this; the Ulster Catholics, being committed to the overthrow of the State, were in effect regarded as traitors. Nor did James Craig (later Sir James Craig, and later still Lord Craigavon) make any bones about the way he intended to run Northern Ireland. He openly referred to it as 'a Protestant State for a Protestant people' and set about ensuring that it would remain so by allowing the boundaries to be gerrymandered—particularly in the case of local government elections—to ensure that wherever Catholics were in a majority they would not be adequately represented. Rateable valuation was the basis for franchise in the local government elections and since most of the property in Northern Ireland was in Unionist hands this tended to shore up the Unionist Ascendancy. The Government of Ireland Act had stipulated that elections were to be on a system of proportional representation—which tended to give minorities a voice in Parliament and which was the system adopted by the Free State—but within a few years Craig had got rid of proportional representation because he believed the system was so complicated that there was a grave danger the voters might make a mistake and wake up one morning to find themselves under the heel of a Dublin Parliament.

Apart from the sporadic outbreaks of violence to which I have referred, the Northern Ireland Government now settled down, behind the Border, to administer its tight little Protestant state in the best interests of those who had proved loyal to her ancient 'freedom, religion and laws'. By its relentless intransigence the Orange Order had succeeded in detaching six counties of Ireland from the remainder and, through the

Unionist Party, was now free to run the sub-province, with the full support of the British Government, exactly as it wished. It is true that Northern Ireland had never wanted Home Rule in any shape or form; but once the Stormont Government had been set up, there was born a new and fanatical loyalty to Stormont, to the British connection, and to the 'Constitution' of Northern Ireland—which consisted of no more than a few clauses in the Government of Ireland Act, and also included one which provided for the suspension or termination of the Stormont Government at the will of Parliament at Westminster. And this is what happened, in March 1972.

Nevertheless, the very creation of the 'state' of Northern Ireland was a triumph for the Orange Order. With one exception, the Unionist members of that first Stormont Parliament were Orangemen, and there were 40 Unionists against about 10 abstaining Nationalists; so were all twelve members at Westminster. Every Corporation and County Council in the new State—even in predominantly Catholic areas like the city of Derry—was 'packed' with Orangemen. The RUC and B Specials were Orangemen, so to speak, to a man. If the new state was not run by the Orange Lodges, at any rate it spoke with an unmistakeably Orange accent,* and since no crack appeared in this monolithic structure until the winter of 1968/69 this is a good moment to turn aside from history and take a look at the Orange Order itself during the past fifty years—a period well within the lifetime of many of the older members of the Order.

* * *

* The Rev S. E. Long puts it this way in his essay in the most recent official history of Orangeism: 'From the outset of the campaign the Orange Order had taken a responsible part. There was a high standard of leadership utterly dedicated to the service of the Unionist and Protestant cause. The Grand Masters had been men of consequence, namely the Earl of Enniskillen, the Earl of Erne (25 years), Sir James Stronge, W. H. Lyones and Sir Edward Archdale. They presided over brethren who responded to good leadership and who were concerned to back that leadership against all enemies. It is certain that without the Order the fight for the maintenance of the Union would have been lost . . . Time has brought many essential changes to the country, but one attitude remains constant, the Orangeman's determination to keep Northern Ireland British'.

Some folk sing of mountains and valleys,
Where wild flowers abundantly grow,
And some of the foam-crested billows
That surge in the waters below,
But I'm going to sing of a river,
And I hope in the chorus you'll join,
Of the deeds that were done by King William
On the green, grassy slopes of the Boyne.

Then Orangemen remember King William,
And your fathers who with him did join,
And fought for our glorious deliverance,
On the green, grassy slopes of the Boyne.

—From *The Green, Grassy Slopes of the Boyne,*
a traditional Orange ballad.

XIV

The Loyal Orange Institution of Ireland

The administrative headquarters of the Orange Order are situated in a small office at 65, Dublin Road, Belfast, which has a modest Union Jack beside its front door. From this office are issued copies of the Laws and Ordinances of the Institution, currently bound in a blue cover—though an old copy which I picked up in a second-hand bookshop in Belfast is bound in resplendent, almost iridescent orange. Entry forms, which *are* currently printed on orange paper, stipulate that the applicant for membership must be 'born of Protestant parents, brought up as a Protestant at . . . school' and include a statement that the applicant is a believing *and practising** member of the Church.

Copies of the current Laws and Ordinances are available only to members of the Order, but I am assured that the rules are not greatly different from those set out in the copy I have, which is dated 1885. The Grand Secretary did give me the first page from the current Laws and Ordinances, carrying the Basis of the Institution, which is word for word as it was in the 1885 edition, except that the House of Windsor has been substituted for that of Brunswick. It runs as follows:

> The institution is composed of Protestants, united and resolved to the utmost of their power to support and defend the rightful Sovereign, the Protestant Religion, the Laws of the Realm, and the Succession to the Throne in the House of Windsor, BEING PROTESTANT† and united

* The italics are the author's.
† The capitals appear in both versions of the text.

> further for the defence of their own Persons and Properties, and the maintenance of the Public Peace. It is exclusively an Association of those who are attached to the religion of the Reformation, and will not admit into its brotherhood persons whom an intolerant spirit leads to persecute, injure or upbraid any man on account of his religious opinions. They associate also in honour of KING WILLIAM III,* Prince of Orange, whose name they bear, as supporters of his glorious memory.

Next follows a list of general qualifications which also have survived unchanged from the 1885 edition of the Laws and Ordinances. Before a candidate can be elected, the Master and Members of the Lodge concerned must satisfy themselves that he possesses the following qualifications:

> An Orangeman should have a sincere love and veneration for his Heavenly Father; a humble and steadfast faith in Jesus Christ, the Saviour of Mankind, believing in him as the only Mediator between God and man. He should cultivate truth and justice, brotherly kindness and charity, devotion and piety, concord and unity, and obedience to the laws; his deportment should be gentle and compassionate, kind and courteous; he should seek the society of the virtuous, and avoid that of the evil; he should honour and diligently study the Holy Scriptures, and make them the rule of his faith and practice, he should love, uphold and defend the Protestant religion, and sincerely desire and endeavour to propagate its doctrines and precepts; he should strenuously oppose the fatal errors and doctrines of the Church of Rome, and scrupulously avoid countenancing (by his presence or otherwise) any act or ceremony of Popish Worship; he should, by all lawful means, resist the ascendancy of that Church, its encroachments, and the extension of its power, ever abstaining from all uncharitable words, actions, or sentiments towards his Roman Catholic brethren; he should remember to keep holy the Sabbath day, and attend the public worship of God, and diligently

* The capitals appear in both versions of the text.

> train up his offspring, and all under his control, in the fear of God, and in the Protestant faith; he should never take the name of God in vain, but abstain from all cursing and profane language, and use every opportunity of discouraging those, and all other sinful practices, in others; his conduct should be guided by wisdom and prudence, and marked by honesty, temperance and sobriety; the glory of God and the welfare of man, the honour of his Sovereign, and the good of his country, should be the motives of his actions.

If these lofty sentiments seem difficult to reconcile with some of the Orange ballads and some of the more extravagant toasts and sermons—even such recent outpourings as the Rev Dr Paisley's fulminations against the abomination of the world and his references to the Pope as 'old red socks'—I can only repeat that there is a double-think running right through the fabric of the Orange Institution which blinds its members to the fact that their written aims, objects and aspirations bear little relationship to the actions of some, at any rate, of their members. Of course, Paisley is no longer a member of the Orange Order; he left, of his own volition, about ten years ago. 'Paisley never cared very much for being in any organization he doesn't personally control', an Orange Order official drily remarked. 'He has his own personal Order now, and wears a collarette not unlike an Orange one.'

After the general qualifications, the Laws and Ordinances of the Order list some specific qualifications. In place of the sworn oath, it is nowadays required that the Master and members of the Lodge concerned ascertain 'that the candidate will be faithful and bear true allegiance to Her Majesty Queen Victoria (in the old copy which I bought, presumably now changed to Elizabeth II) and to her Protestant successors; that he will, to the utmost of his power, support and maintain the Laws and Constitution of the United Kingdom, and the succession to the Throne in Her Majesty's illustrious house, BEING PROTESTANT.'

They also must ascertain 'that the candidate is not, and

never was, a Roman Catholic *or Papist*,* or married to one', that he is not, and never was, and will not become a member of any Society or body of men who are enemies to the lawful Sovereign, or the glorious Constitution of the realm, as established in 1688; and that he never took, and never will take any oath of secrecy, or any other oath of obedience, to any treasonable Society.

I inquired whether this meant that no convert could ever join the Orange Order. Apparently it is possible, but very difficult for a convert, however sincere, to be accepted for membership. 'He would have to be a convert of several years standing,' I was told, 'and we would screen his background very carefully before admitting him.' His acceptance would also have to be authorized by the Grand Lodge. It is even more difficult for a convert to gain admission to the inner circles of the Orange Order; in the Black Preceptories, for example, no convert can be admitted if either of his parents is still living, in case pressure might be brought to bear on his parents by the Roman Church; I even heard of a convert who for many years has been a Protestant clergyman, but was 'blacked out' because one of his aged parents was still alive.

The next section in the list of particular qualifications for membership concerns giving assistance to the magistrates and civil authorities when called upon to do so, fidelity to brother Orangemen and includes the condition that the candidate will not, in any manner, communicate or reveal 'any of the proceedings of his Brother Orangemen in Lodge assembled, nor any matter or thing therein communicated to him, unless to a Brother Orangeman, well knowing him to be such, or until he shall have been authorized to do so by the Grand Lodge'.

'People outside the Order make a lot of fuss about this so-called secrecy code,' an Orange official told me, 'but it's the same with most trade union meetings, isn't it? You wouldn't communicate what goes on behind the closed doors at a union

* The italics are the author's. It is interesting that the people who frame the rules feel that Roman Catholic is not sufficiently specific, but need to add the slightly pejorative 'or Papist'.

meeting to anyone who wasn't a member of the same union, would you?'

My own impression, after talking around the subject with a wide variety of Orangemen of all sorts, is that most of the proceedings of the Orange Lodges would not be of any great interest to anybody outside the Order, but what goes on behind the closed doors of the Lodges I shall deal with later.

Admission of members is normally by ballot, one month after the candidate has been formally proposed and seconded, with one black bean in seven to exclude.

The Institution is organized on a system of Lodges, similar to the Masonic Society. There are four types of Lodge: the Private or Primary Lodge, the District Lodge, the County Lodge and the Grand Lodge. Every Orangeman first joins a Private or Primary Lodge. Members of the District Lodge are drawn from the Private Lodges in the District; members of the County Lodge are drawn from the District Lodges; and the Grand Lodge consists of members (usually officials) from the County Lodges. The average Lodge consists of about thirty members who meet monthly in the local Orange Hall, or, if there is no Orange Hall in the area, in a hotel room. The old practice of meeting in public houses is no longer permitted. The minimum fee on initiation is £1 and the average subscription is around 25p per month.

It has never been the practice of the Orange Order to issue—or even, as far as I could ascertain, to record—details of membership. They have never made a survey of their membership or attempted to break it down into what the advertising world describes as 'A, B, C or D readership'. I have been using phrases like 'an Orange official' and 'a prominent Orangeman' because in general the people to whom I talked did not want to be quoted, and would talk more freely if they were assured that they were not going to be mentioned by name. At the same time, I must say that I was everywhere received with the utmost courtesy and given every assistance that they possibly could give me without breaking their own rules; and although I told them all that I was writing what I hoped would be a completely objective book about the Order, and warned them that their idea of an objective book about Orangeism might be very different from mine, and that I would probably say things about the Order that would horrify them, they still gave me every possible assistance.*

Walter Williams, the Grand Secretary, estimates the current membership in the Six Counties as roughly 100,000 members, organized in about 2,000 Lodges, and including members of the Women's Lodges and the Junior Orange Lodges, for boys between eight and seventeen years of age. He reckons that a breakdown into categories—white-collar workers, professional men, factory workers, etc.—would roughly correspond with a breakdown of the population of the Six Counties as a whole. Other officials are inclined to think that 100,000 would be far more realistic for the country as a whole, including what the Ulstermen call 'the three lost counties' and the Republic, and are convinced that the Institution has a much higher proportion of working-class members and nothing like a representative ratio of professional men.

Some Lodges seem to have a higher status than others, and fees are higher, though not much—up to £5.25 on initiation and up to 50p a month subscription. This, I was told, would reflect the fact that the Lodge's expenses—in providing entertainment, refreshments and so on—were higher and would not be designed to discourage working-class members. 'In the cities, it is natural that professional men should want to join a Lodge where they would meet their own sort,' I was told, 'and equally, a ship-yard worker wouldn't feel at home among a lot of white-collar workers.' So in the cities the Lodges tend to consist more or less of men from the same class of the community. In the country, things are much more democratic. There is normally only one Lodge in a country district, so the local landlord may be found sitting down with his own head gardener.

Because they have never kept records of their membership, they were unable to help very much on the question of whether the membership is waxing or waning. There seems to be a

* One reason for this could be that they see nothing wrong with their Institution and genuinely believe that anyone who suggests giving Catholics a fair crack of the whip needs his head examined.

general feeling that the Institution has gained ground since the present troubles started, but this could be wishful thinking. 'Numerically we are stronger than before the war,' Walter Williams assured me, 'and we had a four-figure increase last year. In one month last year, I remember issuing entry forms to over 1,000 candidates.' The membership, he said, tended to be static around the early 'sixties, and the intake of new members about balanced the wastage from death, drop-outs, and expulsions. 'We have never been concerned about the drop-out rate,' he said, 'and the expulsion rate is negligible.'

In what circumstances are members expelled? According to the Laws and Ordinances, members who dishonour the Institution by marrying a Roman Catholic are automatically expelled. Members can also be expelled—though they not necessarily are—for attending a Catholic religious ceremony. It is widely believed that Phelim O'Neill, ex-Unionist M.P., was expelled because he attended a Catholic service as part of a general ecumenical movement that was going on at the time. The Order say that he was expelled because he refused to acknowledge their authority. Phelim O'Neill, who is related to Lord O'Neill, confirmed this. 'I joined the Orange Order for political reasons,' he said, 'like many other people in this part of the world. When I attended a Catholic service which was part of a general community effort that we were trying to get off the ground at the time, I refused to go and be disciplined because I knew exactly what would happen. They would let me off this time but warn me not to do it again, and as I had no intention of giving any such undertaking and the Orange Order had outlived its usefulness to me—in fact being a member had become an embarrassment to me—I let them sack me.'

Other grounds for expulsion include moral and criminal offences. If you are tried and found guilty of a criminal offence in court, you are automatically expelled. But men can be expelled for offences with which they have not been charged in court. Homosexuality, immorality or any 'conduct unbecoming to an Orangeman' can lead to a member of the Order being charged by the members of his own Lodge. If he disagrees with the verdict of his Brother Orangemen in Lodge, he has the right to appeal to the next Lodge above, and in fact an appeal can be carried right up to the Grand Lodge, but it stops there; no member can question the ruling of the Grand Lodge.

I asked for an example and was told that if a member of an Orange Lodge should find himself in the Divorce Courts, whatever decision the court reached the Lodge might decide that he had been guilty of immoral conduct. He could then be tried and possibly expelled. Expulsion from the Orange Order may not seem a very grave sentence, and probably it isn't any more; but during the fifty-odd years when the state was rigidly run by the Orange-controlled Unionist party it could ruin a man's career, at worst, or cost him his job, at least. And there is no chance of nipping around the corner and applying for membership of another Loyal Orange Lodge; for one of the qualifications for membership is that the candidate has not 'to his knowledge or belief, been proposed in and rejected by, or been expelled from, any other Orange Lodge, and that he is not under suspension from one'.

The top Orangemen seem satisfied that they are getting as many young recruits as ever. The normal minimum age for joining the Order is eighteen, but members of the Junior Orange Lodges can become Orangemen at seventeen. There seems to be little doubt that whatever is true about the adults, membership among the young is limited to a certain educational level. The Institution has—and its officials freely admit this—almost no recruits from the universities. Long hair was another obstacle which had to be overcome, but the Orange Order solved this one by relaxing the rules on the wearing of bowlers, etc., and by accepting long hair as a necessary evil if they wanted to attract young recruits. In the absence of any breakdown of the membership into age groups it is impossible to give any firm statistics on this matter, but from looking through the photographic files of half-a-dozen newspapers, both in the Republic and in Belfast, it seems to me that there are as many young—i.e. eighteen to twenty-four years of age—members in the Order as ever there were.

The Lodges, as I have said, meet as a rule about once a month, and a quorum is normally five. At Lodge meetings, the members mostly wear a miniature collarette, far lighter and less obtrusive than the large collarette worn for parades. Although they are obliged to wear whatever formal dress the Lodges have decided upon during public parades, dress is informal at Lodge meetings. 'We have a slightly secret system,' I was told by one prominent Orangeman, 'by which we can tell whether all the people in the room are bona fide members of the Order.' Another equally prominent Orangeman scoffed at this. 'We have passwords,' he said, 'which are changed from time to time. But if you don't know the password, all you do is whisper to the man next to you "What's the password this month, mate?", or if you want to use traditional Orange phraseology, you say: "What's the password this month, brother?" And he'll tell you, and in you go.'

The practice of detecting intruders is known as 'tyling' and there is a special tyler's ritual. His 'obligation' runs as follows; 'I, . . . do solemnly declare that I will be faithful to the duties of my office and I will not admit any person into the Lodge without having first found him to be in possession of the Financial Password, or without the sanction of the Worshipful Master of this Lodge'. The use of secret signs by which Orangemen may recognize a brother in a crowd—more or less as Masons recognize one another—has, I am told, fallen into disuse. In the early days of the Order, various grips, the wearing of such symbols as a five pointed metallic star as a watch pendant, and even gestures supposedly based on the injury King Billy received on the eve of the Battle of the Boyne were widely used but I was assured by a solemn phalanx of top Orangemen, including the Grand Master, John Bryans, J.P., the Grand Secretary, Walter Williams, J.P., and one of the official Orange historians, the Rev S. E. Long, A.L.C.D., that they had no way whatever of knowing whether anybody might or might not be a member of the Orange Order unless, of course, he was already known to them.

When the tyler has decided that nobody other than bona fide members of the Orange Order are present, the meeting starts with a prayer and a hymn. Then the minutes of the previous meeting are read and signed. New members waiting outside for initiation are next brought in by their respective proposers and seconders and one of the minor rituals of the Order takes place. The candidate for membership carries the Bible in his hands, with the Book of Laws and Ordinances placed on top of it. A Chaplain, if present, or in his absence a Brother appointed by the Master, then questions the candidate and his sponsors. The candidate is asked whether it is of his own free will and accord that he seeks admission to the Orange Institution, and his sponsors are asked whether they can answer that he is a 'true Protestant and a loyal subject'. Next follow questions designed to discover whether the candidate has all the qualifications required, as described above, and as late as 1899 the Master then admonished the new candidate thus (and I am assured that the current rules are not substantially different): '. . . and it is also required of you that, should you now or at any future period be in the possession of the electoral franchise, you will support by your vote and interest ORANGE AND PROTESTANT CANDIDATES ONLY, and in nowise refrain from voting, remembering our motto: "He who is not with us is against us." Your neglecting to fulfil these conditions will render you LIABLE TO EXPULSION'.

After further quotations from the Bible, the Master says: 'We receive thee, dear brother, into the Religious and Loyal Institution of Orangemen, trusting that thou wilt abide a devoted servant of God, and a true believer in his Son, Jesus Christ, a faithful subject to our Queen, and supporter of our Constitution. Keep thou firm to the Protestant faith, holding its pure doctrine, and observing its holy precepts, make thyself the friend of all pious and peaceful men, avoiding strife, and seeking benevolence; slow to take offence and offering none, thereby, so far as in thee lieth, turning the injustice of our adversaries into their own reproof and confusion'.

Here the Master shall invest the newly-made Brother with the Insignia of the Order, and then raise him by the hand, which he will hold while he repeats: 'In the name of the Brotherhood, I bid thee welcome, and pray that thou mayest long continue among them a worthy Orangeman—namely, fearing God, honouring the Queen and maintaining the law'.

I have taken this ritual from the Rev H. W. Cleary's book *The Orange Society*, published in 1899, which, as I have said, I was assured by a prominent Orangeman, is remarkably accurate on details of ritual, etc. I should have preferred to use the current ritual, and I asked a group consisting of the three above-mentioned top Orangemen in Ulster, for the texts. They said that it had never been their practice to release their rituals and regulations to non-members because they were so often misrepresented. I suggested that if they had nothing to hide surely the best way to avoid such misrepresentation would be to release the actual forms of current induction ceremonies and other rituals for inclusion in such a book as this. They agreed that a time might soon come when they would decide to do this, but it could only be after a major decision by the Grand Lodge. I mention this merely to forestall any criticism that I am using an out-of-date ritual. So far from being sinister, I think the induction rituals of the Orange Order are harmless, indeed almost childish, in their simplicity and if I was forced by the above circumstances to use a 70-year-old version of the induction ritual, *faute de mieux*, I don't think seventy years will have produced all that many changes in the ritual of an Institution that is already three centuries behind the times.

Nevertheless, outside the ranks of the Order, the idea persists that the initiation of new candidates involves painful or possibly frightening experiences. I mentioned this to a number of Orangemen and was assured that although there may have been some sort of test of a man's courage in the very early days of the Order, these days the initiation is a very simple affair, based on Gideon's Chosen Few in the Old Testament, and that nothing happens at an initiation ceremony which does not appear in the Laws and Ordinances of the Institution. (A frequent charge against the Orange Institution, throughout its history, has been that its practices frequently differ from its written Laws and Ordinances. To take one example, it is said that long after the Oath had been dropped from the Laws and Ordinances it was still administered; it was simply dropped from the Laws and Ordinances because it was, in effect, against the law to make a man swear not to divulge in any circumstances, even in a law court, anything that takes place in Lodge.)

Following the induction of the new candidates, there would be a lecture and address, and the new candidates would hear an explanation of how the Lodge works.

The Lodge would then settle down to normal business. This might include a discussion on some religious point, but more often than not the 'normal business' of an Orange Lodge concerns matters of community interest—whether the Lodge should use its influence to have a pedestrian crossing erected near the local school or how much money the Order ought to contribute to some local charity. 'You'd be very disappointed at the secret deliberations that go on behind the closed doors in most of the Orange Lodges,' one slightly disgruntled Orangeman told me. 'My Lodge spent the whole of the last three meetings before the Twelfth last year discussing the sort of sandwiches we should bring to Finaghy Field.'

And the meeting ends, as it opened, with a prayer. Here is a typical opening prayer (there are alternatives):

> Gracious and Almighty God! Who in all ages hast shown Thy Almighty power in protecting righteous Kings and States, we yield Thee hearty thanks for the merciful preservation of Thy true religion, hitherto against the designs of its enemies.
>
> We praise Thee for raising up for our deliverance from tyranny and arbitrary power, Thy servant, King William III, Prince of Orange; and we beseech Thee for Thy honour and Thy name's sake, for ever to frustrate all the designs of wicked men against Thy holy religion, and not to suffer its enemies to triumph; defeat their counsels, abate their pride, assuage their malice, and confound their devices. Deliver, we pray Thee, the members of the Church of Rome from error and false doctrine, and lead them to the truth of that Holy Word which is able to make them wise unto salvation.
>
> We beseech Thee to bless every Member of the Orange Institution with all Christian virtues. Bless us with brotherly

> love and loyalty. Take away everything that may hinder our godly union and concord; so that we may henceforth be of one heart and of one soul, united in one holy bond of truth and peace, of faith and charity, and may, with one mind and one mouth, glorify Thee, through Jesus Christ our Lord.
> Amen.

Only one version of the closing prayer appears in my list of Laws and Ordinances. It runs as follows:

> O Almighty God! Who art a strong tower of defence unto Thy Servants against the face of their enemies, we humbly beseech Thee, of Thy mercy, to deliver us from those great and imminent dangers by which we are now encompassed. O Lord! Give us not up as prey to our enemies; but continue to protect Thy true religion against the designs of those who seek to overthrow it, so that all the world may know that Thou art our Saviour and mighty deliverer: through Jesus Christ our Lord.
> Amen.

I have gone through the portions of scripture suggested for use in Lodges and could not find any central link or connecting thread, nor indeed anything that might seem to have any special Orange significance; they vary from extracts from Deuteronomy, Joshua, the Second Book of Chronicles and the Psalms, to such little-known portions of the New Testament as First and Second Peter and First John, but including only one extract from the Gospels: the St Matthew account of the Sermon on the Mount and the Beatitudes.

Here is the official Order of Business at Lodge Meetings, as set out in the Laws and Ordinances:

1 The Chair to be taken by the Superior Senior Officer present
2 The Deputy Chair by the next in order
3 A Tyler, or Tylers, to be appointed to keep the door
4 A Steward, or Stewards, to preserve order
5 The Opening Prayer to be read by a Chaplain (if present), the Brethren standing

6 A portion of Scripture to be read
7 Proceedings of the last meeting to be read and confirmed
*8 General Qualifications to be read
9 Preliminary communications to be read or made
10 Dues and payments to be collected
†11 Appeals relating to Elections to be heard and decided } (At Meetings for elections)
12 Election of officers } (At Meetings for elections)
13 Letters and other communications (if any) to be read
14 Business arising out of either of the latter
*15 Election of candidates according to 2nd and 3rd Law
*16 Admission of the Candidates of last meeting
†17 Appeals (not against Elections) to be heard and disposed of
†18 Reports from inferior Lodges to be heard and decided
19 General Business to be transacted
*20 Names of candidates for next meetings to be read
21 The CLOSING PRAYER to be read in the same manner as the Opening one.

It all sounds rather dull and I believe it is dull, which may explain why many of the Lodges find it difficult to get a quorum except in the immediate vicinity of July 12th. Throughout history, the Orangemen have always been far keener on marching than on meeting.

The halls in which these meetings take place are mostly dour, brick buildings, daunting in their dingy Victorian austerity. I was proudly shown over what was described to me as 'the Hampton Court of Orange Halls' at Scarva, scene of the Sham Battle. It was built in 1908 on a piece of ground donated to the Orange Order for 'as long as water flows and grass grows' by the late Henry Thomson, M.P. for Newry. It has a stained glass window with the Masonic square and dividers and a representation of King Billy on his white charger. Downstairs there is a

* Articles 8, 15, 16 and 20 to be observed in Private Lodges only.

† Articles 11, 17 and 18 to be observed in all EXCEPT Private Lodges. The others to be observed in all Lodges.

band room, and upstairs a large assembly room which is also used for dances and other social occasions. The bare wooden boards are shiny with French chalk and the passage of many feet, and the walls are hung with portraits and old prints, including one of King Billy landing at Carrickfergus.

I was assured that in most country districts the Orange Hall is the centre of community life. It is hard to imagine anything even remotely festive occurring in such grim surroundings. And this was the Hampton Court of Orange Halls. I cannot imagine what the humblest one must be like.

* * *

And when he came into the camp I saw an awful sight,
Two armies there they did prepare for to renew the fight;
A man six cubits and a span his brethren did defy;
None in that place dare face him but that young Shepherd's Boy.

The King says this Goliath does fill our camp with awe,*
Whoever will this monster kill shall be my son-in-law;
Then I will go, and lay him low, the youth he did reply.
Then go, said he, Lord be with thee, my valiant Shepherd's Boy.

Then from the brook five stones he took, and placed them on his scrip;
Undauntedly across the plain, this gallant youth did trip;
At his first blow he laid him low, cut off his head for-bye,
He dropped his sling and they made a king of this young Shepherd's Boy.

Now to conclude and finish off this wondrous dream of mine,
There's none but he who is born free shall ever know the sign;
So fill your glass, round let it pass, for I am getting dry,
And toast with me the memory of this young Shepherd's Boy.

—From *The Shepherd's Boy*,
a traditional Orange ballad.

* In the Orange Order, the Old Testament tales have acquired a new symbolism; thus Goliath can be taken as the Church of Rome and the Shepherd's Boy as King Billy.

XV

The Arch Purple and the Black

I have already referred briefly to Purple Marksmen and to the Black Preceptories within the Orange Order. This is probably the most difficult area for anybody outside the Order to investigate—and those inside the Order will not write much about it because, whatever they may say, a great deal of secrecy still shrouds the inner workings of this curious institution.

The need for an inner circle to screen candidates very carefully and exclude undesirables probably arose, as I have suggested in an earlier chapter, in the period immediately preceding the 1798 rebellion, when General Lake's harsh treatment of suspected United Irishmen, many of them disgruntled Presbyterians, drove many people into the Orange Order for protection. In its early days, the Orange Order was predominantly a Church of Ireland (Established Church) institution, and non-conformists were almost as suspect as Catholics. There seems to be little doubt that the Purple Marksmen within the order—who possessed an additional set of secret signs and recognition signals, passwords and rituals not known to the rank and file Orangemen—were there to exclude persons of doubtful political stability who might be merely using the Orange Order as a cloak or protection, and to see that none of the inner secrets of the Order reached such people.

It has been suggested to me that the Black Preceptories, which seem to have infiltrated the Orange Order very shortly after its formation, could have been yet a further attempt to confine the inner secrets of the Order to members of the Established Church, since the Blacks set great store on belief in the Trinity, which would exclude some suspect non-subscribing non-conformists (non-subscribing, that is, to the Westminster Confession of Faith, the official doctrinal standard of English-speaking Presbyterianism). But the Black Preceptories—or the Imperial Black Chapter of the British Commonwealth, to give the institution its title—claim a succession which goes back to the Knights Hospitallers and the Crusades. I shall go into that later, but initially, as I have said, the Black Preceptories were not recognized by the Orange Order, which permitted only two degrees, the Orange and the Purple. In the early days of the Order, the Purple Marksmen were a small and select few, with more elaborate and testing initiation ceremonies than those to which ordinary Orangemen were subjected. One of the qualifications for admission was an oath 'faithfully to keep all matters confined to him as a Purpleman, *as well from an Orangeman as from one who is not a Member*', and candidates had to swear on oath that they would keep 'this part of a Marksman from an Orangeman as well as from the ignorant'; nowadays all Orangemen of good behaviour become Purple Marksmen more or less automatically after about six months in the Order.

One early (about 1800) oath of Secrecy ran as follows: 'And I do further swear, in the presence of Almighty God, that I will always conceal, and never reveal, either part or parts of this that I am now about to receive, neither write it, indite it, stamp, stain, or engrave it, nor cause it so to be on paper, parchment, leaf, bark, brick, stone, or anything, so that it be known'.

And the initiation ceremonies of this period, particularly to the inner circles such as the Purple and the Black, were, it seems, much more challenging and frightening than the present rituals. In the Rev H. W. Cleary's book *The Orange Society* there are baffling references to a 'ride on a billy goat' as part of the initiation ceremonies to one of the 'degrees' of the Orange Order. I asked about this and was told that it was still not far from the truth. What was the truth? Perhaps that in the earliest days of the Order a ride on a billy-goat might have been one of the tests of manhood, and that in more recent years it had degenerated into a question of being blindfolded and tossed rather roughly in a blanket, or something of that kind.

But even this apparently is not without its attendant dangers: Lord Advocate J. B. Balfour attested that on April 27th, 1895, one Joseph Rankine of Airblies was being initiated into the Purple degree at the Motherwell Orange Lodge when he was blindfolded and tossed so violently in a net or hammock that his spine was dislocated or broken at the neck. He also gave evidence of how, on July 7th 1893, one David Blair, while being initiated into the Purple degree at an Orange hall in Belfast, was likewise blindfolded, and while in the act of mounting a table (or ladder) in this condition, fell backwards and was killed. In Waltham, Massachusetts, a Frank A. Preble, being initiated into the Orange Lodge was compelled to discard most of his clothes and clamber blindfold over a number of rough blocks. He was struck with whips, and posed on a ladder, thrown off it and tossed in a blanket. The initiation ceremonies concluded with his being burned on the breast with a branding iron, which gave him wounds which were raw for some ten days afterwards. A writer in the *Contemporary Review* for August 1896 tells how a candidate for the Orange Order was shot dead at his initiation; he was killed by a bullet from a revolver used in some form of 'Russian roulette' ceremony.

2

The Imperial Black Chapter of the British Commonwealth appears to boast of the fact that its origins are lost in the mists of the early days of chivalry. It claims early references in ancient documents which refer to 'Turks, pagans and infidels' and point to the early days of the Crusades which, the Orangemen conveniently forget, were preached by a Pope—and a French Pope at that. There is supposed to have been a Preceptory at Kilmainham in what is now the Republic—by yet another ironic coincidence it was in Kilmainham Jail that the rebels of Easter 1916 were executed—dedicated to the Knights of the Red Cross, and another Preceptory at Templepatrick, a few miles from Belfast, dedicated to St Patrick.

According to a paper on the subject published in the *Journal of the Royal Society of Antiquaries of Ireland* and written by Aiken McClelland of the Ulster Folk Museum, the Grand Black Chapter apparently owes its origins to the Imperial Grand

Lodge of Knights of Malta and Parent Black Lodge of the Universe—later known as the Imperial Grand Encampment of the Universe and Grand Black Lodge of Scotland of the Most Ancient, Illustrious and Knightly Order of the Knights Hospitallers of St John of Jerusalem. Here McClelland appends a note 'Not to be confused with the Sovereign and Military Order of St John of Jerusalem, of Rhodes and of Malta, usually referred to today as the Knights of Malta', but this surely is a quibble; if the Blackmen trace their origins back to the Knights Hospitallers and the Crusades, then they cannot disclaim some association with the Knights of Malta, however much they may deprecate it.

According to McClelland, in 1796, just one year after the founding of the Orange Order, some Orangemen in Loughgall, County Antrim, added a new degree—the Purple—to the ritual, and for the next thirty years the Orange Order, under the influence of members who were also hedge-Masons* and possibly Knights of Malta, formed an amazing number of degrees. As early as September 1808, Thomas Currins, a member of L.O.L. No. 1162, a military lodge attached to the Royal Regiment of Artillery then stationed in Cork, received 'the Orange, Purple, Royal Mark Black, Scarlet and Blue' while another certificate states that Currins was dubbed and installed as Black Knight of the Most Holy Order of the Orange'.

A Grand Black Orange Lodge of Ireland was founded in 1802—i.e. seven years after the founding of the Orange Order—and existed until at least 1814, while the Royal Britannic Association of Knights of Israel was in existence before 1810. The Britannic Association, which still exists in Canada, was described, according to McClellan, as 'an organization founded or established for the maintenance and propagation of pure evangelical truth, as contained in the written word of God, as well as the dissemination of strict moral ethics; in fact the system, as propounded, may, with truth, be described as religion veiled in allegory and illustrated by signs and symbols'.

* 'Hedge' Masons were Masons belonging to Lodges which for one reason or another—religious non-conformity, for example—were not recognized by the Grand Lodge.

During the inquiries of the Royal Commission on Orange Lodges in 1835, Stewart Blacker referred to the Black Preceptories. 'The Grand Lodge was always desirous of having their two Orders of Orange and Purple perfectly unshackled and unconnected with any other order whatsoever,' he said. 'They had reason to believe that those Black Lodges, over which they had not any control nor the slightest connection, had induced some of their members to enter their body. They had also heard that there were certain rules among them, such as if a brother is struck, any brother who sees him struck is immediately to take up his quarrel, without inquiring if he has a just cause to do so or not. They thought that this might lead to riots at fairs and markets, and also from the frequent admission into those Black Lodges of various improper characters who had been expelled from the Orange Institution for misconduct, they considered it their duty to warn all members in connection with the Orange Institution to avoid their meetings . . .'

When asked about the origin of these Black Lodges, Blacker told the Commission that he imagined 'they arose from the desire of the lower orders to have something more exciting or alarming in the initiation of members; I think it may be a mixture of freemasonry with that of the old Orange system, a species of mummery innocent of itself and originating in the strong desire that vulgar minds in general manifest for awful mysteries and ridiculous pageantry'.

However, despite this and many other disclaimers, it seems that the Orange Order did tolerate the Black Lodges and even accorded them a sort of respect which could have been due to the fact that leadership in the Black Institution was usually drawn from the established clergy and the landed gentry. In the early days, the Black Preceptories were modelled more closely on the Masonic Order, with a pyramid-type structure; that is to say with fewer and fewer members in each of the higher degrees. Nowadays, just as almost all Orangemen more or less automatically become Purple Marksmen, so almost all members of the Black Preceptories make their way through the various Orders within that Institution more or less automatically.

I have heard the Black Preceptories described on several

occasions as 'the poor man's freemasonry' and I think that's about it, though the institution's links with the Orange Order are still very close. You cannot become a member of a Black Preceptory without first being a Purple Marksman in the Orange Order, and if you are expelled from the Orange Order you are automatically expelled from the Black Institution. However, apart from this, and apart from the fact that they are both exclusively Protestant institutions, they insist that they are completely different and separate. The only occasion they have marched together was on the 50th anniversary of Ulster Day, May 8th, 1965—the anniversary of the signing of the Covenant. That is not to say that Blackmen do not march on July 12th, but they do so in their capacity as Orangemen, and wearing their Orange, not their Black regalia.

2

The headquarters of the Imperial Black Chapter of the British Commonwealth is a Victorian Gothic mansion called Brownlow House at the end of Windsor Avenue in Lurgan. Brownlow was the family name of Lord Lurgan and his ancestors, the first of whom was a linen merchant from Nottingham who was granted 1,500 acres of land here in 1609, while his son was granted 1,000 adjoining acres. Over the centuries the family has thrown up some eccentric autocrats. One Lord Lurgan was drunk all day and every day, from early in the morning, and it is said of him that whenever he fell down, as he frequently did, and his friends rushed to help him to his feet, he would wave them away and say: 'Leave me alone. It's all right. I've got people to do that sort of thing for me,' and signal imperiously to his servants. Another Lord Lurgan was a fanatical follower of greyhound racing and coursing and it is said that on one occasion while he was watching a coursing match from the house the kill took place on the far side of a small cottage which obscured his view. He immediately gave orders for the cottage to be pulled down and issued instructions that no edifice was ever to be erected in its place.

In the grounds of Brownlow House there is a large (54 acre)

artificial lake, created to give employment around the time of the Great Famine. The American Forces in Northern Ireland had their headquarters in the current bizarre mansion, and took some of the stained glass back to the States with them. It was bought by the Black Institution to prevent it from falling into the hands of the Roman Catholic Church, which was planning to turn it into a convent, and originally the Institution had ideas about making an orphanage of it. At the moment the eerie, Denis Wheatley atmosphere is heightened by the fact that the shutters are nowadays permanently closed in the downstairs rooms for fear of attacks from Fenian bombs, but it would be a spooky sort of place at the best of times. I shouldn't care to spend a night there on my own.

Unlike the Orange Order, which has branches in many countries, operating independently of the Institution's headquarters in Belfast, the Royal Black Preceptories—and there are 423 Black Preceptories in Canada alone—are all run from an upstairs room in Brownlow House, where Alex Cushnie, the Imperial Grand Registrar, issues certificates, rules and other documents and administers the Institution's finances. The Imperial Grand Registrar is the equivalent to the Grand Secretary of the Orange Order; in the Black Institution all the titles have a more spacious, illustrious ring. Thus the Grand Master becomes the Imperial Sovereign Grand Master. All members of Black Preceptories—Preceptory, incidentally, is merely a grander word for Lodge—are known as Black Sir Knight, a tradition which produces curious effects when the member also happens to be a knight in, so to speak, civilian life; thus you get Black Sir Knight Sir Norman Strong, who was the last Sovereign Grand Master; the current incumbent is Black Sir Knight Mr James H. Molyneaux, M.P. at Westminster for South Antrim.

Between the Purple and the Black, there is a transitional order known as the Arch Purple. The Arch Purple exists as a separate degree of Orangeism in many other countries, but not in Northern Ireland; here it merely represents a transitional stage through which a Purpleman must go before he becomes a member of one of the Black Preceptories. Once he joins the

Black Institution, which has a fairly elaborate ritual—'I think bucolic horseplay with faint scriptural overtones fairly describes what goes on' is how Dr Dewar put it—every member is free to go through the remaining ten degrees, taking a new degree every month or so. There is no formal 'preparation' as such for initiation into the various higher degrees, and no additional initiation rites other than a very formal one.

The degrees are as follows: Royal Black, Royal Scarlet, Royal Mark, Apron and Blue, Royal White, Royal Green, Royal Gold, Star and Garter, Crimson Arrow, Link and Chain, and Red Cross. The emblems for these degrees vary from Preceptory to Preceptory; in the inner sanctum of the Institution at Brownlow House there is a set of illuminated emblems, including three signs which together stand for the Black Institution as such—the twelve apostles, one blacked out; the burning bush of the Old Testament, and a red hand which has nothing to do with the Red Hand of Ulster but something to do, I gather, with the cloud no bigger than a man's hand from the Bible—and nine which indicate higher degrees. These include the six-pointed star of David, a stylized representation of Solomon's Temple and some stones which presumably are being used in its construction; a dove with an olive branch, and a rainbow in the sky, with implements to be used in rebuilding the world after the deluge; David's sling and five stones; a star and garter; an hour glass, balance and chain, the Masonic square and dividers; a heart pierced with an arrow. Over the throne of Sovereign Grand Master (who wears robes with a red cross on the breast which look medieval in design and might well date back to the time of the Crusades) there is a red cross with the lamb and key, and a Masonic square and dividers, this time with the addition of a letter G (for God?) appears on the throne normally used by the Chaplain during meetings of the Preceptory.

Alex Cushnie showed me a certificate which is issued to members of the Institution who go right through all the degrees to the final one, the Red Cross, which normally takes about eighteen months from first joining the Institution, he said. The certificate is all in black except for the red cross and large red seal; and the general crest of the Institution, the skull and cross-bones, appears on top of it. I asked him why the skull and cross-bones. 'We're a black institution,' he said. 'We're in mourning.' 'For whom?' I asked. 'Joseph,' he said. Fighting back the urge to ask 'Joseph who?', I waited and was rewarded. 'When Joseph was sold into slavery in Egypt,' he said, 'he was given up for dead, and it's because of that we're in mourning.' I did not seek further elucidation.

To be a Blackman is slightly more expensive than being an Orangeman but only marginally (50p to £1 on initiation and dues of around 25p per month). Elevation to each succeeding degree entitles members to wear an additional emblem on their black collarettes and some members do wear as many emblems as possible; others, more sophisticated, realize that since you cannot take the degree of the Red Cross without first going through all the others, it is only necessary to wear the emblem of the Red Cross. As well as the traditional walk to the Sham Fight at Scarva every July 13th, the Blackmen march on the last Saturday in August (for no reason other than it happens to be a trades holiday).

My impression is that the Blackmen go in for more secrets and secret rituals than the Orangemen, but most of them are fairly esoteric and devolve around symbolic interpretation of the scriptures, particularly the Old Testament. I also got the impression that the Blackmen are generally less belligerent and less politically-minded than the rank-and-file Orangemen. As to how many Orangemen join the Black Preceptories, I was given three separate and very different figures by three men all of whom should know. One said seventy per cent, one said fifty per cent and one said less than a third. I would guess less than a third, if only for the reason that only men of a certain cast of thought would be prepared to go along with the mumbo-jumbo that membership of the Black Preceptories entails, while membership of the Orange Order as such is essential in many walks of life in Belfast.

It is not the ambition of every Orangeman to join one of the Black Preceptories; in fact, most Orange Lodges have members who are also members of the Black Institution and who canvass for membership of that institution, so theoretically at any rate any member of the Orange Order can, these days, become a Blackman if he wishes.

One of the surprising things about the Black Institution is that it still attracts a large number of young people into its ranks (about 1,000 last year, between 19 and 24 years of age, according to Alex Cushnie). It is hard to see what appeal this extraordinary institution, with its Masonic symbolism and its elaborate biblical ritualism, could hold for young men in their early twenties, but there is no doubt that many of them do join the Blacks; again, there are in the newspaper files plenty of pictures of them marching. In general, they meet in Orange Halls on a different night from the ordinary members of the Orange Order, though there are two Black Preceptories in Ulster with their own halls.

Women are not admitted to any of their functions and there is no equivalent to the Women's Lodges of the Orange Order.

* * *

Are not all who make profession
Of their hatred to Rome's creed,
Protestant in name and doctrine,
Protestant in word and deed?
Tho' perchance some of their number
Do not worship Christ the Lord,
And consider not the spirit
One with I am and the Word.

And tho' others may be tossing
To and fro with every breeze
Of false doctrine, like a vessel
Rolling on the wintry seas,
If they raise their voice still loudly,
In protest against Rome's guilt,
Of the name are they not worthy?
On the rock are they not built?

—From *Who are the Protestants?*
printed in McKeague's *Orange-Loyalist Songs*,
1971

XVI

Religion and Politics

To what extent does the Orange Order impinge upon politics and everyday life in the Province of Ulster? I had heard that, for example, it was a great deal easier to get an overdraft or a mortgage on a house if you happened to be a member of the Orange Order than it would otherwise be, if only for the simple reason that most bank managers and building society officials happen also to be members of the Orange Order and tend to trust fellow-members of the institution more than outsiders.

In Belfast I was assured by one member of the Orange Order that this was not true for the reason that while the Orange Order always attracted both the clergymen and landlords at the top level, and grass-roots working-class members and farm labourers at a lower level, it had never achieved much success with the middle classes. Within ten minutes I was being assured by another equally eminent member that while in general this was true, in recent years the middle classes have been joining the Order in large numbers and that now it probably would be far easier to get an overdraft or a mortgage if you happen to belong to the Orange Order.

In a recent—May 18th, 1972—article in *This Week*, an Irish news magazine, Robert Cooper wrote about conspiracies in the North, including the Orange Order. 'One of the most commonly believed conspiracies,' he wrote, 'concerns the Orange Order. The theory runs that this is an enormously powerful, cohesive force which meets in every townland or parish in Northern Ireland bringing together all able-bodied Protestant men to plot the downfall and destruction of the Catholics. It dominates and controls the Unionist Party, business and commercial life and the Civil Service. (Incidentally, the Catholic Church is also believed by many Protestants to control the Civil Service, and in particular the Post Office and Inland Revenue.)'

I don't know whether this is true, but I do know that an Irish Catholic girl living and working in Belfast, who told me that she wasn't even aware that she was a Catholic as distinct from a Christian until the troubles started in 1968, assured me that it used to be said in Belfast that the reason Catholics couldn't get or hold down jobs in Belfast was because they were that much less reliable and efficient than the Protestants. 'Yet', she said, 'the two branches of the Civil Service still run from Westminster—the Inland Revenue and the Post Office—have a ratio of about fifty-fifty Protestant to Catholic staff including senior officers, while in the other Government departments, to which appointments are made by Stormont, the proportion is about 80–85 per cent Protestant, and exclusively Protestant in the top jobs.'* I asked her whether she ever thought of 'emigrating' to the Republic and she replied: 'No. I sometimes think about it, and I suppose from a sentimental or patriotic point of view it would be nice if it were all the one country again. But I don't want the IRA shooting people on my behalf and telling me it's to give me my freedom. I've got all the freedom I need, and I'd think twice about going in with the Republic unless they could guarantee me the same benefits.'

This is a pretty widespread reaction in Northern Ireland; the aggressively Conservative and Unionist Stormont Government showed little reluctance to accept the British Labour Party Welfare State 'benefits' and the Catholic Nationalists in Northern Ireland were equally content to accept them—which may explain why there has been no widespread Nationalist emigration from Northern Ireland to the Republic since the war, though there has been to England. Before the war there would have been none anyway, because of the unemployment level in what was then the Free State.

To revert to Robert Cooper's article, he goes on: 'The

* According to *The Northern Ireland Problem*, by Denis P. Barrit and Charles F. Carter, the ratio of Catholics in the 'Imperial' Civil Service is 33 per cent in the Inland Revenue, 33–40 per cent in the Customs and Excise, and 50–55 per cent in the Post Office.

Orange Order, it is thought, issues edicts to all Protestants telling them whom they should employ, who should get houses, and how they should vote on every issue. How different is this from the reality. True, the Orange Order sends about one-fifth of the delegates to the Unionist Council and has also seats on most, but by no means all, Unionist constituency associations. This link is indefensible and is one of the major reasons why the Unionist Party got itself into the mess it did . . . It is true that until recently it was virtually impossible for a non-Orangeman to get selected as a Unionist candidate, but this had very little to do with the Orange delegates as such. It had everything to do with the Loyalist scale unconsciously constructed by most Unionist selectors. One point was allocated for having been a member of the Unionist Party; two points for having fought in the war; three points for having a father or grandfather active in Unionist politics; and five points for membership of the Orange Order, five points for membership of the Derry Apprentice Boys and five points for membership of the Royal Black Preceptory.

'Many non-Orange candidates found in the past that it was not the Orange delegates who held their non-membership against them, but the non-Orange delegates who felt it impossible to believe that a man could become a Unionist Member of Parliament without wishing to be a member of the Orange Order.

'The Orange Order would only have been the sinister conspiratorial force which many believed it to be if most if not all of its members had joined for the same reason—a desire to plan together to defeat Roman Catholicism. Certainly many joined the Orange Order for exactly this reason, but it is a gross over-simplification to imagine that it was universal. There is many an Orangeman who joined the Order not to gain anything out of it, nor out of any enmity towards his Catholic neighbour, but simply because the Order, the colour, the bands, the banners and the Twelfth were all part of his traditional way of life. His father had been an Orangeman and walked on the Twelfth, as had his grandfather and great-grandfather before him, and joining the Order was as automatically a part of his growing up as Baptism or Confirmation.'

Robert Cooper adds that an Orange acquaintance told him that at the first six meetings of the year in his Lodge the major topic of conversation was whether there should be ham or corned beef sandwiches at Finaghy Field on the Twelfth—precisely what I had heard from another source. The other six meetings consisted of prolonged debate on whether the decision they had taken on this momentous issue was the right one or not. Another Orange friend of his attended three successive meetings before the Twelfth and in this Lodge the controversy centred on whether the members of the Lodge should march round the walls of the local convent three times or whether twice would be enough.

Traditionally, the Ulster Unionists have always been Protestant extremists. In 1931, the Ulster Protestant League was formed; this was an overtly anti-Catholic movement whose policy was 'neither to talk nor walk with, neither to buy nor sell, borrow nor lend, take nor give or have any dealings at all with them, nor for employers to employ them nor employees to work with them.' The following year Lord Craigavon (formerly Sir James Craig, one of the founders of the State) assured an Orange gathering that 'Ours is a Protestant Government and I am an Orangeman', and in 1934 he told the Commons:

> 'I am very proud indeed to be Grand Master of the Orange Institution of the loyal County of Down. I have filled that office for many years and I prize that far more than I do being Prime Minister. I have always said that I am an Orangeman first and a politician and a member of this Parliament afterwards . . . all I boast is that we are a Protestant Parliament and a Protestant State.'

Sir Basil Brooke, later Lord Brookeborough, who became Prime Minister in 1943, went even further. In 1933 he told an Orange demonstration: 'Many in the audience employ Catholics, but I have not one about my place. Catholics are out to destroy Ulster with all their might and power. They want to nullify the Protestant vote, take all they can out of Ulster and see it go to hell'.

The following year, he returned to this theme:

> 'I recommend those people who are Loyalists not to employ Roman Catholics, ninety-nine per cent of whom are disloyal . . . usually there are plenty of good men and women available and the employers don't bother to employ them. You are disfranchising yourselves in that way. You people who are employers have the ball at your feet. If you don't act properly now, before we know where we are we shall find ourselves in the minority instead of the majority.'

During the bad years, in the 'thirties, when unemployment in the Six Counties was around the 28 per cent mark, it was 41 per cent among the Catholics; this was partly the result of the discrimination shamelessly preached by Sir Basil Brooke. And shameless is literally the word; the Orangeman feels no shame whatever at discriminating against the Catholics who, he believes, are disloyal rebels who stand for the dissolution of the State. There was trouble at Stormont in the early 'forties when it was reported that of thirty porters employed there, twenty-nine were Catholics. John M. Andrews, then Prime Minister, himself inquired into the situation and was able to report that he had made a check on this and was happy to say only two of the porters were Catholics and 'they were both temporary'.

One of the most alarming features of the bigotry of the Orangemen is that it is completely unconscious. They believe that they are the chosen few, singled out for special privilege by a Protestant God, and that they owe the privileged position which they hold in the state, and are determined to maintain at all costs, to a combination of industry, sobriety and devotion to the Protestant cause. When I asked one of the top Orangemen how he felt about the ecumenical movement, he replied that the Orange Order had always really been in the vanguard of the ecumenical movement in so far as it had been instrumental in bringing members of the various branches of the Reformed Churches together. Ecumenism, in the Orange Order is, however, strictly confined to the Reformed Churches; it does not extend to the Church of Rome.

At its lowest level, when Orangemen set out—as they still do from time to time—to taunt and provoke their Catholic fellow-citizens into hostile reactions they use horrifying catch-calls like 'your Virgin Mary was the biggest whore in Bethlehem', seemingly unaware that precisely the same Virgin Mary was the mother of the 'Protestant' Jesus Christ, their own 'Only Mediator'.

And it would be a mistake to think that fear, mistrust and contempt for Catholics is confined to the lower intelligence levels within the Order. Lord O'Neill, then Captain Terence O'Neill—even at a time when he was, as he claimed, trying to 'build bridges' between the Protestant and Catholic communities in the Six Counties, and when his tentative moves towards making the Six Counties a more prosperous place for all, so that Catholics would want to play a larger part in the life of the state, had led to his overthrow—was capable of making, in a radio interview, a reference to Catholics almost stupefying in its tone of condescension:

> 'The basic fear of the Protestants in Northern Ireland is that they will be outbred by the Roman Catholics. It is as simple as that. It is frightfully hard to explain to a Protestant that if you give Roman Catholics a good job and a good house they will live like Protestants, because they will see neighbours with cars and television sets. They will refuse to have eighteen children. But if the Roman Catholic is jobless and lives in a most ghastly hovel, he will rear eighteen children on National Assistance.
>
> 'It is impossible to explain this to a militant Protestant, because he is so keen to deny civil rights to his Roman Catholic neighbours. He cannot understand, in fact, that if you treat Roman Catholics with due consideration and kindness they will live like Protestants in spite of the authoritative nature of their church.'

This is the kind of attitude that is sad and frightening because it is quite unconscious. O'Neill genuinely believed he was being progressive and broad-minded. I have met him and talked with him; he would be horrified to be considered a bigot.

In 1959, the question of admitting Catholics to membership of the Unionist Party was seriously discussed, and Sir Clarence Graham, chairman of the standing committee of the Ulster Unionist Council, said that he would not rule out the possibility that the day might come when many members of the Nationalist Party would wish to join the Unionist Party, confusing, as so many Ulster people do, the terms Catholic and Nationalist. After the matter had been debated at length, the Unionist executive committee issued a statement which set out the party's position:

> . . . the policy and aims of the Unionist Party remain unchanged and are as laid down by Edward Carson and James Craig, namely:
> (1) to maintain the constitutional position of Northern Ireland as an integral part of the United Kingdom and to defend the principles of civil and religious liberty.
> (2) to improve social standards and to expand industry and agriculture: and
> (3) to welcome to our ranks only those who unconditionally support these ideals.

This was far too vague for the then Grand Master of the Grand Orange Lodge of Ireland, Sir George Clark, who said that in no circumstances would the suggestion that Catholics be admitted to membership of the Unionist Party be countenanced by the Orange Order. He went on:

> 'I would draw your attention to the words "civil and religious liberty". This liberty, as we know it, is the liberty of the Protestant religion . . . In view of this, it is difficult to see how a Roman Catholic, with the vast differences in our religious outlook, could be either acceptable within the Unionist Party as a member or, for that matter, bring himself unconditionally to support its ideals. Furthermore, an Orangeman is pledged to resist by all lawful means the ascendancy of the Church of Rome . . .'

All evidence points to a weakening of the links between the Orange Order and the Unionist party in recent years. Despite

Sir George Clark's warning, Major James Chichester-Clark, who succeeded Lord O'Neill as Premier, announced that he would welcome into the party Roman Catholics who wished to be associated with Unionism, and not just as voters but as active party members, with equal rights to office. In his book *Northern Ireland: 50 years of Self-Government*, Martin Wallace writes:

> 'The direct influence of the Order appears much reduced in recent years, despite its substantial representation on the Ulster Unionist Council, but its indirect influence is substantial in that a large majority of Unionist M.P.s and Senators belong to the Order, as do many party members. However, aspiring Unionist politicians feel it less necessary than in the past to join the Order, and when Dr Robert Simpson was named as Northern Ireland's first Minister of Community Relations on September 25th, 1969, he immediately announced his resignation from the Order. He said he took this action to avoid the suggestion, however ill-founded, of improper influence. At this time, two other members of the Cabinet were not Orangemen; one had resigned when a member of his family had married a Catholic, while the other had been expelled for attending a Catholic service held as part of a civic week in his community.' [That would be Phelim O'Neill, who, as we have seen, was not, strictly speaking, expelled for attending a Catholic Service but for refusing to be disciplined by the Order after doing so.]

2

The hostility between the two communities which followed the pogroms and disturbances during and in the immediate wake of the Civil War in Ireland continued to a greater or lesser degree to cause problems in certain areas—notably the maintenance of law and order, education and, to a lesser extent, National Health—throughout the fifty-odd years of Stormont's existence as a separate Parliament. And to the extent that they represented and still represent the most intransigent and intractable element in Ulster Protestantism the Orangemen must bear much of the blame for creating situations which did not and could not conceivably occur in any other part of the United Kingdom.

The Catholics must also bear part of the blame for the situation. They set the sectarian pattern, in fact, in the early days of the new state, when they refused to have anything to do with a government which they believed would not long survive and which was cutting them off, by force of arms, behind an arbitrary and unfair border (which they felt confident would be completely redrawn by the Boundary Commission) from their fellow countrymen south of the border. This attitude naturally produced a reaction among the Ulster Protestants who, understandably enough, saw no reason why jobs, particularly in the Civil Service and other government-controlled bodies, should be given to people dedicated to the overthrow of that government.

I have already mentioned the fact that Sir James Craig initially reserved one third of the places in the Royal Ulster Constabulary for Catholics, but Catholic recruitment never reached anything like that level. Until their disbandment in 1970, the B Specials were almost exclusively Protestants and *Orangemen*. To maintain law and order in this very unstable situation the Stormont Parliament decided that both police forces should be armed, and introduced a number of repressive measures which would again have been unthinkable elsewhere in the United Kingdom. Chief of these was the Civil Authorities (Special Powers) Act, 1922, originally intended as a temporary measure and, at first, renewed annually; in 1933 it was given indefinite duration. This Special Powers Act, as it is usually called, gave the Minister of Home Affairs (and through him the two armed branches of the police force) almost unlimited powers to 'take all such steps and issue all such orders as may be necessary for preserving the peace and maintaining order' and specifically entitled him to delegate these powers to his Parliamentary secretary or to any officer of the RUC. Any person who does any act of such a nature as to be calculated to be prejudicial to the preservation of peace or the maintenance of order in Northern Ireland, not specifically provided for in the regulations, was deemed to be guilty of an offence against the regulations.

Section Three provides that any alleged offence may be tried by a court of summary jurisdiction. Under Section Six, anyone convicted under the Explosive Substances Act, 1883, of causing an explosion likely to endanger life or attempting to cause an explosion with intent to endanger life *may be sentenced to death.* Until the repeal of Section Five in 1968, punishment by whipping could be imposed for a number of lesser offences concerned with explosives, firearms, arson and demanding with menaces.

Regulations embodied in this Act empowered the Constabulary to enter and search buildings without a warrant, to stop and search vehicles or persons. The Act gives the Government power to suppress the publication of literature 'prejudicial or likely to be prejudicial to the preservation of peace or the maintenance of order'. An RUC officer can authorize arrest without warrant and detention for the purpose of interrogation. The Minister can make an order restricting any person's movements or providing for his indefinite internment; it is under the provisions of this Act that the internees are held at Long Kesh.

This Act has proved a continuous embarrassment to the British Government, particularly in recent years since it is contrary to the provisions of the European Convention of Human Rights, to which Britain is a signatory.

But the Stormont Government introduced other measures designed to enable them to cope with the special circumstances in Northern Ireland, including the Public Order Act (NI) 1951 and the Public Order (Amendment Act) (NI) 1970, designed to give the authorities some power to control local processions, particularly Civil Rights marches, and the carrying of 'offensive weapons', and also to make it an offence to hinder, molest or obstruct lawful processions. Then there is the Flags and Emblems (display) Act (NI) 1954, which has no British counterpart and which makes it an offence to interfere by force with the display of the Union Jack and empowers the police to remove the Irish tricolour (one third green for the Republic, one third

Orange for the North, and between them a white band, for peace) if they fear that its display may lead to a breach of the peace, which it almost invariably does. By contrast, the Union Jack is frequently flown in the Republic at football matches, shows, exhibitions and even by many international hotels.

3

Another area in which the polarization of the Protestant and Roman Catholic communities has led to misunderstandings is in the field of education.

A committee set up by the first Northern Ireland Minister for Education, Lord Londonderry, under Mr Robert Lynn, to inquire and report on the existing organization and administration of the educational services in Northern Ireland was boycotted by the Catholics. As a result, the great gulf that separates Catholics and Protestants in Northern Ireland begins at school. They are educated separately, though this is largely due to Catholic intransigence and not to Orange sectarianism; the Northern Ireland Government is and always has been prepared to go more than half way to integrate the Catholic schools into the state system, but the Catholics insist on total control of their schools. The result is complete segregation, with the Protestant (State) schools, until recently at any rate, teaching almost no Irish history as such and referring to the Easter Rebellion only in passing as one of the incidents of World War I.

The Government of Ireland Act, 1920, stipulated that the Government would not endow any religion and that no person would be afforded any advantage or suffer any disadvantage on account of his (or her) religious belief, which was interpreted as meaning that public money could not be used to finance any school giving religious instruction.

The Orange Order and the Protestant churches all opposed this. They wanted instruction in and through the Bible to remain a feature of the educational system and they wanted to ensure that Protestant pupils would be taught only by Protestant teachers. Under pressure from the three main Protestant Churches and from the Orange Order, the Government passed, in 1925, an amending Act deleting the offending parts of the earlier Act and advising the adoption of a programme of 'simple Bible instruction' as part of the general school course. In the matter of education, Catholic clergy seem to have been consistently opposed to all attempts at integration—again this is understandable from their viewpoint, but cannot be expected to give members of the Orange Order any confidence that those in charge of the Catholic Church are less autocratic than they were, though the Orange Order would not look any more kindly on a completely integrated educational system if it led to Catholic teachers being charged with the education of Protestant children.

When in 1968 a White Paper appeared setting out the Government plans for Local Education and the Voluntary Schools, the Catholic Bishop of Down and Connor, Dr William Philbin, seemed to be demanding the best of both worlds when he claimed that:

> 'It seems that an application by us to have State aid to Catholic schools brought up to the English level—65 per cent to 80 per cent—has been made the occasion of an invasion of the established system of Catholic School Management . . . We have to take account of the strongly-supported campaign against the existence of our schools in recent years, and to ask ourselves whether the present move is not seen as a first step towards their disappearance. No educational considerations appear to have been operative in this aspect of the proposed changes. The motives have been political and belong to the darker areas of politics, in which religious prejudice is paramount.'

On April 8th, 1966, in a speech on community relations at an ecumenical conference in County Armagh, Captain O'Neill said:

> 'A major cause of division arises, some would say, from the *de facto* segregation along religious lines. This is a most delicate matter and one must respect the firm conditions from which it springs. Many people have questioned, how-

ever, whether the maintenance of two distinct educational systems side by side is not wasteful of human and financial resources, and a major barrier to communal understanding.'

Cardinal Conway, the Catholic Primate, carped at this. He noted that the Prime Minister had spoken on the subject of denominational schools four times in two years, 'suggesting with various degrees of emphasis that it would be a good thing for the community if the Catholic schools were to disappear . . . I find this continuing pressure on Catholic schools by the head of the Government very surprising and, indeed, disquieting'.

There is some evidence—a National Opinion poll carried out in 1967—that the Catholic laity feel that Protestants and Catholics could be educated in the same schools without doing any irreparable harm to the Catholic community, and in 1970 the Unionist Party conference passed a resolution urging the immediate integration of all schools, which was described as impracticable by the Minister of Education.

Incidentally, one by-product of this total segregation is that it makes discrimination in employment that much easier. There is no need to ask a candidate his religion; all that is necessary is to find out where he went to school.

4

A somewhat similar situation arose in relation to one Belfast hospital, the Mater. This hospital, founded in 1883 to provide 'relief for the sick and suffering without distinction of creed', is a teaching hospital associated with Queen's University, which has always been non-denominational. After World War II, the Northern Ireland Government introduced a state national health service, based on the British one. The British Act, however, provided that where hospitals which were linked with a particular religious denomination were being transferred to the Ministry 'regard shall be had in the general administration of the hospital and in the making of appointments to the Hospital Management Committee to the preservation of the character and associations of the hospital'.

This was accepted in England, but it wouldn't do in Northern Ireland. The trouble was that, although non-Catholics had always been treated in the hospital, Catholic medical practices prevailed and there was the added danger of Protestant patients being exposed to such Popish practices as Mass in the wards. As a result, Mr William Grant, the Minister of Health, speaking with an unmistakeably Orange accent, announced: 'They are either coming in one hundred per cent or they are staying out one hundred per cent. There is going to be no half-way stage about this matter'. So the Mater stayed out and supported itself on the proceeds of a very successful football pool, largely drawing its support from the Republic, where the British football pools are not permitted to operate because they would interfere with the revenues of the Irish Hospitals Sweep. And it is interesting that the Northern Ireland Government levies duties on the Mater football pool.

Over the years various attempts have been made to solve the problem of the Mater and its position was one of the many matters under discussion when Stormont was prorogued. In this, unlike the question of education, the Catholics are not digging their heels in; there is no obligation on a Catholic to go to a Catholic hospital, but there is a Canon Law obligation to have all Catholic children educated in a Catholic school.

5

It is probably an over-simplification to say that the Orange Order is responsible for all the discrimination in jobs and housing and the gerrymandering of constituencies to ensure Protestant majorities even in areas where the Catholics are in a majority. (In Londonderry County Borough, right up to the end of the 'sixties, sixty per cent of the seats on the Corporation were held by Unionists despite the fact that sixty per cent of the population was Catholic; this situation was achieved by constructing wards in such a way that Unionist representatives required only a very small majority and non-Unionist representatives were returned with vast majorities in overwhelming

Catholic areas.) But as the Unionist party has been dominated consistently by the Orange Order, and as people who are opposed to the Order can point to a number of extremely bigotted and incautious remarks from people who should know better, such as those I have quoted above and many, many more, and claim them as evidence that it is the declared policy of the Order to discriminate against Catholics, it is hard for the Orange Order to shrug off such accusations. And there have been so many impartial inquiries and commissions of one sort or another into Northern Ireland's affairs recently that the world can no longer be in much doubt that there genuinely was discrimination, particularly in regard to local authority housing; local government appointments, especially to senior posts; manipulation of local government boundaries to maintain Unionist control; and continued refusal by Stormont to acknowledge even the need to investigate Catholic complaints about such discrimination.

6

A persistent belief exists among the Catholics in Ulster that most members of the Orange Order throughout the past fifty years have been armed and would not hesitate to use their arms. The B Specials, as we have seen, were Orangemen almost to a man. They kept their guns at home, just as they had done when they were in the Ulster Volunteer Force—in many cases they were the same guns—and they used them often, savagely and indiscriminately, against Catholics. And although they were disbanded in 1970 and obliged to hand in their 'official issue' weapons, the 10,000 strong force is believed still to have weapons of all sorts—shot guns, .22 rifles and many more lethal automatic weapons. There are gun clubs all over Northern Ireland and more people hold firearms licences than anywhere else in the United Kingdom.

I asked a number of Orangemen I met whether many of their members were, in fact, armed. The reply was almost standard: 'Well, of course, I myself wouldn't know which end of a gun to hold,' and then a pause, followed by something like this: 'But

I'd say you wouldn't be far wrong if you assumed that the vast bulk of the members of the Order either have arms or have access to arms. And know how to use them'.

To what extent is Orange thought representative of Protestant thought in the Six Counties? Probably less now than it used to be, despite the Orange Order's claim of an increase in membership since the troubles started. One Protestant to whom I talked—he is not an Orangeman—put it this way: 'If the Orangemen *did* represent Protestant thought in Ulster, we'd all be in the Institution, wouldn't we? And yet they only claim 100,000 members and that's probably an exaggeration. But supposing it's true, that's only one-tenth of the Protestant population. All right, part of that population consists of small children and girls who can't join the order, so give them maybe a sixth of those able to join. It's still only one Protestant in six, out of a total population that also includes one Catholic for every two Protestants anyway. So I don't think they've got anything like the power they claim'.

Finally, to conclude this chapter, I would like to return to the point that although some of the pronouncements of the leading Orangemen have been horrifyingly bigoted and condescending, the ordinary rank and file member of the Orange Order, when not incensed by bands and banners and booze, can be an extraordinarily human and surprisingly humorous species of humanity. I have been told that 'the crack' at Orange Lodge meetings is usually very good, and I don't doubt it for a minute. There have been times, during the fifty-odd years' existence of the State of Northern Ireland, when Ulster Catholics and Protestants got on famously. Something of the attitude that existed between the religions was caught by the County Down poet and novelist, Lynn Doyle (who was not an Orangeman himself, but was a staunch Protestant) in his poem, *An Ulsterman*, from the collection, *Ballygullion Ballads:*

I do not like the other sort,
They're tricky an' they're sly,
An' couldn't look you in the face
Whenever they pass by,

Still I'll give in that here an' there,
You'll meet a decent man;
I would make an exception, now,
About wee Michael Dan.

But, then, he's from about the doors,
An' lived here all his days,
An' mixing with us in an' out,
He's fell into our ways.
He pays his debts and keeps his word,
An' does the best he can,
If only all the Papishes
Were like wee Michael Dan.

A better neighbour couldn't be,
He borrows an' he lends,
An'—bar a while about the Twelfth,
When him an' me's not friends—
He'll never wait until he's asked,
To lend a helpin' han'.
There's quite a wheen of Protestants
I'd swop for Michael Dan.

Of course he'd burn me at the stake,
I know that very well;
An' told me one day to my face
I'm not too safe from hell.
But when I backed a bill for him
He met it like a man.
There's sparks of Christianity
About wee Michael Dan.

So, while I have my private doubts
About him reaching heaven,
His feet keeps purty near the pad
On six days out of seven;
An' if it falls within the scope
Of God Almighty's plan
To save a single Popish sowl,
I hope it's Michael Dan.

And one more story, to illustrate a curious feature of the Orangeman. I have already made the point that although they all know perfectly well that their institution is based on King William III's campaign and the defeat of King James in 1690, they feel that somehow the Order is a far more ancient institution which goes back to the Bible if not to the Garden of Eden—equally, although if they stopped to think about it they must realize that King William was a Dutchman who spoke little if any English, nevertheless he is regarded by the rank and file Orangemen as a wee Belfast man, who even spoke with a Belfast accent.

John Robinson, of the BBC in Belfast, told me that he was being driven home down the Malone Road one night by a taxi-driver whom he knew to be an Orangeman. The driver asked him if he had ever heard tell how the Malone Road got its name. John said he didn't, and the Orangeman told him the following story: 'On his great march from Carrickfergus to the Boyne', he said, 'King Billy passed through the city of Belfast which was only a collection of mud cottages and a bridge over the Lagan in those days.* And as he was approaching Belfast down this very road, which didn't have a name at the time, he stopped and decided to go on a wee bit of a reconnoitre. His batman offered to go with him, but King Billy replied: "You will not. I'll go my lone." And that's how the Malone Road got its name'.

* To quote Macaulay again, King William III met Schomberg at Belfast and 'the meeting took place close to a white house, the only human dwelling then visible, in the space of many miles, on the dreary strand of the estuary of the Lagan'.

* * *

Sons of Ulster, stalwart B Men,
Closed now is your stirring page,
Ended is your valiant story,
To placate an unjust rage.

Half a life-time's blameless record
Cast aside by scheming men,
And the work of years extinguished
By the politician's pen.

Born as Ulster faced the gunman,
Fighting for her very life.
Born as murder stalked the highways,
And our land was torn by strife.

Curfew tolled its sober warning,
And the 'Specials' stood to arms.
At the cross-roads, on the hillsides,
Through the long night of alarms.

Stood to guard the homes of Ulster,
Thwart the hidden killer's aim.
Loyal service marked your history,
Won for you a well-loved name.

Feared and slandered by detractors,
With God's help you kept us free,
Upright, friendly, Ulster B Men,
Cherished will your memory be.

—From McKeague's *Orange-Loyalist Songs*, *1971*.

XVII
What Went Wrong?

As this is a book about the Orange Order as such, and not a history of recent events in Northern Ireland, I am primarily concerned with the extent to which the Orange Order and religious sectarianism generally was involved in the series of events which began with the first Civil Rights demonstration in 1968 and has since escalated into the present situation which is very close to civil war, with 21,000 British troops keeping the peace between Protestant extremists, Catholic Nationalists, two wings of the IRA and a wide variety of Protestant armies of all sorts, with Stormont prorogued, and half the buildings in Belfast and Londonderry in ruins. 'The Province is bleeding to death', an Ulsterman said to me recently. 'Even if it stops to-morrow, it will take us ten years to get back to where we were in 1968.' True . . . but what went wrong?

For a little over fifty years a portion of a Province which had never wanted Home Rule managed to struggle along, under a form of Home Rule which allowed it very little economic autonomy, reserving all the principal taxes on income and expenditure to the Parliament at Westminster, known in Northern Ireland as 'the Imperial Parliament', just as Britain is known as the 'Mother Country'. From time to time British troops had to be sent in to assist the regular Ulster garrison of 2,500 soldiers and the RUC and B Specials to maintain order,* and although theoretically there should have been a contribution from Northern Ireland to cover such expenses as these very Armed Forces, and known as 'the Imperial Contribution', in point of fact it has cost Britain a very considerable sum of money to keep some pretence of a parity in the standard of living between the Six Counties and the remainder of the

* In 1922, 1931, 1933, 1935 and 1969.

United Kingdom. It is hard to get accurate figures as to how much the Six Counties of Ulster actually cost the British Government; I have seen estimates varying between £70m a year and twice that much.

And to the extent that 'what went wrong' revolved around the maintenance of law and order in the province, and that the Orange Order largely dominated the Unionist Party which was responsible for maintaining law and order with, among other forces, the 10,000 strong B Specials, almost all of them Orangemen, then the Orange Order must be held at least partly responsible for what has been happening in Belfast during the past four years.

Again, to be fair, I must say I can see an Orange viewpoint on this, too. When the first Parliament of Northern Ireland sat in 1921 the six Nationalists and the six Sinn Fein members who were elected to the 52-seat assembly refused to attend; there was no formal 'opposition' at Stormont until 1927, and there never was an effective one in any genuine sense in all the fifty years of its existence. The Catholics and Nationalists refused to have anything to do with the new state and whenever IRA raids from across the Border took place it was natural, perhaps, that the members of the Orange Order and the Unionist Party should suspect the Catholics and Nationalists of giving shelter to the enemies of the new state. I don't hold much brief for the B Specials, but if you are sent into an area, say in Londonderry, where your previous experience has taught you that more than half the people are perfectly prepared to try to kill you, you will not react like a British policeman taking details of a minor traffic infringement on the Upper Richmond Road. Equally, you can see why the Catholics and Nationalists resent the treatment they received from the B Specials in what they regard as 'their' country.

Throughout the first fifty years of the existence of the Six County Government, one question was never faced either by the Republicans in the South of Ireland or by the Unionists in the North, but it must be faced now. It is the question posed in an excellent—though anonymous—review of Robert Kee's *The Green Flag* in the *Times Literary Supplement*, dated May 26th,

1972. What the anonymous reviewer asks, in effect, is: How long do you have to establish yourself in a country before you are considered to have a stake in it? This question is particularly apt in relation to the Irish, who become more American than the Americans themselves after one generation, while at the same time denying that the Ulster Planters are in any sense Irish, although they have been there for over 300 years. The *TLS* reviewer writes:

> Nationalism, once its credentials are established, is nowadays accorded full rights at the bar of international opinion. Those who come forward as its champions receive moral approval and may receive material assistance. Those who are seen as thwarting its fulfilment are condemned. It is therefore of more than historical importance to know whether there is for the island of Ireland one stream of legitimate nationalism or two. Are the Protestant Irishmen who are thickly concentrated in the North-East corner of the province of Ulster to be thought of as a minority within the Irish nation who, whether from selfishness, fear, or religious in-breeding, have systematically frustrated the full realization of Irish nationalism? Or are they to be thought of as being in possession of a separate nationalism of their own which, even if 'nationalism' is not exactly the right word for it, is marked by an authentic collective identity and focus of loyalty which entitle it to no less consideration than the sentiment to the south of it?
>
> If the answer to the second question is yes, then the Ulster-Unionists deserve some support in their settled determination not to be absorbed into an all-Ireland republic, and the consequence of coercing them into that position can be confidently predicted as disastrous. If the answer to the question is no, then it becomes a sensible object of policy in the interests of the Ulster Protestants themselves, as much as in those of anybody else, to do what can be done to condition them to acceptance of their historical lot. And the answer to the question is certainly not to be found by simple inspection of the map—'Ah,

yes, a smallish island of convenient shape. Obviously one nation'. Nationality has more to do with people than with territory.

But given all that, what went wrong? Again ironically—and I seem to be using that word throughout this book—it was the first attempt by a Unionist politician, Lord O'Neill, to 'build bridges' between the two communities, which led to the beginnings of the present disturbances.

O'Neill, convinced that the materialism which almost inevitably follows a rise in the standard of living in capitalist terms, believed that if the Catholics in the community were afforded opportunities of keeping up with their next-door neighbours, they would quickly forget about religion and politics and seek to play a 'normal' part in the development of the community. He felt that the economic development of the country was being held back by keeping Partition as the major issue in Ulster politics, and without even consulting Stormont, arranged a meeting with the then Republican Premier, Sean Lemass, in 1965.

This produced two immediate reactions: from the Catholics, a faint hope, which grew into a conviction, that if they pressed their cause they might, at long last, achieve a measure of justice; and from the ultra-Protestants, a violent backlash which found its most able spokesman in the Rev Dr Ian Paisley, who began to organize a series of protests against the growing toleration of Romish trends in religion and the new liberal attitude towards Republican Fenians. Paisley, although no longer an Orangeman (and in those days by no means the smooth, assured, plausible politician into which exposure to the rarified air of Westminster has transformed him) spoke in unmistakeable near-Orange tones when he warned his followers against the dangers of flirtation with the whore of Rome.

Paisley was supported by the Protestant working-class youth (who had jobs because their Catholic counterparts were unemployed and who wanted to keep matters that way) and the small bourgeoisie (who could remain competitive by employing Catholic labour at artificially low rates); and he showed his hostility to O'Neill's regime in the traditional way—by marching and preaching and protesting and ultimately, mob violence.

2

It was at this stage, whether manipulated, as many people say, by agencies specializing in international unrest, or occurring spontaneously as the result of circumstances, a Civil Rights movement also appeared on the Ulster scene. In June 1968, Austin Currie, a Nationalist M.P. organized a 'sit-in' as a protest against the local council's plan to give a council house in County Tyrone to a 19-year-old, unmarried, Protestant secretary of a Unionist politician instead of to a Catholic family. It was also a protest against Stormont's refusal to interfere in what it said was purely a local matter. Encouraged by the publicity the 'squat-in' received in the newspapers and on television, the protesters held a civil rights march at Dungannon in August. It passed off peacefully and the police did not intervene.

In October 1968, another march was planned, this time for Londonderry. It was banned by William Craig, then Minister of Home Affairs at Stormont, and when the 3,000 unarmed marchers went ahead with their parade, in spite of the ban, they were attacked and roughly handled by the RUC. Ninety-six people, including two Labour M.P.s, had to have hospital treatment.

The press and television cameramen had moved into Ulster in strength and for the first time the world became aware that the Irish Question was still not solved. Most of the television coverage and the liberal press came out heavily on the side of the civil rights marchers and the Nationalists, and against Paisley and Craig and the Orange-dominated Unionist Party, and there is no doubt that this contributed to the feeling among the Orangemen that they were once again in danger of betrayal.

As early as 1966 an Ulster Volunteer Force had been formed as a Protestant, Unionist counterpart to the IRA. Other associations of loyalists included the Ulster Loyalist

Association and the Loyal Citizens of Ulster, but by far the most influential at this stage was Paisley's Ulster Constitution Defence Committee and the Ulster Protestant Volunteers which it controlled. It described itself as 'one united society of Protestant patriots pledged by all lawful methods to uphold and maintain the Constitution of Northern Ireland as an integral part of the United Kingdom as long as the United Kingdom maintains a Protestant Monarchy and the terms of the Revolution Settlement' (an aim almost identical with that of the Orange Order).

The law did not always agree that Paisley's methods were lawful and he spent a sojourn in jail after 112,000 of his supporters, armed with scythes, cudgels studded with nails and a couple of revolvers, held a day and night vigil to prevent 6,000 civil rights marchers from passing along a route in Armagh, approved by the police, in November 1968.

The Cameron Commission's report on *Disturbances in Northern Ireland* made no bones about the role of Paisley's movement:

> It is our considered opinion that these counter-demonstrations were organized under the auspices of the Ulster Constitution Defence Committee and the Ulster Protestant Volunteers and that their true purpose was either to cause the legal prohibition of the proposed Civil Rights or People's Democracy demonstrations by the threat of a counter demonstration, or, if this move failed, to harass, hinder and if possible break up this demonstration.'

The People's Democracy referred to in the above extract was a Marxist movement originally started in Queen's University, Belfast, though not restricted to University members. They held a demonstration march from Belfast to Derry on January 1st, 1969, which was intercepted and attacked at several points along the route by Paisley's militant Protestants, armed with stones and cudgels. The RUC stood by and made no move to protect the march which had not been banned and was therefore perfectly legal. During the week-end that followed, the RUC 'invaded' the Catholic Bogside area of Londonderry, batoning Catholic men, women and children in the streets and even in their own homes.

But even before things had reached this stage, O'Neill, the Prime Minister, had warned the Ulster people that Britain would not tolerate this kind of thing indefinitely. He had already had a visit from Harold Wilson, then British Premier, and had announced the first batch of Stormont reforms which included the promise of 1,200 new jobs and 960 new houses for Derry (though not until 1981); the abolition of the company vote in local government elections and a Commission to administer Derry in place of the Corporation and County Council. The Civil Rights marchers regarded these concessions as 'too little and too late', and went on marching and protesting, and the Orangemen among the Unionist backbenchers—genuinely convinced that, if you give a Catholic Nationalist any concessions, instead of being eternally grateful he will merely demand still more concessions, which is perfectly true of any oppressed minority—questioned whether the Government had any mandate to introduce such reforms without going to the country.

O'Neill made a television appeal for an end to violence, warning the people that if they did not face up to their own problems the Westminster Parliament might well decide to act over their heads. Craig, taking the hard-line Orange stand, declared that Northern Ireland would resist any attempts at British intervention in her affairs and was dismissed.

But the disturbances went on, the Unionist Party split for the first time in its long history, O'Neill resigned, to be succeeded by Major James Chichester-Clark and the newsmen and TV commentators moved to Derry for the next potential flash-point, the annual march of the Apprentice Boys around Derry's walls—chanting their Orange songs and throwing pennies down into the Catholic Bogside area as a gesture of their continuing contempt—on August 12th, 1969. 'That day's parade', according to the *Sunday Times* Insight team, 'was no more "provocative" than those of previous years. Indeed it was a model of order and well-stewarded discipline. To discuss it in degrees of provocation, however, is to imply that it is like a students' demonstration in England—a basically pacific event which on occasion may be taken over by wild spirits. The point of the Apprentice Boys' parade is that it is an annual political experiment of the most empirical kind. If the Catholics take the insult lying down, all is well. If they do not, then it is necessary to make them lie down. In August 1969, after nearly ten months of intense political excitement, the Bogsiders were not prepared to lie down.'

It all started with a few Catholic hooligans throwing marbles, stones and bottles at the tail of the procession as it passed one of the entrances to the Bogside. The Bogsiders withdrew behind barricades they had prepared and awaited the onslaught. The RUC with, behind them, gangs of Protestant hooligans anxious to follow the police into the Bogside and teach the Fenians a lesson, penetrated the Bogside and were showered with petrol bombs from the flat roof of a block of flats. The police withdrew, and the Bogsiders declared a 'Free Derry', flying the forbidden Free State Flag and defending their 'No Go' area with petrol bombs and paving stones while the RUC replied with CS gas. (It was, incidentally, the first time CS had been used in the UK.) In the three-day siege, in which B Specials as well as the RUC were involved, six people were killed and 87 injured; and on August 14th British troops were called out to assist the police in preserving law and order.

In Belfast, on the night of August 14/15th, rioting, burning and shooting broke out, and before it was all over ten civilians had been killed and 145 civilians and four policemen wounded by gunfire, which included fire from Shorland armoured cars, and about 150 houses, all Catholic, had been destroyed by fire. Twelve hours later the British Army went into action in Belfast too.

The Insight team quote a Unionist senator as complaining to the Stormont members' dining room at large that 'if only the bloody British Army hadn't come in, we'd have shot ten thousand of them by dawn', and make the point that it was Ian Paisley, and not the Catholics, who first compared the British Army with the SS. Initially, relations between the British Army and the Catholics, whom they were to a large extent protecting from the militant Protestants and Protestant B Specials, were extremely friendly, though in general the soldiers couldn't tell one side from the other, and didn't understand the first thing about the situation.

Lord Hunt—alleged to be descended on his mother's side from one of the thirteen Apprentice Boys who shut the gates against the Catholic forces—was appointed to look into the whole structure of the police forces in Ulster and Sir Leslie Scarman was selected to head a judicial tribunal of inquiry into the disorders.

Hunt reported that the RUC should be disarmed, reinforced with Catholics and run by a British chief officer, and the B Specials disbanded and replaced by a new citizens' militia—later known as the Ulster Defence Regiment—run from Whitehall.

The new police chief, Sir Arthur Young, himself described the effect of these recommendations, which were seen in the Protestant Shankill Road area, on the night of October 11/12th, his first evening in Belfast, as it happened. 'They rose in their wrath to demonstrate against the vile things that Hunt had said about their wonderful police. They came in their thousands down the Shankill Road, appearing like animals, as if by magic. Then they marched to burn the Catholics out of the nearby flats. And as they came down the street, they were halted by a cordon of exactly the police they were marching to defend. The British Army, which was also present, held its fire until twenty-two soldiers had been injured by weapons which included sub machine guns, all fired by Protestants. Then the troops opened fire, killing two Protestants and wounding a great many more.'

What has been described as the end of the British Army's 'honeymoon' with the Ulster Catholics came after a parade of Junior Orangemen at Easter 1970.

Easter—the anniversary of the Sinn Fein Rising in Dublin—is always an uneasy time in Ulster. April 1st, 1970 was Easter Tuesday. Despite warnings that parades into Belfast might cause trouble, a Junior Orange band marched straight up the Springfield Road, on the fringe of the Catholic Ballymurphy estate, and continued to march up and down the road for two hours, it is said, before leaving for a parade at Bangor. When the Orangemen—many of them Junior Lodge members in their early teens—returned to Belfast that night, their bands still playing sectarian ballads, sticks and bottles were thrown at them by an angry Catholic crowd, who also threw stones and bottles equally impartially at the British troops when they appeared in their lorries. The army didn't much like this, and the following night, when rioting again broke out in the Ballymurphy area, 600 troops supported by Saracen armoured cars moved into the district and used CS gas in the narrow streets on rioters and peaceable citizens alike, turning, as so often in the past, many of the don't-knows into violent, anti-British Nationalists.

In further riots during the preparations for the Orange parades on July the 12th, 1970—which had not been banned because everyone in Whitehall was more concerned with the General Election campaign than with events in Northern Ireland—the IRA break-away 'Provisionals' emerged for the first time as a factor in the ever more puzzling pattern, and six more lives were lost in shooting incidents, some of which went on for hours.

When the Tories ousted the Labour party in the General Election, and Maudling replaced Callaghan as Home Secretary, he paid a flying visit to Belfast almost immediately after the riots and his reaction, according to the Insight team, was to remark, as his plane gathered height on his way back to London: 'For God's sake bring me a large Scotch. What a bloody awful country.' Callaghan had already been making plans for direct rule of Ulster from Westminster. He couldn't see the point in all the panoply of Parliament in a place with a population no bigger than that of a few London boroughs. 'They don't need a prime minister over there,' he is reputed to have said. 'They need a good Mayor of Lewisham.'

The grisly details of more recent events are so fresh in everybody's minds that there is no need to reiterate them—the curfews, the pouring in of more and yet more troops, the raids for arms, the interrogations, the internments without trial, which led in turn to indiscriminate bomb explosions in busy shopping centres and crowded public houses, the murder of soldiers, the tarring and feathering of girls, the proliferation of private armies (the Ulster Defence Association, the Vanguard movement and so on), the burnt-out shops and homes, the barricades, the Whitehall 'initiative' which eventually came in March 1972, and prorogued Stormont, officially for a year but, many people believe, for ever.

'The Protestants have turned the other cheek so many times they must be dizzy,' a Catholic Belfast journalist remarked to me. And there seemed to be a genuine feeling in Belfast in May 1972 that only a handful of people on both sides wanted the violence to continue and that such continued Catholic support as there is for the IRA and the mass Protestant support of the Vanguard rallies and UDA demonstrations are the result of intimidation of one sort or another.

There is no doubt that sectarian bitterness on both sides has increased. The writing on the wall, which has always been a safety valve for Belfast's frustrated sectarian copy-writers, has become more menacing, and some of the Protestant hooligans take their sectarian ballads not from the traditional Orange song books but from more recent, unofficial efforts like *McKeague's Orange-Loyalist Songs, 1971*, which includes this particularly nasty effort (designed to be sung to the tune of 'I was Born under a Wandering Star'):

I was born under the Union Jack,
I was born under the Union Jack.
Do you know where Hell is?
Hell is up the Falls,
Kick all the Popeheads and we'll guard Derry's walls.

I was born under the Union Jack,
I was born under the Union Jack.
Falls was made for burning.
Taigs are made to kill,*
You've never seen a road like the Shankill.

* 'Taigs' or 'Taigues'—street slang for Catholics.

I was born under the Union Jack,
I was born under the Union Jack.
If Taigs were made for killing,
Then blood is made to flow,
You've never seen a place like Sandy Row.

I was born under the Union Jack,
I was born under the Union Jack,
If guns are made for shooting,
Then skulls were made to crack.
You've never seen a better Taig than with a bullet in his back.

John McKeague is not a member of the Orange Order—he was at one time, but drifted away from the movement when he moved from Bushmills to Belfast about ten years ago—and so far from approving this collection of 'Orange' songs, the Orange Order seemed to be horrified by it. 'Of course, we can't patent the word Orange,' an official said to me. 'And we can't stop anyone from using it.' Equally, I don't suppose they can stop the more militant of their members from singing such songs, whether they are 'official' or not. Mrs Isabella McKeague, 67-year-old mother of John McKeague, was burnt to death in her son's shop in Belfast in May 1971, but the collection had been openly on sale in Belfast a month before that. A copy of the song book was sent to Maudling along with a copy of the Prevention of Incitement to Hatred Act (N.I.) 1970, and McKeague was sent for trial. He claimed that he had published the collection not to incite hatred but 'for the purpose of fund-raising and to make a record of the popular Orange and Loyalist songs of the period' and was acquitted when the jury failed to agree. The collection is no longer on sale in the streets though I was able to buy a copy without much difficulty.

The winding up of Stormont clearly angered the Unionists and Orangemen, as the tense television appearances of Brian Faulkner (who replaced Chichester-Clark as Premier) and the two-day protest strike organized by Craig's Vanguard movement showed. An interview in the *Sunday Independent* of May

28th, 1972 with four men who claimed to be the men behind the Ulster Defence Association said that the UDA had 25,000 trained men in the greater Belfast area, and that they would shortly have another 7,000, mainly former British servicemen and including some commandos, and many more throughout the province. They were not interested in a United Ireland in any shape or form; their first demand is for a return of Stormont with increased powers.

When asked about their attitude to the security forces—the British Army, the RUC and the Ulster Defence Regiment—one man replied: 'Well, we appreciate the fact that they are only doing a job, but if the day ever came when we had to resist them, we would'. They also emphasized that although undoubtedly they have Orangemen in their ranks they had no interest at all in the Orange Order as such, and that what they stood for was loyalty to Ulster, not to the Protestant faith.

How do the Orangemen feel about the prospect of a United Ireland on some basis or other? One man replied: 'If it takes 18,000 well-trained and well-equipped British troops to contain half a million Catholics in Ulster' [again, note the typical Orange double-think—he had apparently forgotten that the troops were initially brought in to stop rioting caused mainly by militant *Protestant* mobs and marauding RUC men] 'and they are not all of them Nationalists by any means, how on earth could Jack Lynch's puny little army contain a million well-trained and well-armed Protestants?' (Another double-think, by the way; approximately half of that million are schoolchildren, far too young to fight, and of the adults, half are women, which reduces his army in one quick swipe to a quarter of a million, many of them old age pensioners.)

I put the question to Captain L. P. S. Orr, M.P., who is Imperial Grand Master of the Imperial Grand Orange Council of the World. It was just before the Westminster 'initiative' was announced, and I asked him what would be the role of the Orange Order in the unlikely event of Britain pulling out altogether and leaving Lynch to sort out the mess to the best of his ability: did he see the Orange Order as reversing roles with the IRA in an effort to make Lynch's administration of the country impossible? His reply, delivered in cold, measured tones, in that disarmingly gentle County Down accent, was chilling.

'No,' he said. 'I don't see that happening, and I'll tell you why. Because there's a million of us, and we've plenty of arms and we know where we can get plenty more, and we've plenty of money and plenty of friends all over the world. So we'd fight. And we'd probably win. And if we won we'd hand over a united Ireland to the Crown, as a present.

'But even in the unlikely event that we didn't win, it still wouldn't happen, and I'll tell you why. Because there'd be none of us left. We'd allow ourselves to be wiped out, every man, woman and child, like the Essenes, rather than submit to domination by a Dublin parliament.'

How could anybody achieve anything at a conference table faced with such intransigence? And yet the Orangemen know full well that only such intransigence will prevent them being sold down the river; that it was intransigence of just this intensity which saved them from submersion in a Catholic State in 1914. Can there be any final solution?

In a *Sunday Times* review of *Prejudice and Tolerance in Ulster* by Rosemary Harris, John Whale wrote: 'The book shows . . . the idleness of talk about Protestants and Catholics learning to live together. The best they could do in Dr Harris's village was learn to live apart—"to keep the latent hostility latent". Most places in Northern Ireland have a similarly mixed population; and in some of them the hostility is already patent. Neither shifting the border, nor demolishing it, can do anything for them; the two communities will still be side by side, hugging their animosities. This book . . . provides evidence for believing that the Irish Question is not just appallingly difficult, but in the end unanswerable.'

* * *

For the sake of my religion I was forced to leave my native home,
I've been a bold Defender and a member of the Church of Rome,
They swore I was a traitor and a leader of the Papist band,
For which I'm in cold irons, a convict in Van Diemen's land.

Right well do I remember when I was taken in New Ross
The day after the battle as the Green Mount Ferry I did cross,
The guards they did surround me and my bundle searched upon the spot.
And there they found my green coat, my pike, two pistols and some shot.

The reason that they banished me, the truth I mean to tell you here,
Because I was head leader of Father Murphy's Shelmaliers,
And for being a Roman Catholic I was trampled on by Harry's breed,
For fighting in defence of my God, my country and my creed.

—From *The Banished Defender*, a ballad of 1798.

XVIII

Orangeism Outside Ulster

Before considering whether there can ever be any final solution, or speculating as to what future, if any, now lies ahead of the Orange Order, it is interesting to look at what has happened to the various off-shoots of the Order transplanted by Ulster emigrants and missionaries all over the world. There is a Lodge in Canada which now consists almost entirely of Red Indian stock; there are fifteen lodges in Ghana which no longer include a single white face. These latter were founded by Ulster missionaries last century. The missionaries have long since departed but Africa's all-black Orangemen still meet and march, wearing orange collarettes and cuffs, exactly like the Orangemen of Ulster; their banners depict King Billy crossing the Boyne and carry mottos like 'No Surrender' and 'Remember Londonderry 1689'.

The Orange Order is very strong in Eastern Canada; and has strayed thence across the border into the United States, where the Institution now numbers about 3,000 members in 54 Lodges, 58 Ladies' Lodges and 12 Black Preceptories. In Australia, active membership has dropped from 40,000 in the 'twenties to about 2,000 today, and most of the members are in their fifties or older. The order has Lodges in New Zealand, in England, Wales and Scotland—notably in the industrial North and Midlands and in the Glasgow area—as well as in the Republic of Ireland.

Dealing first with the Republic, the Institution's headquarters there is, for all practical purposes, a suburban bungalow in Blackrock, just outside Dublin, where the Grand Secretary, Edward McGuigan, administers its affairs on a part-time, amateur basis. There is what used to be an Orange Hall—now known non-committally as 'The Protestant Hall'—

in Northumberland Road, Dublin, but the Orange Order has so little use for it that the ground floor has been let to a charitable organization devoted to the relief of cancer. The last public parade held in the Republic was in 1936, and even then it was merely a procession from the main Orange headquarters, Fowler Hall in Parnell Square, to Amiens Street railway station, where the Orangemen were entraining for Belfast to join the Twelfth of July 'walk'. Since then, although a contingent under the Dublin and Wicklow banner always marches in Belfast on July 12th, the Orangemen make their way to the railway station singly and in mufti; the decorations are not donned, nor the banners unfurled, until they are safely across the border.

Mr McGuigan reckons that there are about 1,000 members in the Republic—not including Donegal, for some reason—and about one-third of these are in Black Preceptories as well. They are thinly spread through Cavan, Monaghan, Dublin, Wicklow and Leitrim.

It is perhaps significant that their principal building, the Fowler Hall, is now rented to the 'Fenian' Republican Government and is used by a branch of the Department of Posts and Telegraphs. The Institution still attracts a few new members—about twenty young men, aged between 24 and 30, in the last three years—but it has tended to become more and more a charitable institution and less and less a militant religious organization.

There has been some anti-Protestant feeling in the Republic since the current troubles in the North started in 1969, and this has tended to give the Protestant community in some areas a cohesion it formerly lacked. A few Protestant church windows have been broken, and a handful of Protestants have received threatening letters. Where this has happened the indignation has come not so much from the Protestants as from their Catholic neighbours. A Catholic newspaper proprietor who lives near the border in Cavan told me that the local Protestant clergyman had complained to him that some of his church windows had been smashed by hooligans. 'Did you go to the police about it?' he asked. 'No, I didn't bother,' the clergyman said. 'I didn't want to make trouble.' 'Well, you should go,' the newspaper proprietor said. 'You've got exactly the same rights in the community as anybody else, and you should insist on them. In fact, if you don't go to the police about it, I will.' And did.

In England the headquarters of the Orange Institution is in Liverpool, and there are Lodges in Manchester, Birmingham, Bootle, Derby, Corby, Leeds, Sheffield, Cheshire and North Wales, as well as in London, Portsmouth and Sussex. A realistic membership figure would probably be around 10,000—largely working class, as in Ulster—but the principal 'walk' is in Liverpool, where traditionally it has always led to riots and disturbances. Contingents of Orangemen from Liverpool march in Belfast and Glasgow; and conversely, there are contingents of Belfast and Derry Orangemen marching in Liverpool and Glasgow.

It is my impression that in the south-east of England the Orange Institution has developed (or degenerated, according to how you look at it) into a cross between a debating society and a benevolent institution; in the North and Midlands, as in Scotland, it has retained its sectarian character. I asked a Belfast Orangeman living in London what exactly was the function of a society dedicated to the maintenance of the 'constitution' and the Protestant Ascendancy in a part of the British Isles where the constitution was not in any grave danger and where the Catholics hardly numbered more than five or six per cent of the population. 'You're talking about English Catholics,' he said. 'But what about all the Spanish and Italian waiters that are pouring into this country? Not to mention the Catholic Irish and the Pakistanis and the Chinese and the Japs. I'd say the Protestant Ascendancy is in grave danger in England at the moment.'

Another Orangeman—English this time—answered the same question by pointing out that the Protestant Ascendancy was in grave danger because of the wave of ecumenism that was sweeping over England. 'Make no mistake about it,' he said, 'we believe in ecumenism. But only among members of the Reformed Church. There is a very real need for our Institution, at the moment, to ward off any efforts to come to closer terms with the Church of Rome.' He added: 'Mind you, we have nothing against individual Catholics as such. Our quarrel is with the Church. We're determined to resist domination by the Roman Church.' I asked him whether he really believed that there was any serious danger of the Roman Church dominating England in this day and age. 'I do,' he said solemnly. And the discussion ended there.

In Scotland, the Orange Order has always been strong and it follows the same sectarian pattern as Orangeism in the industrial North and Midlands of England. There is a strong attachment between the Northern Irish and the Scots (many of the Northern Irish are descended from Scots Lowland planters; others are Celts who left Ireland for Scotland around or before the Roman conquest of England—the Scotii, as the Romans called them—and later returned to Ulster as Planters) and it shows up in all sorts of ways; the fact that the junior members of the Ulster Defence Association choose to call themselves 'the Tartan Gangs' for instance. And in Glasgow the ancient rivalry of the Catholics and Protestants—which is a rivalry, as it is in Belfast, for jobs and houses far more than on ideological grounds—now expresses itself in the faction fights between the supporters of two football teams, Celtic (Catholic) and Rangers (Protestant and given to Orange banners). One fighting gang of hooligans in Glasgow was always known as 'the Billy Boys', a reference to King William of Pious and Immortal Memory.

2

It is a fact often overlooked that because of a combination of the Irish tradition of mass emigration and the Irish religious fervour the Catholic Church throughout the English-speaking world is for all practical purposes the *Irish* Catholic church. And, because the Irish, Protestant and Catholic alike, tend to take their sectarianism with them wherever they go, the Irish Protestants who emigrated tended to keep up their association with the Orange Order and to form Loyal Orange Lodges on whatever alien soil they found themselves.

In Australia, about a quarter of the population is of Irish descent. Australia's most famous folk hero is Ned Kelly, the bushranger, whose name unmistakably stamps his origins. First as convicts and later as free settlers, the Irish have exerted a powerful influence on the growth and character of the colony.

New South Wales was established in 1788 and within two years a number of Irish political prisoners had been deported there, following the Rising of 1798.

The first Orange Lodge was founded just 47 years after the colony itself. In 1835—the period when the Orange Order was in trouble in England—a Private Andrew Alexander, of the largely Irish 50th Queen's Own Regiment, arrived in New South Wales with regimental Lodge warrant No. 1780 sewn into his tunic. The Lodge met unofficially in a room above a printing press in Sydney, and gradually lost its military status. In 1845 Warrant No. 1780 became Sydney No. 1 and Private Alexander its first Worshipful Grand Master.

Several other Lodges opened around that period but closed down again as their members took off in the rush to the gold-fields. Those which continued to meet did so behind closed doors and there were frequent skirmishes between the Orange-men and their hereditary Catholic enemies. Irish priests organized hurling matches to coincide with the Orange processions on the Twelfth and in Melbourne in the 1840s an Irish priest called Patrick Geoghegan, who was responsible for erecting a new Catholic chapel, was shot in the street by disapproving Orangemen. In 1853, at the goldfields of Bendigo, a party of Orangemen who were celebrating the Twelfth were set upon by Catholics who attacked them with pick-handles and other weapons.

When, in 1868, at Clontarf, a suburb of Sydney, an Irish Fenian called O'Farrell tried to assassinate the visiting Prince Alfred, Duke of Edinburgh, feelings ran very high among the Protestant community, which flocked to join the Orange Order in protest. Membership increased by 30,000 in a few months. A Protestant Association was also formed throughout Australia which was dedicated to excluding Catholics from all positions of power or influence.

It was not uncommon to see advertisements which stated 'No Catholic need apply' and in suburban streets children chanted (as they do in Belfast today) 'Protestant, Protestant, ring the bell; Catholic, Catholic, go to hell'.

The anti-conscription campaign led by the Irish Roman Catholic Archbishop of Melbourne, Dr Mannix, caused much bitter feeling and threatened the unity of the country during World War I. Many firms refused to employ Catholics during the war and the Orange Order boasted that every time Dr Mannix opened his mouth the Institution enrolled hundreds of new members.

In the 'twenties Orange action in Australia was largely limited to issuing manifestoes pointing out the high proportion of Catholic candidates in the Australian Labour Party—60 out of 89 in 1922, for example.

But as Australia grew more affluent the Irish connection—and its religious overtones—began to diminish in importance, and the Orange membership started to fall away. In New South Wales today there are fewer than 100 lodges, and active membership, as I have said, has dropped from around the 40,000 mark in the 'twenties to fewer than 2,000. Most of the members are in their fifties and they complain that no new members are joining. They still meet once a month in dingy hired halls. Headquarters in most states are in unfashionable inner suburbs, though Melbourne is an exception with a headquarters in fashionable Elizabeth street; this HQ has a library and an information centre. Typical of the books and pamphlets available are such titles as *The Vatican Against Europe*, *The Shadow of Rome* and *The Ecumenical Mirage*. Recently the Grand Secretary of the Loyal Orange Institution of Victoria has been in controversy with Dr Ramsay, the Archbishop of Canterbury, over his 'continual seeking of closer association with the Roman Catholic Church'.

In recent years the Lodges have been contributing to a Northern Ireland Relief Fund, to help bereaved Ulster Protestant families. Other activities include the provision of homes for the aged, fighting for free, compulsory secular State schools, supporting Protestant members of Parliament and a recent campaign against a suggestion to drop the Union Jack from the Australian flag.

For the most part, however, the Orange Lodges are scarcely mentioned in the newspapers. Occasionally the march of the Twelfth is reported; the last reference to the Order in the *Sydney Herald*, for example, was in 1968, when the July procession rated a 1½″ single column entry.

In addition to the Orange Institution (in fact there are two in Australia, one in New South Wales and one covering the remainder of Australia, both claiming pure descent from Private Andrew Alexander's Warrant), there is an Ulster Society in New South Wales which has 23 clubs throughout Australia. Its president, George Nelson, who is also an Orangeman, claims that it stands for the 'permanent union between Northern Ireland and Australia to maintain the power and the best traditions of the British Commonwealth' and to maintain an interest in Ulster national life. Some members of the Ulster Society and of the Australian Orange Lodges have indicated that they are prepared to go back to Northern Ireland and fight if necessary, and the same applies to Orange communities in Canada, in Glasgow and parts of Britain.

Mr John H. Gowans, a printer, of Annandale, is Worshipful Grand Master of the Loyal Orange Institution of New South Wales. Recently he told reporters that he was concerned to see that none of the money collected in Australia for the relief of Ulster Protestants would ever fall into Catholic hands. 'God forbid that we are bigoted,' he said. 'We only want to keep our country Protestant. We have no ambitions to change Italy or France or Spain. They can remain Catholic. We didn't oppose the Pope coming out here to see his constituents. We are just against unity.'

3

In Canada, as in Australia, the Orange Order was first introduced by units of the British Army which held Orange Warrants.

Montreal had an Irish Warrant to form Lodges as early as 1825 and issued its own local Warrants under this authority. The first Lodge in Nova Scotia was organized at Halifax in 1847 and by 1848 a total of 83 Lodges were in existence, nine of them in the predominantly Catholic area around Montreal. By 1870 there were over 1,000 Lodges and the membership of the Order totalled 100,000 out of a population of about four millions.

With the opening up of the country and the improvement in transport facilities, Orangeism spread and although some of the smaller Lodges were swallowed up in larger ones the movement as a whole continued to spread, reaching its peak between the two world wars. Before World War I, the Orange institution had 250,000 members; after World War I, that figure may have gone as high as 300,000. Now it is down to about 100,000 and dropping steadily.

A curious feature of the situation is that, although the American War of Independence was partly the work of Scotch-Irish immigrants disaffected with England, Orangeism in Canada has always dedicated itself to resisting all attempts to sever Canada from Britain.

Ogle Robert Gowan, a member of a distinguished Irish family to whom Orangeism meant primarily the retention of the British connection, was one of the prime movers in the development of the Order in Canada. He went there in 1828 and was a founder member of both the British League and the United Empire Association. Gowan gathered his Orangemen from the 36,000 inhabitants of what is now the Ontario district. He formed the Grand Lodge of British America at Brockville, Ontario, on January 1st, 1830, and is generally regarded as the founder of the Orange movement in Canada. He held a Warrant issued by the Duke of Cumberland and was Grand Master for eighteen years.

The Order in Canada consists of one Sovereign Grand Lodge and eleven Provincial Grand Lodges. Then there are, as in Northern Ireland, District Lodges and Primary or Private Lodges. As in Northern Ireland, the Orange Order has produced inner affiliated organizations; one such is the Royal

Scarlet Chapter, a purely Canadian offshoot dating back to 1843. There were Orange cadets marching as early as 1853, and the Cadets became the Orange Young Britons in 1869. There has been an association of Canadian Derry Apprentice Boys since 1861. The Loyal True Blue Association, another offshoot of the Orange Order, claims to be the first such organization in Canada to admit women as members. And a Ladies' Orange Benevolent Association came into being in 1889.

And, of course, Canada has its Blackmen—the Royal Black Knights, formed under a Supreme Grand Black Chapter instituted in 1874. In Canada the Blacks hold their celebrations on August 12th, the anniversary of the Relief of Londonderry.

As early as 1833, Ogle Gowan suggested the formation of an Imperial Grand Orange Council of the World. This organization held its first meeting in Belfast in 1866 and since then has met every three years; more than half of the Council's dignatories have been Canadians.

Throughout the years Orangemen have been prominent on school boards, municipal councils and in the Canadian parliament. The Orange voting strength has always been a factor to be considered in Canadian politics, and in the early days of Canada's parliament it used to be said that 'the Battle of the Boyne was the number one issue' in most election campaigns. The same was true in Newfoundland.

In the province of Quebec there has always been a solid, French-speaking Roman Catholic bloc of voters strongly opposed by the English-speaking Protestants spurred on by the Orange movement. Any extension of the use of the French language outside Quebec has always been vigorously opposed by the Orange Order.

The Order is also against the use of public funds to support private schools, except in areas where there are no public schools, and has opposed efforts of the Catholic Church to secure concessions for its separate schools.

The Orangemen helped to pioneer Canada and their Lodge halls frequently became social centres for pioneer communities. For many years the big social event of the 'fall' season was the oyster supper and dance in the local Orange hall on November 5th, to celebrate Guy Fawkes Night. But the big day of the year in Canada as in Northern Ireland, is July 12th, the anniversary of the Battle of the Boyne. A Canadian Orangeman told me that one former Grand Secretary of the Order had his home and office telephones and his car registration plates all numbered 1690 'to make sure he would never forget the date'. I can believe the story but not the explanation; no Orangeman is ever likely to forget the date of the Battle of the Boyne. It is far more likely that he was merely wearing his colours, so to speak, on his sleeve.

On the Glorious Twelfth, the Canadian Orangemen, led by one of their number mounted on a white charger and wearing 17th century costume, traditionally marched to the music of fife and drum, behind flags and banners and under arches of evergreens decorated with ribbons and mottoes, past homes and buildings adorned with flags and bunting. There would be loyal speeches and shouts of 'No surrender' and, in the evening, banquets with all the loyal Orange toasts and Orange ballads and 'Rule Britannia'. In country districts, community picnics were a popular way of celebrating the Twelfth.

But in Canada, as elsewhere, the day did not always pass off peacefully. In 1827 the Orange celebrations at Kingston, Ontario, were followed by riots in which several people were injured. There were similar outbreaks of violence in New Brunswick and other districts and in 1836, Sir Francis Head, Lieutenant Governor of Upper Canada, was debating whether the best method of securing tranquillity in the province would not be the voluntary—or perhaps, if necessary, the compulsory—dissolution of the Institution. In 1839, his successor, Sir George Arthur, requested the Toronto City Council to ban the annual parade. Mayor John Powell refused and a monster walk was held. It all has a sadly familiar ring. In 1842 the Government passed the Party Processions Act, aimed at ending Orange parades, and a Secret Societies Act which disqualified Orangemen from holding public office or serving on juries. On July 12th of that year the Orange Hall at Kingston was attacked. Riots in New Brunswick in 1849 resulted in at least one death. But the legislation aimed at suppressing the Order actually strengthened it, and when the Processions Act was repealed in 1850 the Orangemen celebrated with a two-mile parade through Toronto, which by then had a twenty per cent Catholic population. As late as 1859 Orangemen were barred from joining the police force or acting on juries, so that although they claimed to have no aim more partisan than the maintenance of the constitution and the link with the mother country, it is clear that the Government, in Canada as in Britain, were highly nervous of the way in which members of the Order in responsible positions might attempt to achieve that aim.

But in Canada there were real battles—as well as sham battles and riots—to be fought, and there as elsewhere the Orangemen proved doughty fighters. In 1866, when the country was half-heartedly invaded by Irish-Americans, Orange Lodges marched as military units to Lime Ridge to defeat the invaders and the annual meeting of the Grand Lodge had to be postponed because nearly every Grand Lodge officer and about 1,000 members were away 'at the frontier'.

The first Orange Lodge west of the Great Lakes was founded in 1870 in the cabin of a schooner anchored in Manitoba's Assiniboine River. The members of the Lodge included soldiers from Ontario who had gone west to suppress Louis Riel's revolutionaries, who had taken up arms against the Canadian Government and were trying to establish a republic on the banks of the Red River. The Riel Rebellion gave the Canadian Orange Order one of its martyrs, Thomas Scott, and his name now appears on many Lodge banners. Another martyr was Thomas Lett Hackett, shot to death in Montreal on July 12th, 1877, on his way from an Orange meeting; the murderer was never found, but was presumed to be a Catholic Fenian.

But despite the Orangemen's readiness to take up arms in defence of the Crown, the Crown and its advisers remained very chary of openly acknowledging the support of the movement. In 1860 the Prince of Wales—later King Edward VII—visited Canada and the Orangemen planned a full turn-out, with banners and regalia, in his honour. However, the Duke of Newcastle, the Prince's private secretary, refused to allow the Prince to land either at Kingston or at Belleville where he knew there would be large Orange parades. And in Toronto, where the Orangemen had erected a vast arch—a replica of the Bishop's Gate in Londonderry—the Duke ordered a re-routing of the march so that it would not pass under the arch. But Orangemen are made of tenacious material; they retaliated by building another Orange arch over the railway tracks at Aurora, just north of Toronto, through which the royal train *had* to pass. The demonstrations that July were the largest on record.

Canada's 1914–18 war effort was directed by an Orangeman, Sir Sam Hughes, who was Minister of Militia and who had Canada's first contingent of fighting men in England within ten weeks of the outbreak of war. It has been estimated that 60,000 of the men in the Canadian Expeditionary Force were Orangemen. During World War II, the Orange Lodges were recruiting centres and throughout both wars some Lodges continued to meet regularly on the battlefields.

In recent years the Orange Order in Canada, like that in Australia, has concerned itself with such matters as an attempt to secure the retention of the Union Jack in the national flag of Canada, and with social services—the provision of children's homes, homes for old people, and insurance schemes; and although the Orangemen still march on July 12th, the movement is running out of steam, and membership, particularly among the young, is rapidly falling away. In 1972, 4,000 Orangemen marched from Queen's Park past the City Hall to the Toronto Island ferry docks. One of the marchers was asked by a *Toronto Star* reporter what it was all about. "It was for King Billy, who won a fight,' he answered. 'It was something about the Irish, but I don't really remember.'

Recent events in Northern Ireland have been very fully covered in Canadian newspapers; the Canadian edition of *Time* magazine led on Ulster week after week around the time of Derry's Bloody Sunday early in 1972. And the Catholic Church is still the same sort of bogey to Protestant Canadians as it is to the Ulster Protestants. I talked with a Canadian Orangewoman who was on holiday in England while I was writing this book. Admittedly, she is getting on in years and her views may not be typical, but she was quite adamant that 'if the Orange Order wasn't there, the priests would tell the people who to vote for and in no time at all Rome would be running Canada—and we all know what would happen then'.

4

Probably because of the massive Catholic emigration to the United States around the time of the Famine, which gave Catholics the upper hand among the Irish communities, the Orange Order has never had anything like the same influence in the United States as it has in Canada, Australia and New Zealand, and has always been far more concerned with social welfare than with sectarianism.

There are Lodges in New York, Pennsylvania, Massachusetts, New Jersey, California, Delaware, Connecticut, Florida, Illinois, Maine, Michigan and Ohio, with a total membership of about 3,000, men and women. The Loyal Orange Institution has about 54 Lodges and the Loyal Orange Ladies Institution about 58; there is also a Royal Black Preceptory with a total of 12 Lodges. Most of the Lodges in the United States celebrate the Twelfth, but more often by picnics and small, local parades than by anything resembling Toronto's two-mile parades.

The movement is governed by a Supreme Grand Lodge instituted in 1868, which is affiliated with the Imperial Grand Orange Council of the world. The Lodge meets every two years in different cities. The aims and objects differ somewhat from those of the Orange Order elsewhere; in the United States, according to Walter C. Wilson, the Grand Secretary, writing from the Supreme Grand Lodge, the Order upholds 'the cause whose object is to support the principles and precepts of the Protestant religion as founded in the Holy Scripture [which is very different from maintaining the Protestant Ascendancy] and to maintain free public schools'.

5

One thread runs endlessly through the mass of literature turned out by Orange Institutions all over the world: it is found in its most concentrated form, perhaps, in a pamphlet published by the Grand Lodge of England in 1917 in what I would describe as a beige cover unless it could be faded Orange. This pamphlet, written by the Rev Louis A. Ewart, D.Sc., Grand Secretary of the Grand Orange Lodge of England, is called *What is the Orange Order?*

In a paragraph headed 'Why the Prince Came', he writes: 'It may be asked why was the Prince of Orange asked to become King, and why the necessity for such an Institution as the Orange Body? King James II, who was a Romanist, had endeavoured to subvert and extirpate the Protestant Religion and the laws and liberties of the kingdom. It was found impossible to maintain civil and religious liberty so long as a Romanist occupied the throne. The Prince came, by invitation, to maintain the Protestant Religion and the Liberties of England, and to secure the Throne for ever against Rome'.

The following paragraph, headed 'Important Act of Parliament' goes on: 'The Act of Settlement of 1688 says: "Whereas it hath been found by experience that it is inconsistent with the safety and welfare of this Protestant Kingdom to be governed by a Papist Prince, or by any King or Queen marrying a Papist—it is enacted that all who may be reconciled to the Church of Rome, or hold communion with the Pope, or shall marry a Papist, shall be for ever excluded from the Crown and Government of England." To maintain this act of Settlement and subsequent Acts confirming the same, is one of the great objects of the Orange Order.'

Under the heading 'Necessity of the Orange Order' the writer continues: 'The principles of the Church of Rome are the same today as they were in the time of James II. The treasonable societies and conspiracies in England and Ireland have all arisen from the teachings of the Romish Church. Even in the present day, wherever it has the power, it will not tolerate a Protestant. It is unceasing in its efforts to undermine the settlement of our Protestant Throne and Constitution, to corrupt our Protestant Faith and to establish again in England the power and authority of the Church of Rome. In all the conspiracies and secret societies in Ireland, Canada and elsewhere, the Orange Order has stood firm to its loyal and Protestant principles, and has proved itself one of the most useful organizations for preserving law and order, and one of the most formidable opponents of the machinations of Rome.'

As it happened, I read the above, plus a lot of other material supplied to me by the Orange Order in Ireland, England and elsewhere, during a brief holiday in Provençe. Some of it, in fact, I read in Orange, looking up from time to time to watch lizards basking in the sun on the remains of one of the finest Roman theatres in Europe. It was hard to imagine any connection, however tenuous, between this ancient, sun-baked, liberal centre of civilization and the bitter brown bricks of Belfast. But—although few Orangemen are aware of it—their Order takes its name from this ancient Roman town, Orange or *Arausio*, near the uppermost limit of the first Roman province in Transalpine Gaul, the *Provincia* from which Provençe derives its name. Orange became a separate principality in Carolingian times as a result of the feudal disintegration of the Kingdom of Arles.

Nor would the Orangemen be too pleased to learn that the titles of those early Princes of Orange were ratified by the Holy Roman Emperor himself. The Orange succession passed in the 16th century to the House of Nassau, which held scattered possessions in the Netherlands and Germany, and William the Silent—an ancestor of King Billy's—became the first Prince of Orange-Nassau. The Orange title has been retained in Holland; as recently as 1908 Queen Wilhelmina decreed that her descendants should be styled princes and princesses of Orange-Nassau.

The tiny principality of Orange was seized by France, and restored to the Orange-Nassau family, and seized again and restored again over the years. In 1623, Maurice of Nassau fortified it as a tiny islet of Protestantism in a great sea of Catholics, but before the end of the 17th century it had finally passed into French hands and all that remained of the old connection was the word Orange in the family name of the Dutch Stadtholders, which passed with King Billy to Ulster and to the Orange Order.

Seventeen miles south of Orange is Avignon, where the palace of the Popes was built during the Great Schism. It is a curious feature of the Orangeman's faith that he appears quite incapable of grasping the fact that even if, in his view, it became corrupt, worldly and over-weighed down with accretions of all kinds, nevertheless it is to the Roman Church that we owe the preservation of a thin thread of civilization and learning through the Dark Ages, and that it is the fact that it was the *Roman* Church, run from its headquarters in the Lateran Palace, one of the ancient palaces of the Caesars, which enabled it to maintain that thread. Because Rome was still associated in men's minds with the idea of civilization, and was regarded as the natural centre of an empire. There probably would not even have been any Christian religion to reform if the Bishops of Rome had not taken over in some measure the mantle of the Caesars, and maintained some sort of continuity with the great days of the Roman Empire. And yet the mainspring and driving force of the Orange Order, for all its talk of civil and religious liberty, has always been, explicitly, antagonism to Rome and everything it believes that Rome stands for.

It would be difficult, I think, to improve on the following as a conclusion to this chapter on Orangeism abroad; it is taken from a pamphlet published by the Orange Institution of Victoria, New South Wales, Australia, and entitled *Why I belong to the Orange Institution.*

> 'If you believe the Roman Catholic Church still clings to the intolerant claim of infallibility and a restoration of temporal power, which claims have never been aband-

oned; if you believe that it is not the lack of inclination that prevents a return to the oppression of the Dark Ages, as judged by those countries where it is still in the ascendancy, and if you believe these assumptions to be disastrous to your country, you should be an Orangeman'.

*   *   *

Then said King William to his men,
After the French departed,
'I'm glad indeed that none of ye
Seemed to be faint-hearted:
So sheathe your swords and rest awhile,
In time we'll follow after'.
These words he uttered with a smile,
The day he crossed the water.

Come let us all with heart and voice,
Applaud our lives' defender,
Who at the Boyne his valour show'd,
And made his foe surrender.
To God above the praise we'll give
Both now and ever after;
And bless the glorious memory
Of William, who cross'd the water.

—From *The Boyne Water*,
a traditional Orange ballad.

XIX

Jesuits in the Jam?

Can there be any solution? And if a solution can be found, or patched up, or imposed on the present ghastly mess, what will become of the Orange Order? Will it develop into a mild debating society, an association of old comrades who will meet occasionally for the sake of old times and discuss the stirring events of the late 'sixties and 'seventies? Or will it stiffen its sinews and continue to fight the good fight against the encroachments of a church that is turning the most undignified somersaults in its efforts to hold on to a few of its rapidly disappearing adherents in a world in which the telly-pundits have long since taken over from the priests and the prelates?

But you will never convince an Orangeman of that possibility any more than you will convince him that a Dublin-based parliament would now be prepared to give the Ulster Protestants all the guarantees they might require to allay their fears about integration into an all-Ireland state. Or rather, he will believe that if Dublin did offer such guarantees it would withdraw them again as soon as the Border was gone.

I happened to be in Northern Ireland when the report of a working party under the Rev Enda McDonagh, Professor of Theology at the Seminary of Maynooth, was published, recommending certain changes in the Irish Constitution and the laws of the Republic. These included deleting the religious preamble to the Constitution; deleting the sub-section recognizing the 'special position' of the Catholic Church as the religion of the majority of the Irish people; deleting the article which prohibits divorce legislation; amending the laws which prohibit the importation and sale of contraceptives, and the dissemination of information about birth-control; and removing a section of the Adoption Act to allow partners in mixed marriages to adopt children legally. I asked several members of the Orange Institution whether the fact that this recommendation, coming as it did from a working party headed by a Catholic priest who is also a Professor of Theology, did not indicate that the winds of change were howling through the corridors of the Vatican. The reaction was that this was all window-dressing. In the first place, it probably wouldn't be implemented—'Rome would never let them put that through', one man said—and there was a feeling that even if it were implemented there was nothing to stop the Republic from changing the Constitution yet again, as soon as the Border was removed. 'They've changed their Constitution once already, in less than fifty years,' one man remarked to me. 'We've had ours ever since 1688. That's almost three hundred years, and we're determined to see to it that it's not changed for the next three hundred years either.'

Equally, the Catholics do not believe that there is any motive in the minds of the members of all the Protestant Associations and armies other than a determination to keep them down. When I pointed out that a spokesman for the Ulster Defence Association had specifically stated in an interview in the *Sunday Independent* that all the UDA wanted was loyalty to Ulster, not to the Protestant faith, and had even made the point that loyalty is not Protestantism, the reaction was that they were only saying that for effect.

There is also growing evidence, after fifty years of almost monolithic unity, of a split—or even more than one split—within the fabric of the Orange Order. Mr William Craig, the Vanguard leader, has not always been consulted by the UDA, which he set up a steering committee to control; the UDA itself is concerned with fringe elements 'climbing on the band-wagon' and turning out in masks and para-military uniforms, but acting independently of the UDA; and a new force has recently emerged, also largely ex-servicemen, known as the Orange Volunteers and rapidly growing in strength, who first marched in Belfast in June, 1972.

Many Ulster Catholics still believe that the Orangemen swear a secret oath to do all in their power to exterminate the Catholics of Ireland. Nobody trusts anybody else in the current situation in Ulster. The reason why the Civil Rights movement went on marching, even after Stormont had promised the reforms which had been demanded, is that the marchers didn't believe that Stormont had the slightest intention of implementing the reforms. The reason why some Orangemen are threatening to take up arms is that they don't trust Westminster. We sometimes forget that there are three nations involved in the affair—if you can call a people so diverse in their origins as the British a nation—not two. Or perhaps there is just one; perhaps the basic unit, after all, is the British Isles, which the Irish—having proved their ability to exist, and even to prosper, under native management—might be tempted to rejoin on some sort of federal basis. But whether even this would be acceptable to the Orangemen is another matter. One reason, as I have said, for their intransigence is that they have never trusted the British not to do a deal with Dublin behind their backs. Their loyalty, as they constantly emphasize, is to the Crown, not to any politicians, or any political party, in Britain.

At the same time, now that it has all come out into the open, Britain cannot possibly allow them to have what they want and continue to be an integral part of the United Kingdom. For what they still want is a tight little Protestant state, in which they will have the say-so as regards jobs and houses, and in which the disaffected rebel Catholic Nationalists will be kept in their place by an armed police force, all or almost all of whom are Orangemen—the B Specials, in fact.

In an issue of the *Police Review*, early in 1972, Sgt. P. J. Welling appealed to the Police Federation and the Home Office to press for legislation prohibiting a serving police officer from taking an oath in any secret society. He was referring to Freemasons, but there is no doubt that there is a strong feeling among the British police that membership of any society which involves any sort of oath or promise not to divulge matters which occur 'in Lodge', except to other members of that society could interfere with the 'impartiality and solidarity' of the police force. And certainly, the British Government would never tolerate a return of the B Specials in any shape or form any more than it could tolerate the IRA in Ulster.

So, if they don't get what they want, what will the Orangemen do? Will they, as Captain Orr suggested, fight to the last man? I met quite a few Orangemen who felt that this was a distinct possibility, but many more who felt that such a suggestion was largely a political bluff. 'The Orangeman is a tough fighter,' one man said to me, 'but he is also a hard worker. Whatever we may say while the matter is still in doubt, I think if it came to the pinch we'd make the best of whatever situation we found ourselves in. And if we did find ourselves forced to go in under a Dublin parliament, I think most of us would accept it, and get what we could out of it. We've all good business heads on us, too. They'd probably find that within ten years we'd be running all their industries for them down there.'

There is a widespread feeling that Craig's massive Vanguard rallies are also very largely a bluff. Most people feel that the numbers supposedly attending these rallies are grossly exaggerated; the *Irish Times* did an analysis from an aerial survey of the crowds which turned up to welcome one of the ships used in the Larne gun-running, the *Clydevalley*, back to Belfast Lough—a Craig promotion—and found the real attendance was far less than had been estimated.

There is a feeling, too, that currently the Orange Order lacks leadership, certainly leadership of the calibre of Sir Edward Carson and Sir James Craig, and that without leadership of such calibre in Ulster it has not much of a chance of making a successful stand in an increasingly liberal world. Dr Paisley, ever a man to be reckoned with, has changed his tune, if not his spots, in recent years and has been playing what might be described as the working-class solidarity ticket rather than the old Orange one. It is doubtful if he would support any movement that would inevitably lead to further destruction and unemployment.

I quoted earlier the anonymous *Times Literary Supplement* reviewer of Robert Kee's *The Green Flag* who made the point that somebody must decide whether the Ulster Protestants are a separate 'nation' or not; and if so, accord them some support in their determination not to be absorbed in an Irish Republic, and if not, do whatever can be done to condition them into acceptance of their lot. He concludes the review as follows:

> Some explanation is required of the fact that the Ulster Protestants alone of all the invaders, planters and settlers of Ireland have not been drawn into the mainstream of Irishness. Are they a peculiarly recalcitrant national minority, or are they extra-national? John Redmond said: 'Irish nationalists can never be assenting parties to the mutilation of the Irish nation; Ireland is a unit . . . the two nation theory is to us an abomination and a blasphemy.' Strong epithets, however, do not settle the question of the theory's truth. Nor is its truth settled by the superior attraction for the cultivated mind of the winding caravan of Irish nationalism with its poets, assassins, scholars, crackpots, parlour revolutionaries, windbags, mythopoeic essayists, traitors, orators from the scaffold, men of action, emerging from so long and so great suffering of the people to impart an almost mystical quality to their often futile and often brutal deeds—the superior attraction of that to the hard, assertive, obsessive, successful self-reliance of the Ulster Protestant which has about as much poetical imagination as is contained in a bowler hat.

I have tried, in this book, to answer the question posed at the beginning of that extract; and I believe that the relative unattractiveness 'to the cultivated mind' of the Orangeman is a factor in the 'siege' mentality which has contributed to the present situation. When I was researching an earlier book, an Ulster Unionist M.P. at Stormont put this very bluntly. 'The Ulsterman is basically unattractive, both to the Southern English and to the Southern Irish,' he said. 'The Southern English get on far better with the Southern Irish than they do with us. That's why we're always terrified that the English are going to do a deal behind our backs with those people down south.'

And if Britain ever does do a deal with those people behind the Orangeman's back—or to his face, for that matter—the reviewer's final reference to 'as much poetical imagination as is contained in a bowler hat' might well explain why it may prove extremely difficult to condition some Ulstermen to acceptance of their lot, whatever that turns out to be. For whatever it turns out to be can no longer include any possibility of a restoration of the *status quo*—the Orangemen 'walking' on the Twelfth with their Lambeg drums to demonstrate their ancient ascendancy and the B Specials handy to keep the 'Taigs' in their place.

Whatever happens, my own guess is that the Orange Order will probably survive the present situation on two, or even three, levels. I imagine the Blackmen will disengage themselves from their more politically-minded brethren and turn themselves into an esoteric, eclectic debating society, dedicated to proliferating the rituals and to interpreting events in Irish history in terms of the Old Testament prophecies. At the lowest level, the Orange Order, I imagine, will continue to march on the Twelfth, as the Orangemen still do in Liverpool and Glasgow, and, from time to time, incite disorderly behaviour. They will certainly continue to look for 'Jesuits in the jam'.*

And, in between, there will be a considerable body of moderate Orangemen who will steadfastly work to contain the arrogance of Rome and its attempts at world domination. How long it will take the latter to realize that they are, in fact, tilting at rusty windmills, is anybody's guess; I reckon a long, long time.

In the meantime they will all meet at regular intervals and drink the loyal toasts and sing the Orange songs, rejoicing still—was it all for nothing, then?—in the stalwart courage of their forefathers:

On Derry's Walls once stood a gallant few,
Whom famine, war or death could not subdue;
Loud raged the siege, yet still each bold defender
Gave up the ghost, and sighed out 'No Surrender'.

* I was assured by a Prominent Orangeman that when an Ulster Protestant woman buys her son a new pair of boots and he walks through the puddles in them, as boys everywhere invariably do, she doesn't warn him that the water will ruin the boots, but says instead: 'Watch out—there be wee popes in those puddles'.

Acknowledgements

Much of the material in this book was obtained through conversations and obviously it would be impossible to list all the people concerned. But some acknowledgements are essential.

I am grateful to the authors and publishers of all the books listed below from which I have gleaned various facts, items of background information and occasionally a few brief quotations. For two rather longer extracts, my special thanks are due to Constantine Fitzgibbon and his publishers, Michael Joseph Ltd., for passages from *Red Hand: The Ulster Colony* and to Patrick Riddell and his publishers Hamish Hamilton Ltd. for passages from *Fire Over Ulster*. I should like to acknowledge my gratitude to Alan M. Montgomery and to his daughter Wynn for permission to use Lynn Doyle's poem, *An Ulsterman*, from the collection, *Ballygullion Ballads*, published by Duckworth; and to Mrs George Bambridge for permission to quote from Rudyard Kipling's poem *Ulster 1912*.

As I hope I have made clear in the text, I received the utmost courtesy and co-operation from the Orange Institution everywhere and would particularly like to thank, for their assistance, Captain L. P. S. Orr, M.P., Imperial Grand Master of the Imperial Grand Council of the World; Mr John Bryans, J.P., Grand Master of the Grand Orange Lodge of Ireland; Mr Walter Williams, J.P., Grand Secretary of the Grand Orange Lodge of Ireland; the Rev M. W. Dewar, M.A. Ph.D., and the Rev S. E. Long, A.L.C.D., both official historians of the Orange Order; Mr Alex Cushnie of the Royal Black Preceptory at Lurgan; Mr Edward McGuigan of Blackrock, Co. Dublin, Grand Secretary of the Orange Institution in the Republic; Mr W. H. Wilkes of Liverpool, Grand Master of the Loyal Orange Institution of England; the Rev G. E. Fiawoo, Grand

Secretary of the Orange Lodge of Ghana at Anloga; Mr Gordon Keyes, Grand Secretary of the Grand Lodge of Canada in Toronto; and Mr Walter C. Wilson, Supreme Grand Secretary of the Supreme Grand Lodge of the Loyal Orange Institution of the United States of America, Inc.

I should also like to express my thanks to a number of fellow-journalists and friends who helped me in London, Dublin and Belfast; they include Norman Bridges of the Ulster Office in London; Henry Kelly and Tony Lennon of the *Irish Times*; John Robinson of the BBC in Northern Ireland and Aiken McClelland of the Ulster Folklore Museum.

For the material on Orangeism overseas, I am indebted to a number of people. First I would like to thank two very old friends of mine who helped to point the way towards suitable sources: Gordon Carroll in Connecticut and Dubarry Hillman in Toronto. The material on the United States came from Walter C. Wilson, Supreme Grand Secretary of the Loyal Orange Institution of the United States; the Canadian material from Wilson McConnell of Toronto, and the Australian material from Lenore Nicklin of the *Sydney Morning Herald*. I am extremely grateful to all of them.

Tony Gray
July, 1972

Suggestions for Further Reading

The early period of the Orange Order, from the late 1790s until the scandal of the Cumberland 'plot' in the 1830s, is extremely well-documented; far more fully, in fact, than the Institution's more recent history. This could be due to the existence of the massive reports of two parliamentary inquiries into the activities of the Order presented in 1835—three volumes, totalling 4,500 pages—which have provided researchers with a wealth of detailed background material.

Both R. M. Sibbett in *Orangeism in Ireland and throughout the Empire* and Hereward Senior in *Orangeism in Ireland and Britain, 1795–1836* draw heavily on these reports, as did the Rev H. W. Cleary in his book *The Orange Society*. Cleary's book is extremely thorough and contains details not found in any other printed material on the Orange Order that I have come across; but, as it was written and initially published in Australia, a lot of the material is Australian-orientated. Also, it is not easy to come by. Sibbett's two-volume book, originally published in 1914 and also hard to come by, is verbose, confused and so partisan that it makes very heavy going. Hereward Senior's book is well-documented and rather more readable.

Orangeism: A New Historical Appreciation—from which I have drawn substantially as it consists of essays by three of the Orange Order's official historians and carries the history of Orangeism right up to the present day—is not available through the book trade nor have I been able to find it in any library in Britain (not even the library of the Ulster Office in London). Copies are available from the Orange headquarters at 65 Dublin Road, Belfast.

Much of the material in my book was obtained, and could only be obtained, through conversations with people, and through picking up what I could glean from various pamphlets, Laws and Ordinances and other material published over the years by the Orange Institutions in Ireland and elsewhere. The Orange ballads I have quoted appear in various collections published over the years, and many of them also appear in anthologies of street ballads, etc. They are very flexible and many different versions of each ballad may be found.

For general reading on Northern Ireland and its present problems, there is no shortage of material, and many of the books I have listed below include both a general run-down on the historical background to the current troubles and various references to the Orange Order. I have listed here only books which refer specifically to Northern Ireland, and not the many standard works on British history and various aspects of Irish history which I have consulted, e.g., Thomas Pakenham's marvellously detailed account of the rebellion of 1789, *The Year of Liberty*.

The following list is alphabetical, according to the authors' names, and not in any way in the order of their usefulness:

The Northern Ireland Problem, by Denis P. Barritt and Charles C. Carter. London: Oxford University Press, 1962.

Holy War in Belfast, by Andrew Boyd. Anvil Books, Tralee, Co. Kerry, 1969.

Orangeism: A New Historical Appreciation, by the Rev M. W. Dewar, the Rev John Brown and the Rev S. E. Long, with an introduction by Capt. L. P. S. Orr, M.P., Imperial Grand Master of the Imperial Grand Orange Council of the World. Belfast: The Grand Lodge of Ireland, 1967.

The Orange Society, by the Rev H. W. Cleary. London: Catholic Truth Society, 1899 (reprinted from tenth Australian edition, 1897).

Red Hand: The Ulster Colony, by Constantine Fitzgibbon. London: Michael Joseph, 1971.

Ulster 1969: The Fight for Civil Rights in Northern Ireland, by Max Hastings. London: Victor Gollancz, 1970.

Whitehall Diary, Volume III: Ireland 1918–1925, by Thomas Jones. London: Oxford University Press, 1971.

Fire Over Ulster, by Patrick Riddell. London: Hamish Hamilton, 1970.

Governing Without Consensus, by Richard Rose. London: Faber, 1971.

Orangeism in Ireland and Britain, 1795–1836, by Hereward Senior. London: Routledge and Kegan Paul, 1966.

Orangeism in Ireland and Throughout the Empire, by R. M. Sibbett. London: Thynne and Co., 1939. (Originally published in Belfast by Henderson and Co., 1914; the 1939 edition is considerably enlarged and appeared without the author's name.)

The Ulster Crisis, by A. T. Q. Stewart. London: Faber, 1967.

The Battle of the Bogside, by Russell Statler. London: Sheed and Ward, 1970.

Ulster, by the *Sunday Times* 'Insight' Team. A Penguin Special, 1972.

Northern Ireland: 50 Years of Self-Government, by Martin Wallace. Newton Abbot: David and Charles, 1971.

Index

A Specials, 188
Abercorn, 2nd Duke of, 163
Act of Settlement, 35, 270
Act of Union, 82, 85–6, 98, 100, 105, 111, 136
Adoption Act, 275–6
Adrian IV, Pope, 29
Agriculture, 44, 148
Alexander of Tunis, Lord, 27
Alexander, Private Andrew, 261, 263
Alfred, Prince, Duke of Edinburgh, 261
America, 138–9, 148, 154, 175, 177–8, 180–1, 215
American War of Independence, 45–7, 49, 264
Ancient Britons, 67–8, 89
Ancient Order of Hibernians, 16, 164
Andrews, John M., 163, 225
Andrews, Thomas, 163
Anglo-Norman rule, 29–30
Antrim, Lord, 36
Apprentice Boys,
  London, 8
  Londonderry, 36–7, 58, 223, 247–8
    association in Canada, 265
Archdale, Sir Edward, 190
Armagh Outrages, 59–63, 66, 79
Army, British, 129–30, 168–9, 175, 181, 184, 241, 248–50, 253
Arthur, Sir George, 266
Asquith, H. H., 165, 169, 177–8
Athlone, great gun of, 22, 24
Atkinson, Dr William, 75
Atkinson, Wolsey, 75
Auxiliaries, 181

B Specials, 188, 190, 229, 235, 241–2, 248–9, 280
Balfour, A. J., 163
Balfour, B. J., 210
Bannerman, Sir Henry Campbell, 165
Barrington, Sir Jonah, 77
Barry, Kevin, 181
Bastille, Fall of, 49
Beers, Francis, 142
Beers, William, 142
Beresford, John C., 82, 86
'Better Government of Ireland' Act, 179–80
'Billy Boys', 260
Black and Tans, 180, 185, 188
Blacker, William, 58, 75, 77, 109, 111, 117, 136, 156
Blair, David, 211
Bloody Sunday (1920), 181
Bloody Sunday (1972), 268
Bonar Law, A., 167–8
Border, the, 182, 188, 275–6
Boundary Commission, 186, 229
Boyd, Andrew, 151
Boyne, Battle of, and celebration of, 7, 9, 14–15, 20, 39–40, 44, 48, 57, 62, 94, 201, 238, 257, 265–6
  ban on celebration of, 103
Brehon laws, 29, 31
Brian Boru, 136
British League, 264
Brooke, Sir Basil (later Lord Brookeborough), 224–5
Brown, Rev John, 49, 55, 57, 59–60, 82, 87, 117, 142, 150, 152, 156, 189
Browne, Peter, Bishop of Cork, 23
Brownlow House, 214–16
Brownrigg, Major, 122
Brunswick Clubs, 111
Bryans, John, 201
Burnet, Dr Gilbert, 39

C Specials, 188
Cameron Commission, 246
Cameron, Hon. John Hillyard, 268
Campbell, J. H. (later Lord Glenavy), 166
Canada, 148, 156, 212, 268
Carlton Club, 123, 125–6
Carrickfergus, 38, 238
Carson, Sir Edward, 165–7, 169, 174, 179, 227, 278
Casement, Sir Roger, 175
Castlereagh, Lord, 70, 116
Catholic Association, 100–1, 104–6, 110

Catholic Emancipation, 61, 82, 84, 86–7, 92, 97, 101, 105–6, 109–11, 115–6, 122, 153
Catholic Emancipation Act, 106, 112
Catholic Relief Act, 75, 81
Catholic Truth Society, 23
Charlemont, Lord, 59
Charles II, 34, 45
Chetwoode, C. E., 91, 111, 122
Chichester-Clark, Major James, 228, 247, 252
Church of England, 45
Church of Ireland, 147, 149–51, 156, 209
Churchill, Lord Randolph, 159–60, 162, 167
Churchill, Winston, 166–7, 179
Citizen Army, 173, 175
City of London Guilds, 31
Civil Authorities (Special Powers) Act, 229
Civil Rights movement, 245–7, 277
Civil War, England, 34–5
Civil War, Ireland, 183, 186, 228
Clan-na-Gael, 154
Clark, Sir George, 227–8
Cleary, Rev H. W., 23, 203, 210
Collins, Michael, 177–8, 180–3, 186
Conscription, 178, 180
Conservative Party, 141, 159–60
and Unionist, 160, 162, 250
Conway, Cardinal, 233
Cooke, Dr Henry, 115–16, 150
Cooke, Under-Secretary, 63–4, 82
Cooper, Robert, 221–4
Cope, Arthur, 181
Corn Acts, 148
Cosgrave, William, 186
Covenant, the Solemn League and, 214
Craig, James (later Lord Craigavon), 16, 166, 168–9, 179, 187, 189
Craig, William, 144, 165, 186, 224, 227, 229, 245, 247, 252, 276, 278
Crawford, Major Fred, 163, 166, 169
Crawford, Robert Lindsay, 164
Cromwell, Oliver, 23, 34, 157
'Croppies', the, 71
Crossle, John, 75
Crozier, Archbishop, 167
Crusades, 29, 210–12, 216
CS gas, 248, 250
Cuchulain, 27
Cumberland, Duke of, 92, 110, 112–14, 117, 122–3, 125–6, 128–30, 132, 141, 264
Currie, Austin, 245
Currins, Thomas, 212
Cushenden, Lord, 38, 161
Cushnie, Alex, 215–16, 218

Dail Eireann, 178, 180, 182, 186, 252
Davidson, Abraham, 74
Defenders, the, 48, 50–1, 56, 59–63, 65, 75, 85, 128
Derby, Lord, 181
Derry, Siege of, 37
Despard, Colonel, 131
de Valera, Eamon, 174, 177–8, 180–2, 186
Devlin, Bernadette, 27, 164
Devlin, Joe, 167
Dewar, Rev Dr M. W., 20, 39, 57, 216
Diamond, Battle of the, 50–2, 55–7, 63, 66, 75, 89, 91, 157
Dillon, James, 167
Dissenters, 45
Dolly's Brae, 141–3
Downshire, Marquis of, 115
Doyle, Lynn, 236
Drew, Rev Dr Thomas, 150–1
Drogheda, Marquis of, 77
Dublin Castle, 33, 60, 63, 65, 68, 78, 84, 97, 100–1, 105, 112, 117
Dublin Corporation, 100
Duigenan, Patrick, 75, 86
'Dungannon Plan', 64
Dutch Blue Guards, 40, 76

Easter Week Rising, 50, 170, 175–6, 178, 183, 211, 231, 249
Education, Northern Ireland, 231–3
Edward, Prince of Wales, (later Edward VII), 267–8
Elizabeth I, 30–1
Emigration, 43, 45, 83, 137–40, 260, 269
Emmet, Robert, 84, 131
Rising, 85, 97
Emmet, Thomas Addis, 65
Encumbered Estates Act, 148
Enniskillen, Earl of, 112–13, 141, 153, 156, 190
Erne, Earl of, 156, 198

European Convention of Human Rights, 230
Evangelists, 109
Ewart, Rev Louis A., 270
Explosive Substances Act, 230
Eyre, Robert Hedges, 112

Fairman, William Blennerhasset, 122–124, 130
Famine, the Great, 136–40, 147–8, 150, 215, 269
Faulkner, Brian, 252
Fenianism, *see* Sinn Fein
Fitzgerald, Earl, rebellion, 30
Fitzgerald, Lord Edward, 65
Fitzgerald, Vesey, 105
Fitzgibbon, Constantine, 47, 50–1, 67–8, 92–3, 115, 160, 185
Flags and Emblems Act (N.I.), 230
'Flight of the Earls', 31–2
France, 43, 47–8, 64–7, 69, 71, 84, 99, 109
  Revolution, 49–50, 65, 121
Free State, 186–7
Free State flag, 248
Freedom of worship, 99

Gaelic Celts, 27–32
Gaelic language, 29–31
Geoghegan, Patrick, 261
George III, 62–3, 82
George IV, 101, 122
George V, 182
'German plot', 178
Germany, 175–6
Giffard, Harding, 77, 80
Giffard, John, Dublin Castle agent, 67
Giffard, John, civil servant, 97
Gladstone, W. E., 149, 155–6, 159, 161, 165, 177
Gordon, Duke of, 123, 128
Gough, General Hubert, 169
Government of Ireland Act, 90, 182, 189–90, 231
Gowan, Ogle Robert, 264–5
Gowans, John H., 263
Graham, Sir Clarence, 227
Grant, William, 234
Grattan, Henry, 46, 61, 66, 75, 97
Graves, Robert, 40
Gray, Sam, 111
Grey, Lord, 121
Griffith, Arthur, 173, 177, 180, 182, 186
Gun clubs, 235

Habeas corpus, 66
Hackett, Thomas Lett, 267
Hall, Private, 94
Hamilton, Gustavus, 38
Hancock, John, effigy of, 118
Hanna, Rev Hugh, 150–2, 160
Hart, William, 75
Haywood (or Hayward), of Sheffield, 130
Head, Sir Francis, 266
Health service, 233–4
Heath, Edward, 165
'Hedge' Masons, 212
Hell or Connaught, 59–60, 68, 79
Henry II, 29
Hill, Sir George, 103
Hitton, John, 122
Hoche, General, 66
Home Rule, 136–7, 160–1, 163–5, 167–8, 173, 177–8, 182, 190, 241
Home Rule bills, 149–50, 159, 161–4, 166, 169, 179
Home Rule Party, 156, 163
Hughes, Sir Samuel, 268
Hunt, Lord, 249

Imperial Black Chapter of the British Commonwealth, *see* Order, Black
Independent Orange Order, 164–5
Industrial Revolution, 90, 93, 98
Innes, Cosmo, 127–8
Inquisition, the, 86
Insurrection Act, 97
Internment, 230
Irish Constabulary, 102
Irish Hospitals Sweep, 234
Irish Question, the, 28, 81, 84, 98, 100, 106, 178–9
Irish Republican Army, 17, 181–6, 222, 241–2, 245, 250–1, 253, 277
Irish Republican Brotherhood, 154, 173–7

Jacobites, 46
James II, 9, 15, 21–2, 35–6, 39–40, 44, 238, 270
Johnston, William, 153, 155–6

Kee, Robert, 242, 278
Kelly, Ned, 261
Kennedy, John F., 139–40
Kenyon, Lord, 95, 122
Knife, Rev J. F., 79
Knights Hospitallers, 210–12
Knights of Malta, 212
Knox, Thomas, 64

Labour Party, Australia, 262
Labour Party, Belfast, 164
Ladies Orange Benevolent Association, 265
Lake, General, 67–9, 73, 75, 209
Lambeg drum, 7–8, 14, 84, 87, 280
Land Acts, 148–9
Land owners, 30, 43, 60, 98, 102, 106
Land reform, 85
Land War, 147–8, 156
Lawless, John, 111–12
Lees, Sir Harcourt, 109–10
Leinster, Duke of, 65
Lemass, Sean, 244
Liberal Clubs, 105, 110
Liberals, 163–4, 167–8
Liberators, 110–11
Liverpool, Lord, 100
Lloyd George D., 178–80, 182
Londonderry, Marquis of, 95, 115–16, 123
Long, Rev S. E., 164, 167–8, 189, 201
Louis XIV, 40, 44
Loyal and Benevolent Institution of Ireland, 109–10
Loyal and Friendly Society of the Blew and Orange, 57, 89, 92
Loyal Citizens of Ulster, 246
Loyal Orange Institution, 269
Loyal Orange Ladies' Institution, 269
Loyal True Blue Association, 265
Luddite troubles, 92
Lundy, Governor of Derry, 36–7
Lurgan, Lord, 214
Lynch, Jack, 17, 253
Lynn, Robert, 231

Macaulay, Lord, 36–7, 238
McClelland, Aiken, 20, 211–12
McComb, Rev Samuel, 12
McCracken, Henry Joy, 69
MacDermott, Sean, 176
McDonagh, Rev Enda, 275–6
McDonald, Sir John, 156
McGuigan, Edward, 257–8
McKeague, Mrs Isabella, 252
McKeague, John, 252
MacMurrough, Dermot, King of Leinster, 28
MacNeill, Prof. Eoin, 173, 175–6
Manchester Martyrs, 155
Manchester riots, 90–1
Mannix, Dr, Archbishop of Melbourne, 262
Marlborough, Duke of, 41
Martial Law, 177
Mary I, 30
Mary II, 35–6, 39, 41
'Massacre of the Protestants', 33–4, 78
Maudling, Reginald, 250, 252
Maurice of Nassau, 272
Maxwell, General, 176
Militia, 51, 60, 63–8, 76–9, 84, 89, 101
Milner, Lord, 169
Milton, Lord, 103
Mitchell, John, 139
Molesworth, Sir William, 130
Molyneaux, James H., 215
Montgomery, Viscount, 27
Munro, Henry, 69
Musgrave, Sir Richard, 77, 86

Napoleon, 81, 98
National Vounteers, 175
Nationalism
  Catholic, 222, 241, 245, 247, 250, 253, 277
  Irish, 18, 29, 153, 155
  Ulster, 154
Nationalist Parliamentary Party, 165, 167, 174, 178, 180, 186, 190
Nelson, George, 263
Newcastle, Duke of, 268
Newport, Sir John, 95
Niall of the Nine Hostages, 31
Nixon, Rev Ralph, 90–2, 94
'No Go' area, 248
'No surrender', 37
Northern Ireland, State of, 15–16
Northern Ireland Relief Fund, 262
Northern Ireland Security Forces, 188
Northern Star, 67
Northern Whig Club, 49
Nucella, Brother, 131

Oakboys, 48
Oath of Allegiance, 182
O'Brien, William Smith, 139, 141, 154
Occasional Conformity Bill, 45
O'Connell, Daniel, 99–102, 104–6, 109–11, 115, 117–18, 137, 143, 153
  effigy of, 154
O'Connor, Rory, 183
O'Donnell, Hugh, Earl of Tyrconnell, 31
Ogle, Rt. Hon. George, 86
O'Neill, Hugh, Earl of Tyrone, 31–3
O'Neill, Owen Roe, 27, 33
O'Neill, Phelim, 199, 228
O'Neill, Lord (Captain Terence O'Neill), 31, 226, 228, 232, 242–3, 247
Orange, Principality of, 271–2
Orange Boys, 52, 55–6, 58
Orange Marksmen, 76
Orange Order
  branches in Ireland,
    before Partition:
      Grand Lodges, 75, 77, 79–82, 92, 103–4, 112, 117, 122, 132, 135–6, 140–1, 143, 150, 156, 227
    after Partition:
      Northern Ireland
        Grand Lodge, 187, 196, 200, 203
      Republic of Ireland, 257–9
  branches outside Ireland,
    America, 257, 269–70
    Australia, 13, 251, 261–3, 268–9
    British–America, 156, 264
    Canada, 13, 215, 257, 263–9
    England, 89–94, 101, 111–12, 122–7, 141, 147, 257, 259–61, 263, 270
      Grand, 131, 135
    Ghana, 257
    New Zealand, 13, 257, 269
    Scotland, 91, 123, 127, 257, 259–60, 263
    Wales, 257
  insignia, 8–9, 18, 202
  Laws and Ordinances, 24, 193–6, 199, 202–5
  meeting, 201–7
  membership, 194–200, 236
  Orange Toast, 22–3
  organisation
    Grand Orange Conference, 156
    Imperial Grand Orange Council of the World, 253, 265, 269
    lodges:
      Grand, 76, 83, 86
      Imperial Grand, 112
      Junior, 198, 200, 249–50
      military lodges, 89, 131
      Royal, 95
      Royal Cumberland, 123
      Royal Gordons, 123
      Women's, 198, 218
    (*see also* under individual names)
'Orange Plot', 70
Orange Volunteers, 276
Orange Young Britons, 265
Order, Arch-Purple, 215
Order, Black, 19–20, 39, 76, 80, 101, 196, 209–11, 213–18, 257–8, 265, 280
  Grand Black Orange Lodge of Ireland, 212
  Royal Black, 39, 153, 155, 223, 269
Order, Purple, 76, 80, 153, 209–13, 215
Order, Red Cross, 216–17
Order, Scarlet, 101
  Royal Scarlet, 101
Orders:
  origins, 55–61
    Freemasons, 15, 52, 55–7, 81, 87, 197, 201, 206, 213, 216, 218, 277
Orr, Captain L. P. S., 253–4, 278

Paine, Tom, 48–9
Paisley, Rev Ian, 16, 27, 195, 244–5, 248, 278
Parliament, Irish
  before Partition, 29, 34–5, 43, 46–7, 49, 61, 66, 73, 81–3, 105–6, 168
    dissolution, *see* Union of England and Ireland
    proposed revival, 153, 160–1, 177
  after Partition
    see Dial Eireann, Stormont
Parliament, Westminster, 43, 47, 61, 66, 73, 81–4, 91–3, 95, 97, 104–6, 117–18, 121, 124–5, 132, 147–9, 156, 159, 161–2, 165, 169, 177–8, 180, 190, 250, 277
  direct rule from, 165

Parnell, Charles Stewart, 18, 148–9, 156, 159
Partition of Ireland, 162, 182–3, 244
Party Emblems Act, 152–3, 155
Party Processions Act, Canada, 266–7
Party Processions Act, Ireland, 122–14, 117, 141–3, 152–3, 155–6
Peel, Sir Robert, 100–1, 113, 141
Peep o'Day Boys, 48, 50–1, 56, 68, 76, 80
Pelham, Chief Secretary, 63, 70
Penal Laws, 43–5, 47, 61
People's Democracy, 246
Peterloo Massacre, 93
Philbin, Dr William, Bishop of Down and Connor, 232
Pitt, William, 50, 61, 81–2, 86, 147
Plantation of Ulster, 31–4, 243, 260
Pole, Wellesley, 100
Population explosion, 98
Portland, Duke of, 78
Potatoes, 136–8, 140
Powell, Mayor John, 266
Pratt, Colonel, 104
Preble, Frank A., 211
Presbyterians, 31, 45, 47, 58, 65, 112, 116, 147, 149, 151, 156, 209
Prevention of Incitement to Hatred Act (N.I.), 252
Protestant Ascendancy, 9, 15, 56, 59, 61, 70, 73, 82, 93–4, 104, 106, 127, 144, 154, 186, 189, 259, 270, 280
Protestant Patriot Party, 46–9
Provisional Government of Ulster, 168
Public Order Acts, 230
Puritanism, 9–10, 45
Purple Marksmen, 19, 209, 210, 213–14

Radicals, 118, 123–4
Ramsay, Dr, Archbishop of Canterbury, 262
Rabbarees, 44
Rankine, Joseph, 211
Rebellion of 1798, 68, 70, 73, 77, 79, 81, 83, 89, 261
Redmond, John, 18, 165, 167, 174–5, 177–8, 180, 279
Reform bills, 118, 126, 130
  first, 115, 121–3
Reformation, 29–30, 36, 194
Republic of Ireland, 19, 180, 242, 276–8
Revolution of 1688, 35–6
Ribbonmen, 85, 87, 113, 128, 142, 152–3
Riddell, Patrick, 183, 185
Riel, Louis, 267
Riots, Belfast, 19th century, 140, 151–2
Riots, Scotland, 127–8
Robinson, John, 238, 282
Roche, Father, 71
Roden, Lord, 136, 142
Roe, Rev Thomas Wellesley, 150, 152
Roman Britain, 28
Rowan, Hamilton, 65
Royal Britannic Association of the Knights of Israel, 212
Royal Commission on Orange Lodges, 213
Royal Irish Constabulary, 151, 154, 181, 187
Royal Ulster Constabulary, 184, 187, 189–90, 229, 241, 245–6, 248–9, 252

St Ruth, General, 41
Salisbury, Lord, 159, 162–3
Sarsfield, Patrick, 21, 39–41
Saunderson, Col Edward, 164
Saurin, William, 100
Scarman, Sir Leslie, 249
Scarva, Sham Fight at, 20–2, 38–9, 206, 217
Schomberg, 21, 28, 40, 238
Scotland, 27, 31, 147–9
Scott, Thomas, 267
Seaver, Thomas, 75
Secret organizations banned, 92
Secret Service, British, 181
Secret Societies Act, Canada, 266
Senior, Hereward, 57–8, 64, 67, 76, 78, 85–6, 100, 104, 124, 131–2
Settlement of Ireland, 27, 31, 46
Shaw, George Bernard, 177
Sibbert, R. M., 115
Simpson, Dr Robert, 228
Sinn Fein, 16, 99, 154–6, 170, 173, 176–7, 180, 215, 242, 244, 249
Sirr, Major, 77
Sloan, James, 56, 73, 75
  inn, 55–6
Sloan, Thomas, 164–5
Smuts, General, 181
Special Constabulary, 187–8
Special Powers Act, 97
Steelboys, 48

Steller, Russell, 36
Stephens, James, 154–5
Stormont Parliament, 90, 178–9, 182–183, 185–7, 189, 222, 225, 228–9, 234–6, 241–2, 245, 247, 251, 277
  prorogued, 251–3
Strong, Sir Norman, 215
Stronge, Sir James, 190

Talbot, General, 40
Tandy, Napper, 65, 71
Tartan Gangs, 260
Taylor, Colonel, 91
Teagues, 280
Templeton, Lord, 163
Thomson, Henry, 206
Thornton, General, 111
Threshers, 85, 87
Tone, Theobald Wolfe, 48–50, 64–6
Tories, 45, 92, 106, 121
Trade and commerce, 46
Treaty of Limerick, 41, 43
Tyling, 201
Tyrconnell, Viceroy of Ireland, 36

Ulster Constitution Defence Committee, 246
'Ulster Custom', 44, 147–8
Ulster Day, 168, 214
Ulster Defence Association, 144, 251, 253, 260, 276
Ulster Defence Regiment, 249, 253
Ulster Loyalist Association, 245–6
Ulster Protestant League, 224
Ulster Protestant Volunteers, 246
Ulster Society, 263
Ulster Volunteer Force, 235, 245
Ulster Volunteers, 166, 168–70, 173, 175, 186
Union of England and Ireland, 81–4, 136
Unionism, 183, 185, 187, 228
Unionist Clubs, 163, 166
Unionist Party, 92–3, 165–6, 173–4, 179–80, 190, 221, 223–4, 227, 233–5, 242, 245, 247, 252
United Empire Association, 264
United Ireland, 48, 253, 275
United Ireland movement, 49–50, 58, 62–3, 65–7, 69, 71, 84
Unlawful Oaths Bill, 103

Vanguard movement, 144, 165, 251–2, 276, 278
Verner, David, 75
Verner, James, 66, 75–7
Verner, Thomas, 75, 77, 83, 86
Verner, Col William, 112–14, 117
Victoria,
  Princess, 122
  Queen, 131, 195, 268
Volunteers,
  18th century: 47–9, 52, 56–7, 61–2, 64–5, 75, 101
  20th century: 173–6

Walker, Rev George, 37
Wallace, Col H., 166
Wallace, Martin, 228
Welfare State, 222, 226, 228
Wellesley, Lord, 103
Welling, Sgt P. J., 277
Wellington, Duke of, 92, 113, 122
Whigs, 92, 106, 118, 125, 131, 141
Whiteboys, 44, 60, 85
Whitworth, Lord, 101
Wilhelmina, Queen, 271
William III (of Orange), 7, 9–10, 12, 14–15, 20–3, 35–6, 38–41, 47, 57, 62–3, 94, 98, 109, 194, 204, 206–7, 238, 257, 260, 270–2
  statue of, 238, 257
William IV, 122, 130
Williams, Walter, 198–9, 201
Wilson, Harold, 247
Wilson, Field-Marshal Sir Henry, 187–188
Wilson, James, 55–7, 75
Wilson, Walter C., 269
Winter, Dan, 75
  inn, 50–1, 55–6
Wolseley, Colonel, 38

Yarmouth, Lord, 92
Yeomanry, 64–8, 75–6, 78–9, 83–4, 94, 102, 111, 113, 125, 147
  Belfast, 75
York, Duke of, 92–5, 110
Young, Sir Arthur, 249
Young Ulster movement, 163, 166